In a Bad State

In a Bad State

Responding to State and Local Budget Crises

DAVID SCHLEICHER

OXFORD
UNIVERSITY PRESS

OXFORD
UNIVERSITY PRESS

Oxford University Press is a department of the University of Oxford. It furthers
the University's objective of excellence in research, scholarship, and education
by publishing worldwide. Oxford is a registered trade mark of Oxford University
Press in the UK and certain other countries.

Published in the United States of America by Oxford University Press
198 Madison Avenue, New York, NY 10016, United States of America.

CIP data is on file at the Library of Congress

ISBN 978–0–19–762915–4

DOI: 10.1093/oso/9780197629154.001.0001

Printed by Sheridan Books, Inc., United States of America

For Amanda, Charlie, and Nate

CONTENTS

PART IV   THE CONCLUSION, OR WHY
STATES ARE OFTEN BAD

and peers is narrow. Students in my seminar were assigned draft chapters and provided excellent feedback.

Speaking of Yale, there are many people at the Law School I need to thank. Since my first day as a law student, Dean Heather Gerken has been a mentor to me and has provided an example for how to write insightful and important scholarship. I can't thank her enough for all of her support, as a dean, as a mentor, and as a friend. As I mentioned above, Robert Post got this whole project started; he is just a total mensch in addition to being a brilliant thinker. Jennifer Marshall is a terrific assistant. Pascal Matthieu is a wizard with grants. Joe Crosby Joe Crosbied things in the way only Joe Crosby can do. Thank you!

Finally, I want to thank my family. They have had to listen to me talk about things like sales tax bonds or Bridgeport's history of fiscal crisis for years. I can't thank them enough for always doing so with good humor and interest. My boys—Charlie and Nate—are just the best, my favorite people. I can't wait for them to read this. My wife Amanda is amazing, my love and anchor. They are the most loving and fun people I have ever met. None of this would have happened without them.

ACKNOWLEDGMENTS

At a cocktail party in 2015, then-Yale Law School Dean Robert Post introduced me to Dick Ravitch, the former lieutenant governor of New York, chair of the Metropolitan Transportation Authority, a central figure in the New York City fiscal crisis, and the éminence grise of the world of municipal finance. I was, and am, a scholar of state and local government law, focusing mostly on land use, urban economic development, and election law. At the time, I had not written much about state and local fiscal issues. But, after one conversation with Dick, I realized I needed to fix that.

Dick and I started teaching a class together at Yale Law School called "The State and Local Budget Crisis." Doing so has been a great education and pleasure. This book is very much the product of interactions in class with the excellent students, Dick, and the variety of people in the municipal finance world who have joined us over the years. I'm not the first person for whom an encounter with Dick Ravitch was a formative experience, nor will I be the last, but I will be forever grateful for his vision, brilliance, focus, and kindness.

That said, there are ways in which Dick was pushing on an open door. My brilliant wife Amanda Kosonen is an international law expert and knows more than I ever will about sovereign debt and international financial institutions (among many, many, *many* other things). Her views on sovereign debt provided a lens into the municipal debt world that I wouldn't have had otherwise. This book clearly bears the marks of her thinking.

They say when you scratch a scholar's theory, you find a biography. That is certainly true in this case. My parents—my mother Linda Schleicher, my father Bill Schleicher, and my stepmother Ellen Chapnick—taught me to care about local politics and, beyond that, about the people who work for governments and those who rely on government services. Mom and Dad both worked for municipal labor unions in New York City, where the shadow of the 1970s fiscal crisis was ever-present. The human costs of fiscal crises were apparent to me, even at an early age. The other day I told Mom that I was pretty sure she wouldn't agree with everything in this book, but that, no matter what, I always know that she is proud, loving, and supportive of me. A child could ask for nothing more from his parents. (Also, my mother is playing a game with my boys while I write this—thanks Mom!)

While all of the book's flaws are my own, many people contributed to any successes it has. My editor at Oxford University Press, David McBride, identified this project and then did an amazing job working with me and shepherding the book into print. The rest of the team that worked with us—Emily Benitez and Kavitha Yuvaraj particularly—did great work. In addition, my publicist Michelle Blankenship helped so much as well.

A group of brilliant research assistants helped me over the many years I've been working on this book. Many, many thanks are due to Rebecca Brooks, Adam Gerrard, Paul Healy, Adela Lilollari, Steffi Ostrowski, Will Poff-Webster, Anirudh Sivaram, and Talia Stender.

Colleagues and friends provided a great deal of feedback and advice. Steve Teles convinced me to write this as a book, rather than as a series of law review articles, advising me both on the scholarly content and talking me through some of my worries about it. I have been working with my regular coauthor Rick Hills on land use projects for years now; my thinking on all sorts of issues has been deeply shaped by his intense and sometimes manic intelligence. Bob Ellickson has been a mentor, a great commentator, and, perhaps most importantly, a role model for how to do scholarly work. Others who provided extremely useful comments on the manuscript or otherwise provided feedback include Bruce Ackerman, Nicholas Bagley, Vincent Buccola, Aure Chaudhury, Peter Conti-Brown, Justin Driver, Christopher Elmendorf, Brian Feinstein, David Fontana, Brian Galle, Heather Gerken, Clayton Gillette, Edward Glaeser, William Glasgall, Tracy Gordon, Daniel Halberstam, Andrew Haughwout, Daniel Hemel, Don Herzog, Noah Kazis, Daryl Levinson, Adam Levitin, Zachary Liscow, Yair Listokin, Julia Mahoney, Gregory Makoff, E. J. McMahon, Gabe Mendlow, Thomas Meyer, Eloise Pasachoff, Michael Pyle, Roberta Romano, Reihan Salam, David Skeel, Douglas Spencer, Susan Wachter, Benjamin Wallace-Wells, David Zaring, Taisu Zhang, and several anonymous reviewers. I also had several wonderful conversations about the Municipal Liquidity Facility and municipal finance more generally with Kent Hiteshew, which taught me a great deal.

The book also benefited tremendously from comments at workshops at the Antonin Scalia Law School, the Federal Funding Issues Workshop, the Federal Reserve Bank of New York, Johns Hopkins University, the Law and Macroeconomics Annual Conference, the University of Michigan Law School, the Yale School of Management, and the Yale Law School. One of the great pleasures of teaching at Yale Law School is that the distinction between students

PART I

WHY IS IT SO HARD TO GET OUT OF A BAD STATE?

An Introduction to the Problem of State and Local Fiscal Crises

Introduction

Why Is It So Hard to Get Out of a Bad State?

Imagine this: Sometime in the late 2020s, while the President and Congress negotiate over one bill or another, big news drops. The Governor of Illinois and the Mayor of Chicago are going to hold a joint press conference to announce that the state *and* the city are flat broke. They are both going to default on their debts and slash their budgets if Congress doesn't do something quickly to help them out of their dire fiscal straits.

Everyone in DC turns on their TVs to watch the press conference. As soon as it ends, the cable networks go live to protests in Chicago. Schools have closed for the day, disorder reigns, and garbage sits uncollected, as teachers, police officers, and other public sector workers take to the streets to oppose proposed layoffs and pension cuts. On location, reporters interview storeowners in Springfield, Illinois, worried that soon-to-be fired state employees will stop spending money, destroying the local economy. The Twitter hashtags #IllinoIsOver and #ChicaGoAway trend worldwide, as major companies announce their plans to move their headquarters and factories away from the state before severe tax increases kick in.

It's a *disaster*. The President brings her advisers and Congressional allies to the White House to formulate a response.

The Chair of the Council of Economic Advisers goes first: "We can't let Illinois or Chicago cut services to the bone and fire tons of employees," he argues. "It will crush the economy. State and local layoffs will directly lower employment levels, and multiplier effects will mean even more job losses. Not to mention the human suffering caused by lost government services—higher crime rates, 40 students in each classroom, more homelessness, and reduced healthcare! Tax increases will destroy economic activity and encourage people and companies to leave the state. Austerity is not a solution."

A Senator from Texas interrupts: "No, no, no! The worst thing we can do is give federal money to Illinois," she says. "Why should my constituents pay for Chicago's mistakes? The state and the city repeatedly refused to raise taxes or cut spending enough to balance their budgets. If we give aid to Illinois or Chicago, every governor and mayor in the country will know that she can spend wildly without consequences. And lenders will know there is no risk in providing money to irresponsible governments. Let Illinois cut spending or let it default. Either way, bailouts are not the answer."

The Secretary of the Treasury pipes up: "Whatever we do, we can't let Illinois default on its promises. State and local governments build and maintain almost everything useful in this country—roads, trains, sewer systems, you name it. To do so, they need to be able to borrow money. If Illinois defaults, or if Chicago files for bankruptcy, the municipal bond market might collapse. States and cities around the country won't be able to borrow, which will mean they can't invest in infrastructure. The future of the national economy depends on Illinois avoiding default."

What should the President and Congress do?

* * *

This scenario may seem far-fetched, but in March 2020 it looked like we were in for a wave of state and local governmental defaults. When the COVID-19 pandemic hit, a massive decline in economic activity followed.[1] Budget experts predicted both huge state and local governmental revenue losses and large increases in demand for healthcare and other social services because of the pandemic and the recession.[2]

Defaults seemed possible, even likely. The last major recession, the Great Recession of 2008, had been brutal on state and local budgets.[3] State and local governments laid off hundreds of thousands of public employees, a loss of jobs so severe that it substantially extended the length of the recession.[4] Detroit and several other cities were eventually forced to file for bankruptcy; the Commonwealth of Puerto Rico effectively did so as well.

Some jurisdictions had substantially improved their fiscal situations between 2008 and 2020, building up substantial "rainy day funds."[5] But others kept accruing more and more debt, often in the form of underfunded pension liabilities and healthcare obligations for retired public workers.[6] In Connecticut in 2019, almost a third of the tax revenue generated by the state went to making payments on debt and retiree obligations.[7] Connecticut was not alone—debt and pension payments made up a huge portion of spending in states like Illinois, New Jersey, and Kentucky as well.[8]

After what we saw following the Great Recession, the COVID-19 recession seemed sure to produce its own state and local fiscal crises. The media ran story after story about impending disasters in state budgets. Municipal bond markets seized up, creating questions about the ability of state and local governments to borrow.[9] State and local governments laid off or furloughed more than a million public employees, more than they had after 2008.[10] Revenues shriveled for many local governments, particularly those with budgets reliant on tourism, the oil industry, car tolls, or mass transit fares.[11] The State of Illinois and New York's Metropolitan Transportation Authority were forced to borrow money from the Federal Reserve.[12] The leader of the Illinois State Senate asked Congress for a $41B bailout.[13]

But a default crisis did not come to pass. The shock created by the pandemic was very different in type from the crisis that hit in 2008. High-income workers had largely stable incomes during the pandemic and the stock market boomed, leading to consistent or even increasing state income and capital gains tax revenues.[14] Federal aid to individuals and firms helped preserve incomes despite high unemployment.[15] The bond market recovered after the Federal Reserve, with Congress's backing, created a facility for buying municipal bonds.[16] And, over the course of several pieces of legislation, Congress provided an *enormous* amount of money to state and local governments, flooding them with more federal money than they lost in tax revenue.[17] The result was state and local budgets in 2021 were generally in better shape than they were before the crisis; by 2022, many governments had huge budget surpluses.

Despite flush budgets, however, the underlying structural problems of state and local budgets have not been cured in many places.[18] It is possible some state and local budgets will be even worse off in several years than they were previously, if governments expand programs or cut taxes now in ways that will be difficult to reverse when the gusher of federal aid runs out.

The easing of pressure on state budgets, though, provides the country with some time to consider how it should respond to future crises, whether they occur in individual jurisdictions or as part of a national economic crash. This book is an effort to take advantage of this lull to develop some new ideas about how federal officials and voters alike should think about the problem of state and local fiscal stress. The book will also propose some policies that can be enacted to reduce the costs of such crises, acknowledging that state and local fiscal crises will inevitably occur in a country with 50 states and thousands of local governments.

Because a true nationwide state and local governmental default crisis seemed possible, Congress was forced to wrestle with how to respond. At the height of the COVID-19 pandemic and associated recession, there was a great deal of public discussion about state fiscal issues. Ideas like creating a bankruptcy code for state governments and federal aid to states took turns dominating headlines.[19]

But the sides in these public debates often seemed to be talking past one another. Republicans claimed state fiscal aid amounted to "blue state bailouts," despite the fiscal situation being as bad in many Republican-dominated states as it was in Democratic-dominated ones.[20] Republicans also pooh-poohed the macroeconomic and social costs of state and local governmental layoffs, waiting until after November 2020 to allow a vote on a second large state and local aid package, even though a Republican president's re-election chances surely would have been buoyed by a better economy.[21] Democrats argued there would be huge negative economic and social outcomes if state and local aid was not offered, and persisted in these claims well after state budgets had recovered substantially.[22] They also claimed that disaster would unfold if states were given the power to file for bankruptcy, without revealing much understanding of how sovereign bankruptcy might work in practice.[23]

That these debates were unedifying, though, was not the fault of politicians or journalists. Scholarship and elite discussion around these issues has not helped them, missing many of the real concerns created by state and local fiscal distress. Experts have not done a good job explaining the true stakes of a state or large city default, nor have we laid out the full set of options available to federal officials in a crisis of this type.

The goal of this book is to provide a clear theory about the challenges federal officials face when a state or city nears default *from the perspective of those officials*, regardless of their party or ideology. That is, it will try to explain what federal officials faced with a state or local fiscal crisis can and cannot do. The goal is to make federal officials ready when and if such a crisis comes to pass, and, just as importantly, to provide all of us judging their decisions with some perspective. Although it will draw on economics, political science, law, and history, this book will do so in service of providing a practical guide to understanding the difficult choices that federal policymakers face in responding to state and local fiscal crises. Further, looking at the role played by the federal government during state and local budget crises will provide some lessons about how we might reform our federal system more broadly.

Fortunately, or unfortunately, there is a lot of historical material to draw on. Crises much like the one I asked you to imagine above have happened several times in American history (without the cable news coverage or Twitter hashtags!). All three branches of the federal government—the President, Congress, and particularly the federal courts—have played important roles in developing policy toward states and cities on the edge of, or after, defaults.

Some of this history is well known. Federal responses to state fiscal crises generated some of the most famous disputes in American political history. These include the debate over the assumption of state debts in Alexander Hamilton's first financial plan as Secretary of the Treasury (famously captured by Lin-Manuel Miranda in "Cabinet Battle #1" in the musical *Hamilton*) and the fight over Southern state debts at the end of Reconstruction after 1876.

But other federal responses to state and local debt crises, even very dramatic ones, are little remembered. President and former victorious Civil War Union general Ulysses S. Grant threatened to send federal troops to the stalwart Union state of Iowa in the 1870s to force small towns to make good on their bonded debt.[24] In the late 19th century, state legislatures effectively disbanded several major city governments, a practice that became known as "corporate suicide," to help them avoid claims by creditors until the Supreme Court stepped in and stopped the practice. The State of Arkansas once played a role in global capital markets much like the one Argentina does today, defaulting on its debts three times between the 1840s and 1930s.

Other federal responses to local fiscal crises are misremembered. For instance, in the mid-1970s, the *New York Daily News* famously described President Gerald Ford's position against providing aid to New York City as "Ford to City: Drop Dead."[25] While the headline stuck in our collective memory, President Ford supported legislation that provided federal loans to New York City only a few months after that headline ran.

While there have been many state and local fiscal crises in American history, the federal government has not developed a single, consistent formula for addressing them. What history reveals is that the federal government does not have any good options when addressing state and local fiscal crises. As a result, it has cycled between responses that are bad in different ways.

When faced with a state or local fiscal crisis, federal officials generally want to achieve three different things. They want to (1) avoid the macroeconomic and social harms associated with state and local spending cuts and tax increases during recessions; (2) avoid creating an expectation on the part of state and city governments that they will get bailouts in the future, as they might therefore refuse to enforce fiscal discipline, what economists call "moral hazard"; and (3) preserve the ability of states and cities to borrow money in order to build infrastructure and make other debt-financed investments.

But the federal government cannot achieve all three of these things. It can achieve two of them, but not three. That is, it faces a *trilemma*.[26]

Here's what it can do.

The first option the federal government has is providing money to deeply indebted states or cities. The federal government can take advantage of its vast taxing powers, immense borrowing capacity, and ability to print money to just pay off the creditors of a state or city. States and cities that receive bailouts do not need to lay off public workers, cut valuable social programs, or raise taxes, reducing the harm to the broader economy and service recipients. State and local bailouts do not require corresponding cuts at the federal level, because the federal government, unlike states or cities, can easily run deficits in a recession. Bailouts also encourage state and local governments to borrow to invest in infrastructure, as lenders will be comforted by what amounts to a federal guarantee for state debts, and thus be willing to loan to states and municipalities at lower rates.

But providing bailouts has an obvious downside: creating moral hazard among states and localities. State and local officials around the country may think future debts will be paid for by the federal government and be reckless going forward. Bond markets may cease to differentiate between good and bad credit risks, lending to both responsible and spendthrift governments at similar interest rates, as investors increasingly believe that the federal government is providing a backstop for their loans. The easy availability of credit removes pressure from politicians to budget responsibly. Further, residents and politicians from other states may resent having their tax dollars going toward services provided in the state receiving the bailout.

Political scientist Jonathan Rodden has shown that national governments around the world rarely provide bailouts to subnational governments without also imposing severe conditions on their ability to make fiscal policy choices in the future.[27] Otherwise, bailouts lead to too much moral hazard and/or interstate conflict. This was borne out recently. The huge state and local aid package in President Joe Biden's American Rescue Plan in 2021 barred states from using federal funds to cut taxes and put limits on the uses for which the money could be spent (although these limits were challenged in court). Repeated bailouts would lead to subnational governments losing much of their independence as fiscal entities.

Put another way, federalism as we know it is inconsistent with the regular provision of bailouts to states and cities.

The second option the federal government has is to encourage states and cities to pay their debts, using political and financial pressure to overcome subnational jurisdictions' legal protections against creditor lawsuits where necessary. If state and local taxpayers are forced to dig deep to pay their debts, moral hazard ceases to be a concern. And the municipal bond market would be strengthened, as lenders would know that they will get paid back even when times are tough.

But forcing states and cities in a fiscal crisis to pay their debts without federal aid has negative macroeconomic and social consequences. States and cities cannot easily run deficits—they can't print money and they have state constitutional and market-based limits on their ability to run deficits or issue debt. The only way a jurisdiction in fiscal crisis can meet its obligations is to cut important services, lay off public workers, and increase taxes. As most state and local fiscal crises occur during recessions, these cuts are particularly economically painful, destroying jobs and economic activity when unemployment is already high. Further, cutting state and local spending in a recession reduces the availability of redistributive government services when they are most needed, less Medicaid spending and fewer homeless shelters when people are most likely to lose their private-sector health insurance or homes.

State and local austerity can turn recessions into depressions.

The third and final option is that federal government can allow, enable, and encourage states and cities to default on their debts, or in some cases, file for bankruptcy. This makes creditors—bondholders, pensioners, and contractors—bear at least some of the cost of fiscal crises, rather than having current federal or state taxpayers bearing the whole burden. As a result, defaults do not create expectations of future federal bailouts or do as much short-term macroeconomic harm as harsh austerity would.[28]

But defaults reduce the willingness of lenders to finance state and local investments, and thus increase the costs of future infrastructure projects. The United States has always relied on state and local governments to build and maintain most of our civic infrastructure. Because members of Congress are elected from geographically based districts, Congress faces real challenges in directly funding new infrastructure without it devolving into pork-barrel compromises that have little to do with real needs for new investment. Further, the informational burdens associated with making decisions in Washington about the infrastructure needs of a continent-sized country makes federal delivery of new infrastructure difficult. While Congress does pass infrastructure bills, it has never provided a majority of the money spent on infrastructure in this country when operations and maintenance are taken into account. Only rarely, like during the height of the interstate highway system, has the federal government even provided a majority of the capital funding for even particular types of infrastructure like roads. Even when Congress gets it together to pass a large new infrastructure funding bill, as it did in with 2021's Infrastructure Investment and Jobs Act, most of the money takes the form of grants to state and local governments, and often requires state and local governments to "match" federal spending with spending of their own.[29]

Congress's structural challenges force it to rely on state and local governments to build and maintain most of our necessary infrastructure. Building infrastructure requires debt. A state or local government will borrow to pay for the construction of, say, a bridge and then pay the money back over the bridge's useful lifetime, the same way ordinary people take out mortgages to buy houses they plan on living in for a long time.

State and local defaults make lenders less willing to buy municipal bonds, both from the jurisdiction that defaults and from others. The economy depends on our ability to provide transportation, education, and basic services like water and energy. All of those things depend on states and cities being able to borrow at reasonable rates.

Defaults reduce the country's capacity to invest in the future.

In a state or local fiscal crisis, there are three bad outcomes—moral hazard, austerity-induced macroeconomic crisis, and reduced future investment in infrastructure. At best, the federal government can prevent two of them. It has to pick its preferred poison. That's the trilemma.

Over the course of American history, the federal government has made different choices along the trilemma. The federal government provided bailouts in Hamilton's assumption of state debts; to Washington, DC, in the 1990s; and, arguably, to states and localities in 2008 and again in 2020–2021. The federal government did nothing to stop states from (and, at times, actively aided states in) defaulting on creditors in the 1840s and again in the 1870s. The federal government also enacted a municipal bankruptcy law in the 1930s, which cities like Detroit and Stockton, California, used after the Great Recession of 2008. And the federal government forced jurisdictions to engage in painful austerity to pay off their debts in the repeating "railroad bond" crises of the second half of the 19th century and following the State of Arkansas' road debt default of 1932.

Whatever choices the federal government made in each situation had their predicted downsides. Bailouts *did* create moral hazard, largely by encouraging bond markets to lend to state and local governments without much regard for their fiscal soundness. Austerity *in fact* harmed the economy during already painful recessions and produced social costs from declining service quality. State and local defaults *caused* investors to reduce future lending, limiting infrastructure investment and economic growth in whole regions of the country.

That the federal government would choose different options at different times is natural. Partisan politicians will want to make choices that help their friends and not their opponents. Liberals and conservatives will not put the same weights on the downsides along the trilemma. External factors like the state of capital markets or the broader economy often made one choice or another more or less attractive.[30] And the federal government is often not unitary in its response. There are lots of people in the federal government, and they do not always push in the same direction.

There isn't a right answer, only differently bad options.

This book will not seek to explain the politics of why different actors made the decisions they did.[31] Instead, it will show that all of them faced a common set of tradeoffs. The trilemma cannot be avoided. There's no way out of the problem, beyond very radical changes to our constitutional and institutional system.[32] And in a crisis, no one has that kind of time.

So what should the federal government do if an Illinois or a Chicago nears default?

Faced with such a crisis, politicians and voters will have to make decisions about which bad outcome from the trilemma they can live with. How they make those decisions will turn on some very deep questions of political and moral philosophy, like how they weigh the likelihood of benefits in the future against costs today, or how much they value the practical fiscal independence of state governments from federal oversight. Also, there is no reason to believe that there is a single right policy response to all state and local fiscal crises, as the state of the economy and credit markets at the time of a crisis should all factor into whatever decisions the federal government makes. A book like this one can't answer those big moral and political questions, nor can it provide timeless advice in advance of a particular crisis.

Instead, the book will explain what the tradeoffs are, but leave the actual weighing of those tradeoffs for you.

But while this book cannot answer *which* leg of the trilemma policymakers should choose in any given crisis, it can and will provide advice on *how* to design responses. No matter whether they choose bailouts, austerity, or defaults, federal officials can shape their policy responses in ways that are better or worse.

In designing their policy responses, there are four basic principles that should guide federal officials' decisions. These four principles are prudence, balancing, spreading, and resilience. No matter which leg of the trilemma they choose, policymakers should seek to build these four principles into their crisis responses.

Prudence: To paraphrase the movie *War Games*, state fiscal crises are a strange game—the only way to win is not to play.[33] The best way to avoid the costs of the trilemma is for states to budget responsibly. Federal officials should take steps during state fiscal crises to encourage states to be more fiscally responsible going forward. They can do so in a number of ways. For instance, federal officials could empower the bond market to monitor state budgets more closely by changing securities law to require states and cities to provide more information about their budget process to investors. Or the federal government could condition federal aid on changes in the accounting standards states use when passing their budgets. If a city defaults, the federal government can wait to provide aid until after the state government has imposed substantial reforms to the city's budget process going forward.

Whichever tack it takes, the federal government is well situated to encourage greater fiscal responsibility in states. And it has a clear incentive to and justification for doing so, the desire to reduce the size or even the need for future bailouts.

Balance: If a crisis does land on the federal government's doorstep, the President, Congress, and federal judges will all need to make decisions about how to respond. What relatively recent state and local debt crises have shown is that, while the trilemma is unavoidable, the federal government does not have to make stark decisions. Rather than all of one or another, the federal government can encourage states to engage in some austerity, permit limited defaults, and create a little moral hazard through small bailouts. Mixed policies are likely to be superior, as there are increasing marginal harms along each leg of the trilemma.

Federal law has already created some tools for producing balanced solutions, and it could develop more. For instance, municipal bankruptcy law provides a forum for judges and governments to balance the competing interests of creditors and service recipients. Judges in municipal bankruptcy cases are forced to decide whether a city government's services have declined to the point that the city is "service delivery insolvent," making it okay to ask creditors to take losses. Currently, though, bankruptcy is only available for local governments and is infrequently used. Congress could make it easier for local governments to get into bankruptcy court. It should also make it possible for state governments to file. Bailouts that come after bankruptcy filings, or that are conditioned on the creation of fiscal control boards, would help balance the problems of moral hazard and cuts for service recipients.

Spreading: Most Americans are represented by many overlapping subnational governments—a state, a county, a city or town, a school district, and a whole bunch of other special districts governing things ranging from mass transit to mosquito control. When a place suffers from an economic crisis or when groups of local politicians are profligate, often many of these overlapping governments suffer fiscal crises at the same time. In a crisis, these overlapping governments compete for resources, fighting each other for subsidies from higher levels of government and greater shares of the local tax base, rather than trying to solve their common problems.

The federal government can encourage jurisdictions to spread losses across types of creditors and stakeholders by pushing overlapping governments to address their crises simultaneously. As a legal matter, these governments are independent from one another. But, in practice, they are just different agents of a common set of principals (the voters and taxpayers they represent). Rather than letting overlapping governments engage in wasteful competition, the federal government should encourage as many related governments as possible to adopt an emergency footing and to make sacrifices at once. Doing so—by providing aid to many different levels of government at once or through reforms to municipal bankruptcy law that would allow simultaneous and related filings—would reduce the size of the losses any one set of creditors or stakeholders would have to take.

Resilience: Beyond the specifics of responding to a given crisis, the federal government should adopt policies that will make the country more able to deal with inevitable economic shocks and state and local fiscal crises. For instance, the federal government can make defaults in one jurisdiction have less effect on borrowing by other jurisdictions. Much-criticized federal and state income tax exemptions for interest on municipal bonds encourage the development of domestic and state-specific investment pools for municipal bonds. This reduces the "contagion" effect a default in one place can have on borrowing by others.

Also, the economic harm of fiscal crises will be smaller if localized economic crises lead unemployed people to leave declining cities and regions. The federal government can incentivize states to reform their housing and labor regulations to make it easier for poor people (and not just rich ones—who leave regardless) to move to economically thriving cities and regions. The federal government could also nationalize some social welfare programs, like Medicaid, that are currently jointly run with states. Doing so would remove some of the pro-cyclical pressure on state budgets and make mobility across regions easier.

No matter how the federal government responds to a fiscal crisis in an Illinois or a Chicago, many people will be unhappy. But it is possible that the federal government can make a fiscal crisis in a major state or city a painful but manageable problem, rather than an unmitigated disaster. This book will show how federal officials can do just that.

* * *

The rest of the book will be organized as follows.

Chapter 1 will review how scholars have addressed the question of how the federal government should respond to state and local fiscal crises. While there is much high-quality work in the field, the literature has mostly ignored the long-standing federal interest in state and local governments having access to credit to build infrastructure and make other investments. Further, the fiscal federalism literature has not focused on the crucial role played by federal courts in responding to state fiscal crises. This chapter will explain how the trilemma works.

Chapter 2 will discuss two of the best-known state fiscal crises in American history. It will start with Alexander Hamilton's plan for the federal government to assume state debts following the Revolutionary War. And it will then address the default crisis of the 1840s, when Congress decided not to assume state debts, allowing eight states and the territory of Florida to default. It will argue that existing scholarship has not fully explored the implications of these two events. The literature has treated the refusal to provide bailouts in the 1840s, and the state balanced budget rules that followed, as an unmitigated success in the battle against moral hazard. But it has ignored the effect the defaults had on the willingness and capacity of state governments to borrow to build infrastructure.

Chapter 3 will discuss the rest of the 19th century. In particular, it will focus on two key episodes: the local government "railroad bond" crises that recurred regularly from the 1860s through 1880s, and the post-1877 defaults by newly empowered white-dominated state governments of the South on debt incurred by mixed-race Reconstruction-Era governments. The federal government, and particularly federal courts, responded to these two crises in radically different ways. The long-run effect of these different responses reveals how the trilemma works. Many cities and counties were forced by the Supreme Court to pay back the debts they incurred trying to encourage railroad construction. The Supreme Court pushed its powers to their limits in order to protect bondholders. The tax increases and spending cuts needed to pay back railroad debt created lots of economic pain, extending recessions and removing important local services. But these judicially created protections for investors also preserved confidence in the bond market. This set the stage for a period in which cities were able to borrow huge amounts to build world-leading infrastructure, including everything from the reversing the Chicago River to building the Brooklyn Bridge. In contrast, newly white-dominated southern state governments were allowed to repudiate the debts accumulated by Reconstruction-era mixed-race governments. They were aided by an aggressive Supreme Court, this time creating modern sovereign immunity doctrine to protect these "redeemer" governments from having to pay their debts to bondholders. These decisions alleviated economic harm in the short term, but also meant that these states could not borrow easily, making it hard for them to build economically essential infrastructure.

Chapter 4 will take the story forward to 20th century, discussing the lack of bailouts in the Great Depression, the creation of municipal bankruptcy law, the Arkansas road debt crisis of 1932, and the New York City and Washington, DC, fiscal crises. These stories will show that rather than choosing one answer to the trilemma, the federal government adopted policies that mixed elements of all three approaches.

Chapter 5 will discuss the Great Recession and the municipal bankruptcies that followed. Its central argument will be that the mixed federal policies we saw in the 20th-century crises were extended and given institutional and ideological shape after the Great Recession, with policymakers and bankruptcy court judges wrestling with the tradeoffs of the trilemma directly.

Chapter 6 will discuss federal responses to state and local fiscal distress following the COVID-19 pandemic and the recession that followed.

Chapters 7 through 11 will develop principles for how the federal government should respond to state fiscal crises. They will show that bailouts, austerity, and defaults are families of policies. Inside each of these umbrellas, there are difficult choices to make about how to structure federal policy. But the four principles of prudence, balance, spreading, and resilience should guide policymakers, no matter how they weigh the harms along each leg of the trilemma.

Chapter 12 will serve as a conclusion, focusing on why structural failures in state politics make fiscal crises more likely.

PART II

WHEN WE'VE BEEN IN A BAD STATE

The Theory and History of Federal Responses to
State and Local Fiscal Crises

What Has Already Been Said about Federal Responses to State and Local Budget Crises?

What Has Been Left Out?

Scholars writing about how the federal government should respond to state and local fiscal stress fall into roughly two camps. One group argues that federal bailouts create excessive moral hazard. Another group argues that federal aid is instead a necessary form of macroeconomic stimulus given the pro-cyclical nature of state budgets. While this debate is important, it is incomplete.

This chapter will show that there is another consideration that has often been the dominant concern in federal responses to state and local budget crises: maintaining the ability of states and cities to borrow to build infrastructure and make other investments. It will explain how these three interests—avoiding moral hazard, stimulating the economy during recessions, and preserving state capacity to borrow—interact, laying out a "trilemma" at the core of federal responses to state and local budget crises.

1.1. State and Local Governmental Moral Hazard or the Problem of "Soft Budget Constraints"

One major school of economists and political scientists studying state and local budget crises focuses on the question of whether state and local governments face "soft budget constraints" or "moral hazard."[1] The basic idea is straightforward. If the federal government provides bailouts to states and cities in crisis, politicians in those jurisdictions and others will begin to expect them, and thus refuse to budget responsibly in the future.

While the idea is simple, the implications are dramatic.

The leading figure in this branch of the fiscal federalism literature is political scientist Jonathan Rodden.[2] The period from the 1980s through the early 2000s featured several national economic and financial crises set off in part by excessive subnational borrowing, most prominently in Argentina and Brazil.[3] Many countries that allowed their provinces to borrow extensively ended up having to bail them out. Countries as varied as Germany, Italy, Nigeria, Russia, and South Africa faced problems due to excessive subnational borrowing.

Why does this problem occur? Rodden notes that many classic arguments in favor of federalism—from Alexis De Tocqueville and the *Federalist Papers* to Charles Tiebout and Barry Weingast—imagine that devolving fiscal authority to subnational entities will result in greater fiscal discipline and wiser spending.[4] If state and local governments are mostly left alone to tax and spend, they will make people happier than if the federal government does it, the argument goes. Subnational governments will not waste as much money because of the threat of exit by overtaxed residents and the greater responsiveness of state and local elections.[5] Under these theories, the national government's proper role is to provide national public goods and to address inter-state externalities. But, otherwise, states and cities should be left alone to provide public services because they will do so more efficiently and popularly.

What these theories about the benefits of federalism leave out, Rodden argues, is the likelihood that, in a pinch, subnational governments will ask the federal government to bail them out.[6] If the federal government shows any real willingness to bail out subnational governments, subnational officials will realize that they do not face a hard limit on how much they can spend. State and local governments can keep spending and/or not taxing, relying on the willingness of the federal government to make up the difference when times get tough. Using economist Janos Kornai's famous term describing the finances of business firms backed by the government in socialist countries and those transitioning to market economies, their budget constraints aren't hard but "soft."[7]

If the federal government offers a bailout to one subnational government, all other subnational governments have an incentive to become fiscally reckless themselves. Not only will they expect a bailout themselves if things go badly, subnational governments will not want their taxpayers to end up being stuck paying for services elsewhere. (Bailouts are paid for out federal government revenue and thus from taxes paid by all residents, even as bailouts only benefit residents of governments who get them.) As a result, bailouts create a need for future bailouts. This is the problem of "moral hazard."

If the federal government offers bailouts, the supposed benefits of federalism will not be on offer. Subnational governments will compete with one another to be more profligate, not to be more prudent. Bailouts—or rather the expectation of bailouts—can bring down the whole system of fiscal federalism.

Seems bad! So why would the federal government ever offer bailouts? The difficulty comes from the fact that many federal officials will want very badly to bail out bankrupt states and cities. After all, the people who live and vote in subnational governments also live and vote in the country as a whole. National-level politicians will not want to see them suffer—failing to bailout subnational governments will mean that their constituents lose services and see higher taxes. Interest groups powerful at the subnational level can also lobby federal officials. And subnational officials are usually part of the same political parties and groups as national-level ones. Turning down a state or local government in need can be quite difficult.

Rodden shows that, to get out of this pickle, after providing bailouts, national governments often take control over subnational governments' fiscal affairs. The national government will pass taxes and then distribute money to subnational governments, rather than letting subnational governments set tax levels for themselves. National governments that offer bailouts also regularly impose strict spending and borrowing limits on subnational governments to reduce the moral hazard problem in the future. These steps address the problem of moral hazard, but mean abandoning benefits traditionally associated with fiscal federalism.

The result, Rodden argues, is that there are two stable equilibria. Either the national government makes a credible commitment not to bailout subnational governments, overcoming the political difficulty of saying no to a suffering state or city,[8] or the federal government does most of the taxing and heavily monitors subnational spending and borrowing, foregoing the benefits of fiscal federalism.[9]

The worst of all worlds is the intermediate case, where the federal government cannot impose discipline on subnational governments but also lacks the discipline itself to refuse to bail out those governments when they run into trouble.

> The real fiscal danger in the twentieth century was not . . . divided sovereignty . . . but rather a murky semi-sovereignty that comes about when a politically-constrained center dominates taxation but not spending and borrowing.[10]

Countries that want the benefits of fiscal federalism need to make firm commitments to not bail out subnational governments and to make these commitments clear to capital markets.

In places like the United States, Canada, and Switzerland, Rodden argues, the national government mostly has refused to bail out subnational governments.[11] As a result, lenders treat subnational governments in these countries like they are independent entities, looking at their tax bases and spending patterns when determining how much to lend and at what interest rates.[12] In contrast, in countries with mostly nationalized fiscal systems, the bond market treats subnational debt the same way it treats debt issued by the national government. Interest rates on subnational bonds are the same as interest rates on national government bonds, because lenders know that the federal government is effectively insuring state and local debt.

Other major figures understand the problem of state and local budget crises in roughly similar terms.[13] Economist Robert Inman argues that the first lines of defense against state governmental profligacy are structural factors like political parties that can constrain wayward state officials, a mature banking system that can differentiate between the credit risks of different states, and a mobile population that can punish wastrel state and local governments. When and where these don't exist, legal limits on state debt issuance in state constitutions and a federal policy of not providing bailouts can collectively help ensure that states don't spend too much and tax too little.

In practice, some combination of these limits has worked in the United States; Inman argues that, at least as of 2010 or so,[14] "U.S. local governments do face a mostly hard budget constraint."[15]

However, legal scholar Michael Greve and others have worried that recent developments mean that hard budget constraints are a thing of the past. According to Greve, the bailout of the banking industry during the Great Recession made arguments against state bailouts more difficult. Further, because a great deal of state debt is now in the form of underfunded public pensions, popular support for public employees makes bailouts more popular, lest states default and destroy the retirements of teachers and cops.[16] Others argue that a state default might create a systemic financial failure, bringing down other institutions like banks or major investors with it, making state bailouts more likely.[17]

Thus, when faced with a subnational fiscal crisis, the federal government may choose to provide bailouts even if officials understand that doing so creates substantial risks.

Notably, in 2020–21, the federal government's tool kit for responding to state and local fiscal pressures created by the COVID-19 pandemic and recession leaned very heavily on state and local aid. The aid did not take the form of jurisdiction-specific bailouts, but rather large amounts of aid given to all states, plus money given directly to cities, counties, school districts, and transit agencies.[18] Aid given to all jurisdictions does not have quite the same potential to create moral hazard, as it does not provide as powerful incentives to be profligate (states get the money regardless of whether they were heavily indebted). But it does reduce the risk of disaster, and thus reduces some incentives to be fiscally responsible.

As Rodden predicted and as will be discussed in Chapter 6, that aid came with substantial conditions, reducing state and local government's fiscal autonomy even as it filled their coffers. The original major aid package, the CARES Act of 2020, included rather strict restrictions on what the money could be spent on.[19] The American Rescue Plan (ARP), passed in 2021 after President Joe Biden came into office, relaxed the restrictions on what the money could be spent on, but included limits on the ability of states to take advantage of the new revenues to cut taxes.[20]

Even so, the aid seems to have created some moral hazard. Lenders have been willing to offer money even to the riskiest municipal borrowers at increasingly good rates, suggesting they believe a continuation of federal aid is likely.[21] Many fiscal experts and politicians have become worried that federal fiscal aid has been a "sugar high," that state and local officials have used to create new programs, continuing spending, or cut taxes, even though the federal aid will run out.[22]

It is worth noting, though, that the extent of moral hazard varies over time and is contingent on the politics of the era. For moral hazard to exist, state or local politicians have to believe that a bailout the federal government provided to some other jurisdiction years ago should influence their budgeting decisions today.

This relies on two assumptions. The first is that state and local officials are far-sighted enough when making spending and taxing decisions to even consider the possibility of a bailout in the future. Often, the explanation for why states and cities get into fiscal trouble in the first place is that politicians have short time horizons. Politicians want to see the benefits of spending or cutting taxes today when campaigning for re-election, but do not expect to be in office when debts come due. But, like the harm of bearing debt, the benefit of a potential bailout will come in the distant future. It is by no means obvious that today's politicians care at all about a potential benefit available that far in the future.

The other assumption moral hazard theories rely on is that state and local politicians must think a bailout given to some other state or local government in the past is evidence that their government will get a bailout in the future. There are reasons to doubt this assumption as well. Places are different from one another, and times change. Maybe a prior bailout came because that government's mayor or governor was in the same party as the president or the speaker of the House. Maybe it came because the federal budget was particularly robust at the time. Or perhaps the majority leader of the Senate at the time just did not believe in moral hazard. Given how contingent decisions to offer bailouts can be, it is not exactly clear what lesson, say, the mayor of Chicago today should take from the bailout of Washington, DC, in the 1990s.

Rodden offers evidence from other countries that bailouts do in fact lead to state and local profligacy. But even this is not determinative, as the time horizons of politicians may change over time and countries are different from one another. However, even if one rejects the idea that state and local politicians have sufficiently long time horizons to care about bailouts or are able to draw clear inferences from past actions, Rodden's argument still has force because of the influence of the bond market on incumbent politicians.

Bailouts limit the degree to which the bond market or other lenders pay attention to governmental budgets when lending.[23] That is, the bond market may pay attention to bailouts even if politicians don't. There is lots of evidence that this is the case. In jurisdictions where bailouts are common, lenders do not demand a premium when lending to fiscally imprudent subnational governments. But, in the United States, lenders differentiate between jurisdictions because they believe that states and cities represent different credit risks. This has an effect on how politicians write budgets. If profligacy leads to increased borrowing costs in the short-run, it creates costs that are on the radar of politicians, even those with short time horizons. Similarly, the risk that credit-rating agencies will create bad headlines for incumbents by issuing downgrades of state and local bonds encourages greater responsibility. In contrast, bailouts reduce bond market pressure on incumbent politicians to be prudent. One can believe that moral hazard exists as a phenomenon even if you don't think politicians take lessons from previous federal bailouts, because of the influence of the bond market.

Even if a bailout for one government does not guarantee a later bailout for a different government, it surely makes it seem a bit more likely, if only by removing the stigma surrounding bailouts. A bailout for one jurisdiction can affect other jurisdictions even if it isn't certain that the next jurisdiction will get a bailout. The increased likelihood of a bailout will affect both the probabilistic beliefs of officials and beliefs among lenders about how much risk they bear. For instance, when Detroit was not given a federal bailout, interest rates on debt for the fiscally troubled Commonwealth of Puerto Rico increased substantially, suggesting markets reduced their beliefs about the likelihood of a bailout, despite the dramatically different situations playing out in each jurisdiction.[24]

1.2. State Fiscal Crises and Macroeconomic Stabilization

The other common way of thinking about federal aid during state and local fiscal crises is that it is a way to achieve macroeconomic stabilization during recessions.

Textbook Keynesian economic theory suggests governments should run deficits during recessions to goose the economy. But states and cities have trouble running deficits. State constitutions require balanced budgets and limit the issuance of debt.[25] States and cities can't print money to finance their debts— only the federal government can do that. And credit markets won't lend to states and cities in the same way they lend to the federal government because state capacity to tax is more limited.[26] In theory, states and cities can save in advance of recessions and then spend down their savings to help alleviate macroeconomic problems. They do this to some extent, but their "rainy day funds" are rarely large enough to fully cover fiscal losses in severe recessions.

As a result, in economic downturns, states are forced to make budget cuts and raise taxes. As macroeconomic policy, this is extremely counterproductive. State and local cuts reduce aggregate demand and increase unemployment, extending recessions. For instance, after the Great Recession, private sector employment returned to its pre-recession peak in April 2014. But public sector employment still had not recovered to its peak until after 2018.[27] These massive losses in public employment help explain why the broader economic recovery following the Great Recession was so slow.

Further, cutting state budgets during recessions harms low-income households as economic conditions worsen. For obvious reasons, people with lower incomes are more reliant on social welfare programs, particularly during recessions.[28] A large part of the federal welfare state depends on state governments picking up part of the bill. The federal government has established a large number of "cooperative federalism" programs for which the federal government and states share funding responsibility—most notably Medicaid.[29] In other policy areas involving redistribution, like services for the homeless or redistribution through schools, states and localities provide either most or almost all of the funding.

States need to balance their budgets when revenues fall during recessions. As a result, they face pressure to cut social welfare programs at the exact moment when they are most needed.[30] Or, because state spending is matched by federal spending in cooperative federalism programs, states end up cutting the rest of their budgets to the bone to pay for the increased demand for social welfare during recessions. Another option is raising taxes, destroying economic activity when it is most endangered by weak demand.

To avoid these bad results, some scholars argue the federal government should be in the business of countercyclically aiding state and local governments, providing money to them in recessions and/or taking over welfare programs.[31]

These arguments apply to the ordinary pressure state and local budgets face during recessions. But solvency crises in individual state governments are just extreme versions of the same story. States and localities almost always face their worst budget pressures during recessions. When forced to the brink, states and cities have to cut the most essential programs—increasing school classes to intolerable sizes, taking police off the streets during crime waves, removing healthcare benefits from those in need at the worst time. Further, states and cities are not necessarily morally blameworthy for their fiscal crises. The national economy lurches for all sorts of reasons completely unrelated to the decisions of state and local policymakers, creating pressure on state and local budgets.[32]

As a result, these scholars argue that we should not think of federal interventions during state and local crises as creating soft budget constraints, but instead as a method for protecting the welfare state and engaging in macro-economic stabilization during recessions.

In theory, of course, the federal government could just offer more stimulus to individuals to counteract any negative effect of state retrenchment, either through more federal spending or through looser monetary policy. The Federal Reserve could just print money and drop it from a helicopter in amounts large enough to counteract the macroeconomic effect of state and local cutbacks. Doing so can even help state budgets. In 2020, aid to individuals and firms helped buoy incomes, which limited the fiscal losses faced by states and cities.

But, as law professor and economist Yair Listokin notes, one cannot simply assume federal fiscal or monetary policy will be sufficient to fight recessions— over the course of history, it often has not been.[33] Further, aid to states and cities is one of the most effective tools of recession fighting, directly supporting em-ployment in ways other forms of macroeconomic policy do not. Such aid may have drawbacks, but so do other types of spending during recessions.

1.3. State Budget Crises, Infrastructure, and Development

These two groups of scholars—those who focus on "soft budget constraints" and those who study the problem of pro-cyclical state spending—both provide a great deal of insight and wisdom. However, both groups leave out a central part of the story: the federal government's long-standing and extensive support for state and local debt.[34]

If the federal government were exclusively concerned with moral hazard, it would be very skeptical of state debt. After all, if states have lots of debt going into recessions, they are more likely to have fiscal crises and ask for bailouts. Similarly, if the federal government were mostly concerned with pro-cyclical state budgets worsening recessions, it would be skeptical of state debt in good times. It would instead encourage states to save when the economy is good, so they have a cushion when the economy is bad.

But the federal government is and has long been *aggressively* in favor of state and local debt. Federal law directly subsidizes debt by making interest on state and local debt exempt from income taxes.[35] The federal government also offers a huge array of subsidized direct loan programs to states and cities.[36]

The federal government's traditional reason for wanting state and local governments to take out debt is its desire to have them build public infrastructure. Both historically and today, states and local governments build, maintain, and own most of our infrastructure—roads, rail, water, sewers, school buildings, and so forth.[37] Even when Congress decides to spend large sums of money on infrastructure, as it did in 2021's Infrastructure Investment and Jobs Act, it does so through grants and loans to state and local governments, and often requires those governments to put up matching funds, amplifying federal spending.[38]

That is, state and local governments make most of the investments that form the backbone of the American economy.[39]

There is a good reason for this. In a country as large as ours, it is difficult for the federal government to determine where and when key pieces of public infrastructure should be built. Bureaucrats and politicians in Washington, DC, just do not know which sidewalks and sewer mains in towns in Oregon and Maine need replacing. As we will see in Chapter 4, the ability of American cities to build infrastructure without asking for permission from DC was an unsung part of the great urban economic growth of the late 19th and early 20th centuries.

Further, political scientists like Barry Weingast and John Ferejohn have long argued that our system of districted elections and state representation in Congress leads to "distributive politics" norms when it comes to infrastructure.[40] Each member of Congress pushes for projects in his or her district. From the early Republic, congressional spending on infrastructure has tended to be spread out among projects in every district or state, rather than providing money for the best projects.[41] Historically, when Congress directly funds infrastructure, it is mostly pork-barrel spending.

Two modern forces have served to alleviate Congress's inability to fund infrastructure. First, powerful and ideologically sorted political parties limit pork-barrel spending. "Distributive politics" is one way to create a majority coalition, buying support with district-specific projects. But strong political party leadership is another, as Mat McCubbins and Gary Cox argue.[42] Rather than providing some projects to everyone, the party that controls Congress may seek to improve the country as a whole and take credit for it as a party.

However, while our modern ideologically sorted Congressional political parties have limited pork in many ways, they have not led to the federal government actually building lots of infrastructure. Part of the explanation for this is congressional gridlock. But even during periods of one-party control of Washington, Congress often finds passing transportation bills difficult. Even when it does, as it did in 2021, federal spending supplements state and local spending, particularly when operations and maintenance are considered.

The other major trend aiding federal infrastructure spending is growing executive power. Congress can and does delegate project selection to administrative agencies, giving the president and expert civil servants the power to choose projects. This helps over overcome the pork problem, as the President has a national, not local, constituency. Indeed, the Infrastructure Investment and Jobs Act put a large sum (although a substantial minority of the total spending) into competitive grants controlled by the Transportation Secretary.[43] But Members of Congress lobby to influence these agency determinations as well. Further, worries that the President will use spending to entrench his political coalition (or not share the goodies widely) reduces Congressional incentives to delegate to the President.

So, while in theory the federal government could fund or build necessary public infrastructure, in practice it cannot do so regularly and well. There are famous exceptions to this, like the interstate highway system.[44] But these are exceptions to a more general rule. The political structure of the federal government is just not set up well to fund or build infrastructure directly.

Although it faces challenges in doing so itself, federal officials often very much want to encourage growth. As a result, Congress needs to find someone to produce needed infrastructure.[45]

The obvious alternative to the federal government building on its own is to let states and cities build infrastructure. Even though state and local governments are in many ways better positioned to plan and build infrastructure, they face challenges paying for it. State and local governments can only tax so much, due to concerns about exit (if taxes get too high, people and businesses may leave).[46]

Further, states and cities not only need revenue to build infrastructure but also need access to credit. Infrastructure is almost always paid for with borrowed money. A bridge lasts a long time. It doesn't make sense to force today's taxpayers pay for the entire bridge, while tomorrow's taxpayers get a free lunch (or rather, a free bridge).[47] Instead, states and cities spread the cost out by borrowing money for construction and then paying it back over time. But states and localities, particularly small ones, can face real constraints on raising capital.[48]

As a result, the federal government can help meet the nation's need for infrastructure, despite its own problems in producing that infrastructure, by working with state and local governments. It can subsidize state and local investments in infrastructure and also ensure that states and cities can finance those investments in capital markets. The main way the federal government does this today making the interest on municipal bonds—debt issued by state and local governments— exempt from federal income taxes. The tax exemption makes the interest rate on state and local bonds cheaper and thus encourages states and cities to borrow and build.

This concern does not go away during state and local fiscal crises. During crises, the federal government has often acted to promote future development and investments in infrastructure by states and cities by protecting creditors.[49] Ensuring that creditors get paid back makes them more willing to lend in the future, and at lower cost. Further, protecting creditors stops the problem of "contagion," or situations where a default in one state or city leads lenders to refuse to lend to other states or cities. If loans are regularly paid back, even when things look dire, lenders are more likely to offer credit at lower rates to more places.[50]

To understand how the federal government has behaved during state and local budget crises, it is essential to recognize that concerns about infrastructure development have often been a central part of federal policies toward states and localities in fiscal crisis. The need for state and local governments to build public infrastructure has been a real policy concern, just as worries about moral hazard and pro-cyclical fiscal policy have been.

1.4. Avoid Moral Hazard, Alleviate Recessions, and/or Build Infrastructure: Pick Two, But Not Three

The three goals of the federal government during state and local fiscal crises—avoiding moral hazard, alleviating recession, and promoting future infrastructure investment—present inherent tradeoffs. In economic crises, policymakers have to make choices about which goals to prioritize and which to sacrifice. As a theoretical matter, one can understand the problem facing federal officials looking at state and local budget crises as presenting an inescapable trilemma.

A graphical representation of the trilemma can be seen in Table 1.1.[51]

When faced with state and local budget crises, the federal government has three basic options.

If the federal government wants to avoid creating moral hazard problems or macroeconomic headwinds, it can refuse to offer bailouts and either encourage or provide a mechanism for the writing down of debt. That is, it can make creditors eat the losses. The downside of doing so is that it will roil municipal bond markets and reduce the willingness and capacity of governments to borrow.[52] Defaults will make it harder for states and local government to build infrastructure in the future, and make the cost of future projects more expensive.[53] This roughly describes the federal policy response to the 1840s state default crisis. The federal government can go even further, and aid states in resisting

Table 1.1 **The Fiscal Federalism Trilemma**

Federal Policies	**Goals** Avoid moral hazard among states and localities	Fight recessions	Promote future infrastructure investment by states and localities
Provide bailouts to heavily indebted states and localities	No	Yes	Yes
No bailout; make state and local taxpayers pay (i.e., help bondholders recover debts)	Yes	No	Yes
No bailout; encourage states and localities to write down debt	Yes	Yes	No

creditor pressure by creating new legal immunities for state governments, as the Supreme Court did in the 1880s and 1890s.

Or the federal government can seek to avoid bailouts while also encouraging future borrowing and lending. But doing so requires state and local governments to engage in massive cuts to their budgets and to raise taxes. As fiscal crises often come during economic crises, this will mean making recessions worse. This, give or take, describes the federal response to the "railroad bond" crisis faced by local governments in the second half of the 19th century. This also was how the federal government responded at first to several other crises, including the Arkansas Road Bond default of the 1930s and the New York City fiscal crisis of the 1970s.

The final option for the federal government are bailouts, which reduce recessionary pressures and encourage future subnational government borrowing. But bailouts for insolvent state governments create concerns about moral hazard, soft budget constraints, and state independence. Alexander Hamilton's assumption of state debts is an example of this strategy. The bailout of Washington, DC, in the 1990s is another example, and, to some extent, so were the federal responses in 2009 and over the course of 2020–21. At other times, the federal government changed its tune during the middle of a crisis, offering some limited financial support to places like Arkansas in the 1930s and New York City in the 1970s, after first pushing austerity or allowing defaults.

This only lays out the theory of the trilemma. The next few chapters, which review the history of state and local budget crises, will reveal how the trilemma has worked in action.

However, that there is a trilemma and that different choices have been made over time does not explain *why* officials choose different options. As we will see as we go through the history of federal responses, sometimes external conditions drive federal decisions. The long period of insufficient demand and low inflation after the Great Recession led Presidents Trump and Biden to support massive amounts of state aid in 2020 and 2021. The limited fiscal capacity of the federal government made bailouts unlikely in the 1870s.

Also, unsurprisingly, the ideological commitments of officials explains how they weigh these tradeoffs. Alexander Hamilton's goal of creating a strong national government led him to worry less about the centralization that would likely follow bailouts for states. Dislike of financiers in the post-Jackson Democratic Party led officials to refuse to bail out states and their bondholders in the 1840s. Support for westward expansion and economic development (and particularly for railroads) led the Supreme Court and politicians to support bondholders against localities during the railroad bond crisis of the 1870s. The broader federal effort to support Southern states after the Compromise of 1876 at the end of Reconstruction was reflected in the Supreme Court's holdings about sovereign immunity in the 1880s and 1890s.

Further, institutional factors influence these decisions. Politicians in Congress are generally very attuned to short-run economic factors. Officials not facing elections, like federal judges or officials of the Federal Reserve, are often (although not always) more attuned to the effect policy can have on long-run factors like investment infrastructure or moral hazard, but less sensitive to short-run suffering.

The chapters that follow will not take hard stances on what the "right" approach was to past state and local budget crises. Instead, they will simply lay out the policy tradeoffs that officials faced. For policymakers of any ideological stripe, it is necessary to have a clear-eyed view about the likely effects of any given response. For that, understanding the tradeoffs faced by officials in the past is crucial.

1.5. Appendix to Chapter 1:
Three Methodological Notes

Before proceeding, it is necessary to discuss three not-at-all obvious decisions about the methods employed in Chapters 2–6.

First, Chapters 2–6 will discuss federal responses to fiscal crises in local governments and fiscal crises in state governments using roughly the same analytical approach, even though there are obviously differences between states and cities.

The most important difference is that federal responses to local governmental fiscal crises are intermediated. That is, there is another government, namely the state government, that has both the most responsibility and the greatest powers to respond when a city or county faces a fiscal crisis. In addition to the tools available to the federal government, states can more directly command cities. Local governments are creatures of state law. The Supreme Court and state courts have held repeatedly that—outside of independent constitutional violations, like racial discrimination—individuals do not have a right to a particular set of local governmental boundaries, powers, or services.[54] States can change the boundaries of local governments or take away their powers. In crises, as will be discussed in Chapter 5, states will often seize control over local governments, displacing their elected officials with financial control boards or emergency managers.

There are other differences as well. Notably, the Constitution protects state governments and their instrumentalities from lawsuits with sovereign immunity but does not protect cities from their creditors.[55] There are other types of immunity that make it hard for creditors to recover against cities, but they are not as powerful as sovereign immunity.[56]

Even so, the federal government has often been forced to respond to local governmental fiscal crises. When doing so, it has faced a very similar set of tradeoffs as it has faced when addressing state governmental defaults. For much of American history, local governments were large relative to state governments, meaning that the capacity of states to provide bailouts was very limited. To this day, many local governments are big enough that, from a national perspective, their problems are of a kind with state crises. New York City's budget is roughly the same size as the budget of the state of Florida.[57] Los Angeles County, California, has 10 million residents, more than all but nine states.[58]

Also, the federal government can either supplement or oppose state responses to local fiscal crises. In some crises, states have acted on behalf of local governments to make creditors take losses, policies that the Supreme Court in the mid-19th century and the president in 1932 found objectionable and challenged. In other local crises, the federal government has worked with state governments. The state of Michigan provided aid to the city of Detroit during Detroit's bankruptcy case, which was being heard in a federal court under the federal municipal bankruptcy law. Congress provided loans to New York City to supplement New York State's response to the city's crisis.

While local governmental fiscal crises do present different questions from state fiscal crises, the policy choices facing the federal government—whether to provide bailouts, enable defaults, or encourage austerity—are relatively similar. Similar enough, at least, that it makes sense to study them together. However, each discussion of local governmental crises in the chapters that follow will bring into the discussion state governmental institutions, like state legislatures and state courts.

Second, Chapters 2–6 treat federal courts as policymakers on a par with Congress or the president, despite the fact that courts make decisions in different ways and face different limits on the scope of their authority. Courts are most often interpreting authoritative legal texts like the Constitution and legislation, not making policy on their own. Also, judges are not generally understood to be part of political coalitions in the way that elected officials are, but rather to stand somewhat outside of them. Many studies of federal responses to state and local fiscal crises, particularly those written by economists and political scientists, treat federal courts as if they mechanically apply easily understood legal rules.

But that is a very odd way of looking at how federal courts behave in this context (and, honestly, in most contexts). Courts face limits, but also have a great deal of discretion. In many state and local budget crises, federal courts have used this discretion to impose their policy views forcefully. As will be discussed in Chapter 3, federal courts regularly relied on their now-abdicated general common-law powers to adjudicate cases involving local defaults in the late 19th century, invoking policy concerns in a relatively free-form fashion. The Supreme Court refashioned sovereign immunity doctrine in the late 19th century, in concert with evolving federal policy about the end of Reconstruction. Contemporary municipal bankruptcy law delegates to courts huge amounts of discretion to shape law and make policy.[59]

One does not have to be particularly cynical about courts to believe that it makes sense to think of federal courts as part of the policymaking apparatus for responding to state and local fiscal crises.

Third, the history and examples in the book are all from the United States. As Rodden has shown, subnational governmental budget crises are common throughout the world. Even so, I decided to limit the scope of the project to American subnational governmental crises and federal responses. Telling the story in a purely domestic way highlights the historical roots of each major approach to fiscal crises and allows things like the role played by the structure of Congress to become apparent. That said, the solutions in Part III of the book are heavily influenced by the study of international examples, particularly the experiences and difficulties of international financial institutions like the International Monetary Fund and the World Bank in providing aid during fiscal and financial crises facing national governments. But to make things a bit simpler (there are already a lot of moving pieces in this narrative), I mostly left the international examples on the cutting room floor.

State Debt Crises through the 1840s

If you know anything about federal responses to state debt crises, you know about Alexander Hamilton's plan to assume state debts during the First Congress. But for scholars of state debt crises, the really crucial event came in the 1840s, when Congress considered something called the Johnson Report, which called for once again assuming state debts following defaults by eight states and a territory.[1] The federal government decided not to follow Hamilton's example, rejecting the recommendations of the Johnson Report and not intervening when eight states and the territory of Florida defaulted on their debts. This decision not to offer aid established a precedent with deep implications for fiscal federalism going forward.

This chapter will discuss the consequences of federal responses to these crises. Federal responses to state fiscal crisis in the 1790s and 1840s reveal how two of the three legs of the trilemma work.

Hamilton's bailouts preserved state budgets and created capacity for them to borrow, allowing states to build important infrastructure, like the Erie Canal. But the assumption of state debts also seems to have encouraged states to issue excessive amounts of debt. The bailouts gave lenders the impression that the federal government stood behind state bonds, encouraging lenders to finance what became untenable levels of state debt. That is, bailouts created moral hazard.

In contrast, the rejection of the Johnson Report really did lead to a reduction in moral hazard. Recognizing that they would have to pay off their debts themselves, state taxpayers pushed for, and won, state constitutional limits on the issuance of governmental debt. Further, some of the direct harms of defaults were borne by foreign investors rather than domestic taxpayers (although states, both those that defaulted and those that didn't, also raised taxes aggressively). But states found it harder to borrow going forward. When combined with state constitutional limits on borrowing, this meant state governments were not as heavily involved in infrastructure development for 80 or so years, with only local governments available to pick up the slack. Defaults led to reduced investment by state governments in infrastructure.

2.1. Hamilton, the Assumption of State Debts, and Moral Hazard

Because the story of the First Congress's debt assumption deal is familiar to anyone who has taken an American history course or seen the Lin-Manuel Miranda's musical *Hamilton*, I will only provide a brief summary. After the Revolutionary War, one of the central economic questions facing the country was what to do about the large amount of debt issued by Congress and by the state governments to fund the war effort.[2] The money was owed not only to the soldiers and suppliers who were paid for their services during the Revolutionary War but also to speculators who had bought those debts from the original creditors.

As part of his *Report on Public Credit*, Hamilton proposed that the federal government assume the debts incurred by states during the Revolutionary War.[3] The plan was for the federal government to convert both federal and state debt into newly issued federal bonds and pay them back in full over time. Hamilton argued that the federal government was in better position to raise money to pay

Statue of Alexander Hamilton, US Department of the Treasury, iStock image—© istock/ Joel Carillet

debt than states were, in part because state taxes would cause capital and population to leave jurisdictions that enacted them. Further, state debts during the
Revolution were incurred for the common defense of the new nation, not state-
specific projects.[4] Creating a larger stock of new federal debt also would stimulate
the economy by providing merchants with a medium for exchange, crucial for a
cash-starved country.[5] And having a substantial body of debt would enhance the
prominence of the new federal government, particularly among creditors who
would now rely on it for payments. Because it would have to tax to pay the debts,
assuming of state debts would be a powerful force for the strengthening of the
federal government. As Hamilton stated: "[I]t would cement more closely this
union of states."[6]

States that had already paid their debts—particularly Virginia, which had it,
as Miranda puts it, "made in the shade"—and Members of Congress opposed to
increased federal authority objected vociferously.[7] Many Members also objected
to making full payments to speculators, who stood to gain substantially despite
not having contributed their bodies and supplies to the war effort.[8]

Ultimately, a deal brokered between Hamilton, Thomas Jefferson, and
James Madison had the federal government assume state debts incurred for the
common defense during the Revolutionary War, but made changes in payments
between the states and the federal government that helped Virginia (and
also ensured that the location of the national capital would be in what is now
Washington, DC).[9]

For our purposes, the debate over debt assumption is less important than
its downstream effects. Hamilton's plan was a bailout for states. Replacing state
debts with federal bonds that were paid back over time and that could trade as
currency was a form of economic stimulus. As we will see in the next section, the
bailout made it easier for states to borrow going forward, allowing them to make
investments in infrastructure and state banks.

However, debt assumption by the federal government also had the effect
of creating a belief among officials and lenders Congress would aid states in
the future. The federal government again assumed state war debts from the
War of 1812 and those of Washington, DC, in 1836.[10] Many lenders developed a belief that debt assumption was going to be federal policy going forward, that the federal government provided what amounted to insurance for
state bonds. Further, bailouts had the effect of reducing the independence
and power of state governments to some degree, which was indeed what
Hamilton intended.

This is the trilemma at work. Unsurprisingly, this planted the seeds for the
next the next set of state fiscal crises.

2.2. The State Debt Crises of the 1830s and 1840s

In 1843, the federal government made a decisive break with Hamilton's policy of assuming state debts. Just as Hamilton's policy involved real tradeoffs—both gains and losses—so too did the new federal government's new policy.

To understand what happened in 1843, though, a little windup is necessary. In the early Republic, the federal government built very little infrastructure. In 1808, President Jefferson's secretary of the treasury, Albert Gallatin, proposed a substantial system of internal improvements. But outside of the National (or Cumberland) Road, Congress largely decided not to raise funds for them.[11] What infrastructure the federal government did build largely took the form of small projects spread across many districts, like lighthouses and navigation improvements.[12]

A reason for this is that Congress was ill-suited to build infrastructure. Gallatin's plan was rejected when some members of Congress attempted to turn it into a bill that only funded projects in one region.[13] President James Madison helped push an internal improvements bill that, to ensure passage, ended up spreading money around on improvements across states around the country. But Madison then turned around and vetoed it when it came across his desk, citing vague constitutional concerns, suggesting his offense at the kind of pork-barrel politics necessary to get an infrastructure bill passed.[14] President James Monroe was able to win passage of the General Survey Act of 1824, which gave the Army Corp of Engineers the power to designate specific high-value infrastructure projects, theoretically overcoming Congress's collective action problem by delegating project selection to the president.[15] But giving the president this much power sat uneasily with western populists, who worried that presidents controlled by eastern financial interests would be able to use control over infrastructure projects to build political support.[16]

When Andrew Jackson assumed the presidency, he took Madison's inconsistent opposition to the constitutionality and advisability of internal improvements and hardened it into a well-specified policy and legal vision, starting with his veto of the Maysville Road project.[17] Jackson and his successors opposed federal subsidies for private transportation companies, which were central to all infrastructure plans at the time, and all federal aid for roads and canals within states' territory.[18] Part of the justification for this position was constitutional; no clause of the constitution specified that Congress had the power to build internal improvements that were local or regional in scope. But it was also political, as Jackson believed federal spending was inevitably infected by inefficient logrolling and eastern banker influence.

As a result, state governments took the lead on American infrastructure development.[19] The first and most famous of these efforts was the Erie Canal, which transformed New York State's economy, creating huge amounts of wealth upstate and helping cement New York City's status as the nation's leading port and financial center.[20] It also led to huge shifts in population, with many people moving to upstate New York and Midwestern states, as produce and commerce could more easily travel between those areas and east coast markets.

In addition to being an engineering marvel and economic success, the Erie Canal was also an important innovation in municipal finance. The bonds issued to build the canal were among the first important municipal bonds in the United States, with tolls on the canal and an array of taxes set aside to repay debt.[21] The first set of Erie Canal bonds were purchased by ordinary merchants in New York, much like today's municipal bonds.[22] But as the Canal started to succeed, there was healthy demand for these bonds, both among wealthy American merchants and, crucially, from British and Dutch investors. Hamilton's assumption of state debts created confidence among foreign investors about the soundness of American state debt.

Toll revenue from the Erie Canal ended up being so abundant that the taxes were not even needed to pay back the money borrowed.[23] The revenue was so substantial that the Erie Canal fund became a "development bank" for New York State, making loans to support all sorts of state industrial policy, from extending credit to millers in Buffalo to helping rebuild New York City after a major fire in 1835.[24]

Many states attempted to replicate the success of the Erie Canal.[25] But unlike the original Erie Canal financing, many of these projects were backed exclusively by what historian John Wallis calls "taxless finance," or borrowing supported not by new taxes, but solely through expected future tolls or grants of monopoly for services along the project.[26] Aided by a surfeit of capital in London and Amsterdam and the good experience investors had in getting repaid during the Revolutionary War and the War of 1812, there was money available to borrow.[27] In the 1820s, Ohio, Pennsylvania, and Maryland built expensive canal networks. In the 1830s, Indiana, Illinois, and Michigan followed suit, while New York and Ohio built their systems out further as well, mostly without sufficient taxes to back the bonds.[28] Other states borrowed to fund different kinds of infrastructure and to establish state banks, particularly in the South.[29] The revenue projections used to support the projects were very aggressive, but investors went along.

State governments ended up taking out $193M in outstanding debt, more than 12% of the nation's GDP.[30] A few states went as far as abolishing state property tax systems, instead relying on other sources of revenue and debt.[31] Other states—particularly western ones like Ohio, Indiana, Illinois, and

Michigan—made extremely aggressive assumptions about how much property values would increase (and thus how much revenue would increase) to justify issuing large amounts of debt.[32]

The Panic of 1837, a major financial crisis, shook the nation's economy. States continued to borrow, though, aided by the efforts of Nicholas Biddle.[33] Biddle had been president of the Bank of the United States, which had just seen its charter expire (and not renewed by Biddle's enemy, President Andrew Jackson). The Bank had been reformed as the United States Bank of Pennsylvania, with Biddle still serving as president. Biddle worked hard to convince British investors to continue to buy state bonds. That the former chief banker of the United States was making representations about the safety of state investments surely helped create an impression of federal support for state bonds.

Within a few years, however, this borrowing became untenable.[34] Alabama, New York, Ohio, and Tennessee came close to defaulting, only pulling themselves back from the brink with aggressive tax increases and spending cuts.[35] Arkansas, Indiana, Illinois, Louisiana, Maryland, Michigan, Mississippi, Pennsylvania, and the territory of Florida all defaulted on their debts between 1840 and 1842.[36]

States responded differently to their defaults. Pennsylvania and Maryland, with substantial commercial economies, were able to resume payments on their debts by raising taxes.[37] Western states facing collapsing property prices were not able to do the same. Illinois and Indiana negotiated with creditors to reduce their debt service, and eventually resumed payment.[38] (These states weren't happy about it, though; Illinois officials at one point took to burning the bonds in question in a huge bonfire in front of the state house.) Arkansas, Florida, Michigan, and Mississippi, in contrast, repudiated a combined $14M in debts, either due to a lack of resources or an unwillingness to raise taxes.[39]

It was only a few generations after Hamilton convinced Congress to assume state Revolutionary War debt, so the idea that the federal government might come to the aid of states was not considered outlandish.[40] Foreign creditors began pushing Congress to bailout states, arguing that there was an implicit federal guarantee behind state debt.[41] In 1842, the federal government tried to borrow for itself but could not, as foreign investors responded to state defaults by treating the United States as a whole as a bad credit risk. Tensions were sufficiently high that former President John Quincy Adams thought that a failure to assume state debts might lead to war with Britain.

Despite this, the federal government refused to bail out the struggling states. In 1843, Congress received a major report by Congressman William Johnson proposing that the federal government assume some substantial portion of state debts.[42] Congress rejected it, declining to assume any state debts. Members of Congress worried that once again assuming state debts would encourage state profligacy and simply be too expensive for the federal government. States were left to figure things out themselves.[43]

This event—the rejection of the Johnson Report's recommendations— has been pointed to by scholars as *the* central moment in the history of fiscal federalism.[44]

If members of Congress rejected the Johnson Report in order to reduce moral hazard, they succeeded. States responded to the crises of the 1840s by blanching at the idea of ever again becoming excessively indebted. During the 1840s, 10 states adopted constitutional changes that restricted the capacity of state government to issue debt; another 8 did so between 1850 and 1860.[45] These restrictions took different forms. Some states adopted strict limits on how much debt could be issued.[46] Others required new debt to be covered by specific streams of tax revenue. State constitutional amendments also included limits on the use of state funds to buy shares of stock or the loaning of credit to private businesses.[47] Many also required bond issuance to be approved by a pop- ular vote. As John Wallis argues, these limits were largely successful in stopping states from relying on "taxless finance."[48]

In one branch of the fiscal federalism literature, these debt limits are seen as the sweet fruit of the Congress's decision not to bail out state governments.[49] Upon realizing the federal government would not help, states had to come to terms with the fact that they faced a hard budget constraint and had to take care of themselves. They adopted policies like debt limits and limits on spending to ensure they would be able to do so in the future.

Further, lenders really did face losses, particularly for more speculative loans to southern and western states. In other places, taxpayers bore more of the brunt, with states raising taxes sharply to cover their debt. But if the goal was to make British and Dutch lenders pay in part for encouraging the profligacy of state governments, federal policy worked.

But the federal refusal to bail out states also had the effect of reducing state in- vestment in infrastructure. Lenders punished defaulting and repudiating states, driving up their borrowing costs or, in some cases, cutting them off from credit markets entirely for decades.[50] And debt limits and the politics that produced them substantially limited the role of state governments in funding internal improvements.[51] It would be more than half a century before state governments became heavily involved in producing infrastructure.

During the state debt crises of the 1840s, the federal government did not try to encourage repayment or provide funds to repay lenders. That is, it chose the leg of the trilemma that harmed bondholders and risked future limits on lending and borrowing. And while this provided benefits, it also had a cost: state governments were increasingly out of the internal improvements game.[52] In a world where the federal government was not going to fund these projects, the fact that states were no longer doing so raised questions about who would actually build the civic infrastructure needed by a growing country.

Into that void stepped local governments.[53] But they too eventually faced fiscal crises. As will be discussed in Chapter 3, the next time the federal government would not allow a series of defaults to cause a decline in funding for civic infrastructure.

The Dual Debt Crises of the Second Half of the Nineteenth Century

The stretch from the end of the Civil War to the titanic election of 1896 is not considered by many to be one of the most exciting periods in American history. High school history classes regularly skip from the Civil War, tarrying for a much-much-too-brief period on Reconstruction and its demise, to the tumult of the Progressive Era, when figures like Teddy Roosevelt and Woodrow Wilson dominated politics.[1] To the extent this era registers as part of traditional popular historical narratives at all, it is private-sector robber barons, pervasive racial segregation, big-city political bosses and their machines, and mass immigration, rather than action in Washington, that receives the most attention.

But this period was a very active one for the building of the American state through large investments in infrastructure.[2] Railroads were built, with huge public subsidies, across the country. And cities planned and built much of our most famous public infrastructure, from the Brooklyn Bridge to the reversal of the Chicago River. Huge systems of newly built public works, from streetcars to aqueducts, made the fast urban growth of this era possible.

During this period, there were two major state and local debt crises. Rather than an Alexander Hamilton–like executive branch figure or a Member of Congress playing the lead role in responding to them, the Supreme Court emerged as the most important federal institution in allocating losses during these crises. Other federal officials played a part as well, but the Court played the decisive role.

In one of these crises, the repeating "railroad bond" crises that raged repeatedly from the 1860s through the 1890s, the Court stretched its powers in order to protect municipal bond investors when they sued defaulting cities and counties. That is, the Court regularly favored creditors over local governments. The Court's decisions were intended to keep capital flowing to railroads and other infrastructural projects. This was consistent with the broad strokes of federal policy under the then-dominant Republican Party coalition, pushing for the development of the West and knitting together the internal market of the country through trade facilitated by railroads.

In the other, the repudiation of Reconstruction-era debt by newly empowered white-only Southern state governments in the 1870s and 1880s, the Court made a series of decisions in hotly disputed cases that protected state governments against the holders of state bonds. Here, the Court favored state governments over their creditors. This too was consistent with broader federal policy, in this case, the desire to end Reconstruction after 1876.

Neither post-Reconstruction Southern state governments nor local governments received bailouts, but federal policy about who had to bear the costs of heavy indebtedness was radically different. And, as suggested by the trilemma, the effects were very different as well.

Court decisions forcing cities and counties to repay their railroad bond debts created substantial short-term economic harm and suffering. But they also set the stage for the cities to borrow to build world-class roads, bridges, aqueducts, and public buildings. Southern state governments' debt repudiations, enabled by the Court, allowed them to offload costs on to creditors, reducing short-term economic harm. But it also meant these states faced challenges borrowing during the period in which the rest of the county built so much important civic infrastructure.

3.1. The Railroad Bond Crises

The period after the defaults and state constitutional reforms of the 1840s was marked not by a decline in subnational governmental borrowing, but by a change in the identity of the borrowers. In 1840, total local governmental indebtedness was around $25M and state indebtedness $175M. By 1880, things were reversed, with local governments owing $821M and states only $275M.[3]

This huge increase in local governmental borrowing led to both glories and crises. Much important infrastructure was built, but many jurisdictions ran into serious trouble. There were a huge number of municipal defaults in the period from before the Civil War to the turn of the century, including major cities like Mobile, Alabama (1839 and again in 1873); Detroit, Michigan (1841); Bridgeport, Connecticut (1843); Chicago, Illinois (1857); Philadelphia (1857) and Pittsburgh, Pennsylvania (1861 and 1877); Savannah, Georgia (1876); Memphis (1870s) and Nashville, Tennessee (1870s); New Orleans, Louisiana (1870s); and San Antonio (1870 and 1894) and Houston, Texas (1875 and 1887).[4]

Most municipal defaults were associated with railroad bonds.[5] Railroads were built up rapidly in the mid-19th century, particularly after the Civil War.[6] The railroad was the most important technology of the period, drastically reducing shipping costs and allowing the country to develop a truly national economy. Support for a national railroad system was a central piece of the policy program of the Republican Party political coalition that dominated American politics during and after the Civil War. The railroad was a crucial tool for promoting their goals of facilitating trade among the states, creating a truly national internal market, and westward economic expansion.[7]

Congress heavily subsidized the intercontinental railroads, largely with giant land grants.[8] Federal support for railroads was a major break with Jacksonian-era hostility to federal spending on internal improvements.[9] The federal government ended up granting, in aggregate, an amount of land almost the size of the state of Texas to support railroad construction.[10]

The transcontinental and other major lines were not the only important railroads built during this period. Railroads expanded across the whole country, building a network for transporting crops and goods. While the goal was a national market, the specific routes through which railroads ran had huge implications for which places prospered. Cities rose out of cornfields wherever railroads developed hubs.[11] Final goods producers moved near train hubs, and intermediate goods producers and service providers moved near factories. As economists put it, during this period there were huge "agglomeration" gains from this phenomenon of co-location by firms.[12] Even with the development of railroads, shipping costs were still remarkably high relative to what we see today. Businesses co-locating in railroad hubs addressed shipping costs in two ways, by reducing shipping costs among firms in the same city (because they were close to one another) and by the costs of inputs and of sending out final goods (because they were next to the railroad). The cities that became hubs for the major railroads during this period, most famously Chicago, grew extremely quickly.[13] Many less famous cities wanted to achieve the same types of gains on a smaller scale.

Understanding the potential for growth and dreaming of grandeur, local governments issued large amounts of municipal debt to buy shares in railroad companies or to otherwise offer them subsidies to encourage them to come through town.[14] Local governments often had more access to capital markets than private companies did (although such projects usually combined both public and private money, often raised from subscriptions by local residents.)[15]

But there were obvious problems with this rush to spend local governmental money on rail, though. To start, with canny rail companies all around the country promoting the possibility of fast economic growth to rural towns, there was a huge amount of fraud. Many cities and counties that offered subsidies were left holding the bag for rail projects that were never finished.[16]

More importantly, not all of these cities could achieve even smaller versions of Chicago-like gains, almost definitionally. Firms wanted to cluster together near railroad hubs to reduce shipping costs. But if firms cluster, there can only be so many winners.[17] And railroads, which face huge fixed costs from constructing lines, are prone to financial collapse when there is lots of competition. Competition drives down the price of shipping to the marginal cost of providing the service, leaving firms without enough money to cover the debts associated with constructing the line.[18] A report to Congress in 1886 found that the economic problems of the railroads were in large part due to overbuilding, which was itself driven by government subsidies.[19]

When economic downturns occurred in 1857 and 1873, many railroads failed, throwing local governments into financial distress.[20] Many local governments defaulted and/or repudiated their debts. After 1873, somewhere between $100M and $150M of municipal bonds were in default (out of about $800M in total municipal debt).[21]

These efforts ran into a huge stumbling block: the Supreme Court. The Court decided hundreds of cases involving municipal bonds and local defaults during this period, more than it did on any other subject.[22] Its decisions were aggressive, forcing municipalities to pay their debts on railroad bond cases to ensure continued investor interest in the broader municipal bond market.[23] At times, the Court engaged in jurisprudential gymnastics, abandoning established precedent and disregarding fraud and malfeasance, in its zeal to force municipalities to pay their debts.

The Supreme Court's determination to enforce the debts of fiscally distressed municipalities during painful economic times caused real suffering across the country. The harsh reductions in services and sharp increases in local taxes needed to resume payments on local debts created social harms and worsened recessions. Further, the Court's decisions in this area completely transformed federal law, for better or worse, and caused a huge revolution in state constitutional law as well.

But these decisions also came with benefits. The Court's support for municipal bond markets paid off, helping set the stage for an astounding expansion of public infrastructure during the end of the 19th century. Put another way, the federal government—largely through the Court but also the rest of post–Civil War Republican Washington—adopted a policy along one leg of the trilemma, one that avoided bailouts and harm to the municipal bond market. But it did so at the cost of making recessions far worse.

3.1.1. Railroad Bonds in the Courts

Following the decline in state investment following the defaults and near-defaults of the 1840s, supporters of new infrastructure, and particular railroads, turned to local governments.

State courts were forced to resolve many questions about the constitutionality of local governments offering subsidies to, and buying stock in, railroads.[24] In 1853, in *Sharpless v. Mayor & Citizens of Philadelphia*, the Supreme Court of Pennsylvania described the issue as "the most important cause that has ever been in this Court since the formation of the government" because of the importance of the railroad to economic development.[25] *Sharpless* upheld local subsidies despite worrying that many investments in railroads would fail, meaning "a burden would be imposed on certain parts of the state, as the industry of no people has ever endured without being crushed."[26] But the state constitution did not explicitly bar such subsidies, the court reasoned, and thus the legislature could authorize cities to issue debt to support railroads.

Pennsylvania was not alone; courts and legislatures around the country also allowed local governments to issue debt to buy stock or otherwise support railroads.[27]

But, after the Panic of 1857, many cities had trouble making payments on these railroad bonds. State courts started reversing themselves, writing opinions holding that debt issued to benefit railroads violated state constitutions and therefore did not need to be paid back.[28] The pressure on state court judges, most of whom were directly elected, to do so was immense. The taxes and public service cuts necessary to pay off these bonds after the Panic were brutal and were creating substantial economic and social duress.[29]

Faced with adverse state court decisions and local repudiations, debt holders—mostly foreign or from the east coast—sought refuge in the federal courts.[30] The same thing happened following crises for the next 30 or so years.

Iowa was an early epicenter of the railroad-mania-induced debt crisis. In 1853, in *Dubuque County v. Dubuque & P. R. Co.,* the Iowa Supreme Court read a clause in the state constitution that banned the use of public money to purchase shares in companies to only apply to the state government itself, and not to local governments.[31]

Cities or counties were free to invest in railroads to their hearts' content. And boy did they. With cities providing huge amounts of subsidies, the state went "railroad crazy."[32] Iowa went from having 68 miles of railway track in 1855, to 891 in 1865, and 2,683 in 1870, a nearly 40-fold increase in 25 years.[33]

Following the 1857 crash, a lot of railroad investments went bust. Localities across Iowa began defaulting on their debts,[34] In 1862, in *Burlington & Missouri Northern R.R. v. Wapello,* the Iowa Supreme Court reversed its prior ruling in

City of Dubuque (which was only nine years old) and found bonds issued by local governments to purchase shares in railroads to be unconstitutional and thus unenforceable.[35]

Capturing the obvious, the *Wapello* court noted that finding the bonds unenforceable "at this late date" might "expose ourselves and our people to the charge of insincerity and bad faith."[36] Despite this, the court argued that bondholders could still appeal to the "moral sense and a public faith" of Wapello County residents to encourage them to pay their debts.[37]

Bondholders understandably did not feel particularly reassured by this argument. Legal scholar Joan Williams notes that "[t]he Iowa bond repudiation sent shock waves through the American business and financial community, which feared widespread repudiation of municipal debt and disruption of national credit markets."[38]

One of the bondholders' key antagonists was the pride of the bar of the city of Keokuk, Iowa: Samuel Freeman Miller.[39] Keokuk, like many places in Iowa, subsidized railroads in an effort to grow and, in its case, to preserve its role as an important shipping node on the Mississippi River.[40] But it never quite became a railroad hub, and railroads that ran across bridges over the Mississippi diminished the importance of its river port.[41] After the Panic of 1857, the city's economy collapsed, and the government could no longer service the heavy debt load it had undertaken to try to get railroads to come to town. Properties fell into delinquency and had to be seized and auctioned. Services were cut to the bone and, absent money to pay for enough police, a crime wave struck the city.[42]

Miller, the city's leading lawyer, became an "antibond warrior," representing towns challenging the legality of their debts and becoming a political celebrity in Iowa.[43] President Abraham Lincoln appointed Miller to the US Supreme Court in 1862.

Despite the fact Justice Miller is now best known for his opinion in the *Slaughter-House Cases,* cabining the influence of the Privileges and Immunities Clause of the Fourteenth Amendment, Miller's crusade against the enforceability of municipal debt was the issue to which he was most committed during his tenure on the Court. His antibond activism on the Court made him sufficiently popular that he was almost nominated for president in 1880 and 1884.[44] As historian Michael Ross shows in his terrific biography of Miller, his best efforts were in vain; Miller was unable to push the Court to adopt his position.

The issue came to a head in 1863. Foreign creditors frustrated by state court decisions in Iowa turned to the federal courts. Cities, unlike states, could not invoke sovereign immunity to keep themselves out of federal court, although they did have other defenses.[45] And bondholders faced a problem in these suits. They had bought bonds issued by Iowa cities that were governed by Iowa law.

"Antibond Warrior" and Supreme Court Justice Samuel Freeman Miller, the Pride of the bar of Keokuk, Iowa, Brady-Handy Photograph Collection from the Library of Congress Prints and Photographs Division, public domain. Courtesy of Wikimedia Commons.

Iowa courts, not federal courts, have the power to decide the meaning of Iowa law. Iowa courts had already told the bondholders that their bonds were illegally issued and thus unenforceable. Further, just a year earlier in 1862, in *Leffingwell v. Warren*, the Supreme Court held that it was bound to apply state courts' "latest settled adjudication[s]" about the proper interpretations of state statutes and state constitutions.[46]

Things seemed stacked against bondholders. In *Gelpcke v. Dubuque*, the Supreme Court had to answer the question of whether holders of municipal bonds found invalid due to the state court's *Wapello* decision could enforce them in federal court.[47] While Iowa courts had changed the law for investors, there seemed to be no reason for a federal court to upset the decision of a court of sovereign state about the legal status of bonds issued by that state.

One possible argument for the Supreme Court's holding in favor of the bondholders might have been that Iowa had violated the Contract Clause of the US Constitution, which forbids states from passing any "Law impairing the Obligation of Contracts."[48] The *Wapello* decision certainly impaired contracts. But the Supreme Court had been very clear that the Contract Clause applied only to "laws" or legislative impairments of contracts, and not to judicial changes about how to interpret or apply contracts.[49] So that argument was out.

But the Court ruled in favor of the bondholders nonetheless. The Court used its common-law powers, applicable here because the case involved litigants from different states. Under the reading of the Rules of Decision Act in the famous case of *Swift v. Tyson* (no longer good law), the Court had the power to determine for itself what law should govern in the case in the absence of state statutes. And then it found that the Iowa Supreme Court could not retroactively find that bonds were illegally issued and unenforceable if it had previously allowed such bonds to be issued.[50]

In a rhetorical flourish, the Court acknowledged that it was creating this legal rule despite the Iowa Supreme Court's contrary interpretation: "We shall never immolate truth, justice, and the law, because a State tribunal has erected the altar and decreed the sacrifice."[51]

Miller dissented to no avail. He noted that the majority's decision directly controverted existing precedent. He also made an argument that presaged what the Supreme Court would do 75 years later in *Erie R.R. v. Tompkins*. In *Erie*, the Court reversed *Swift*'s interpretation of the Rules of Decision Act and foreswore its general common-law powers in cases with diverse parties, instead giving state supreme court rulings the same power in federal court that they have in state court. Just as the Court would later argue in *Erie*, Miller argued that the majority's approach in *Gelpcke* created two overlapping legal rules, one applicable in state court to cases filed by Iowan creditors against Iowa towns and the other applicable in federal court to cases filed by non-Iowans.[52]

But legal niceties—like the nature of the federal system or *stare decisis*—could not stop the Court from enforcing debts and protecting bondholders.[53] After *Gelpcke*, the Court went on to decide case after case involving railroad bonds in favor of bondholders.[54]

One key issue courts were asked to resolve was whether questionably issued municipal bonds were "negotiable securities." If they were negotiable securities, bona fide purchasers—people who bought them on the open market in good faith—could recover against cities even if there was some reason the bonds should not been issued in the first place.

In *Knox County v. Aspinwall*, the Court held that municipal bonds were subject to the bona fide purchaser rule and enforceable even when the public record revealed errors in their issuance.[55] In *Mercer County v. Hackett*, the Court held that where municipalities had the power to issue bonds, such bonds were to be treated as negotiable securities in federal court even if a state court had ruled that they were not.[56]

The epidemic insanity of the people, the folly of county officers, the knavery of railroad "speculators," are pleas which might have just weight in an application to restrain the issue or negotiation of these bonds, but cannot prevail to authorize their repudiation, after they have been negotiated and have come into the possession of bona fide holders.[57]

But why make taxpayers, rather than bond purchasers, responsible for the "insanity," "folly," or "knavery" of bond issuance? In later cases, the Court was very clear that its goal was to encourage and protect investment in the municipal bond market.[58] If "distant purchasers were under obligation to inquire before their purchaser . . . whether certain contingencies of fact had happened before the bonds were issued," the bonds' "market-value would be disastrously affected."[59] In one case, the Court wondered whether a requirement that purchasers check the public record before buying bonds would keep any "sane person" from participating in the bond market.[60]

The Court also worked hard to get local governments to actually pay creditors back, over the objections of local officials, who did not want to raise taxes during painful economic times. Federal courts began issuing *mandamus* orders to compel city and county officers to levy taxes to pay back bonds. They did so even when state laws limited cities' taxing authority. For instance, in *Von Hoffman v. City of Quincy*, the Court found that a state law taking away a local government's authority to pass a special tax, passed after bonds backed by that special tax were issued, violated the Contract Clause. It was thus proper for a court to issue a *mandamus* order forcing local officials to enact taxes even though the state government had told them not to.[61]

Perhaps the most notable case of this type was *Butz v. Muscatine*. The Court ordered local officials to levy stiff tax increases even when a preexisting city charter specifically limited property tax increases.[62] Iowa courts had decided that state statutes requiring local governments to pay their debts did not override city charters limiting property tax increases. State courts usually have the final word on the meaning of state laws. The Court just ignored those decisions, substituting its own reading, noting that "there are several adjudications of the highest court of the State more or less adverse to the views we have expressed. We do not deem it necessary more particularly to advert to them."[63]

Local government officials took dramatic steps to avoid these *mandamus* orders. The Supreme Court made a distinction between ordering officials to raise taxes, something they found within their *mandamus* power, and simply raising taxes by court order, which it thought was beyond its authority. Elected local officials took to immediately resigning after conducting official business, leaving the court with no one to order to raise taxes.[64] Somewhat surprisingly, this gambit sometimes worked, depending on whether state law allowed for marshals to be appointed to levy taxes in cases of vacancies. Other local officials just hid from federal officials, holding local meetings "under bridges or in out-of-the-way places" so federal officials could not find them and order them to raise taxes.[65] One court order was only enforced when a court bailiff snuck into a local meeting disguised as a "drunken tramp" and was able to serve papers on city officials.

These *mandamus* orders led Iowa to the "brink of rebellion" according to historian Charles Fairman.[66] Iowa courts began issuing injunctions forbidding local officials from collecting taxes after federal courts issued ruled that they must.[67] The Supreme Court pushed back, holding that state courts could not enjoin tax collectors from following federal court orders.[68] At one point, Keokuk residents offered to indemnify local officials who were fined for ignoring federal court orders.[69]

Cooler heads prevailed, and federal court orders were enforced, but a later flare-up of resistance to federal court mandamus orders in 1870 caused President Ulysses S. Grant to state that "if it becomes by duty to use force to execute the laws of Iowa . . . I shall do so without hesitation."[70]

Just so we are clear, in 1870, five years after the end of the Civil War, President Grant, who had been the most important general of the Union Army during the Civil War, threatened to send the Army to the staunchly union state of Iowa over a dispute about . . . *municipal bonds*. That's how serious this was.

Later cycles of railroad bond collapses led to new avoidance strategies. State legislatures became very creative in their efforts to help localities avoid paying their debt.[71]

One common (if completely ridiculous) ploy was "corporate suicide."[72] States would create new local governments to govern the same territory as existing, heavily indebted cities. The state would assign to the new entity the exclusive power to tax property in the city. The new city might then buy the assets of the old one. Creditors could attempt to recover against the old municipal government, but they would be left suing an entity without assets or ability to raise money through taxes.

In *Mobile v. Watson*, the Court put an end to this creative form of debt avoidance, holding that "successor" cities were liable for debts incurred by their predecessors, even though they were newly created legal entities with no formal relationship to the old cities.[73] Notably, the Court's decision in *Mobile* (and several other cases[74]) stand in stark contrast with the Supreme Court's long-standing rule that, absent some constitutional violation, states are free to organize and re-organize their local governments as they see fit.[75] (I will return to *Watson* and its implications for financial innovations like New York City's "Big MAC" bonds in the appendix to Chapter 9.)

The Court shot down state and local efforts to avoid creditors at every turn. Miller dissented over and over again. His objection was not jurisprudential, but ideological.[76] In a letter to his brother-in-law, Miller wrote, "It is the most painful matter connected with my judicial life that I am compelled to take part in a farce . . . to give more to those who have already, and to take away from those who have little, the little they have."[77] Miller had very little sympathy for the "gambling stockbroker of Wall Street."[78] Such investors, he said later, "engage in no commerce, no trade, no manufactures, no agriculture. They produce nothing."[79]

The cumulative effect of the railroad bond decisions transformed American law. The Court relied on its common-law authority to make determinations in cases in diversity cases in federal court under *Swift v. Tyson*. But these decisions were not a clear application of the rule of *Swift*. Scholars like Tony Freyer, Randall Bridwell, and Ralph Witten have convincingly argued that *Swift* was understood for its first 20 or so years to be a more modest doctrine keyed to customary practices and largely aimed at avoiding bias against out-of-state interests in state court decisions.[80] The felt need to protect railroad bond investors was one of the central forces that pushed the Court to embrace a more swaggering policymaking common-law authority under *Swift* that was later abandoned in *Erie Railroad v. Tomkins*.[81]

Further, as legal scholar L.A. Powe argues, the approach taken by the Court in these cases led to the development of its freedom of contract substantive due process doctrine in the "*Lochner*-era" of the late 19th and early 20th centuries. Through adjudicating these cases, the Court developed and "became accustomed to a free-wheeling jurisprudence."[82] This openness toward policymaking "left to the Court a legacy of activism which transcended any individual opinion."[83]

What explains why the Court was so willing to push legal doctrines to their breaking point in these cases? Why overcome the strong legal arguments made by Miller and the sympathetic claims of taxpayers to rule in favor of foreign bondholders?

Miller thought the answer lay in favoritism for the rich. While there was some of that to be sure, this can't explain what the Court did. After all, the Court was far from universally pro-investor. In 1876, at the height of municipal bond cases, the Court allowed substantial regulation of the railroad industry and grain elevators by states in the *Granger* cases.[84] The Court also lined up behind Miller to firmly reject efforts to use public money to support private industries *other* than railroads.[85] Miller's contention just does not fit the full set of decisions made by the Court.

Instead, the policy impetus behind the Court's railroad bond decisions is best understood as an effort to protect municipal bond markets in order to promote infrastructure development. Building railroads and other civic infrastructure was a major goal of federal policy. As Powe notes, "[r]ailroad development, the key to opening the country economically, required assistance. The cases fully articulated the special importance of railroads to the country."[86] The Republican political coalition (which had appointed most of the Justices) broadly supported the developmental program of railroad subsidies.

To encourage the building of infrastructure, the Court needed to support the municipal bond market. In the railroad bond cases, the Court focused on preserving the ability of bond purchasers to make investments without being taken advantage of by state courts and local governments. Given the central role played by local investment in expanding the railroad system, the soundness of municipal debt markets was an important national issue. The victory by bondholders was not complete—they still had to negotiate with cities to get paid in fact, often accepting haircuts that reflected local jurisdictions' real ability to pay—but it was far better for them than it would have been had the Court sided with Justice Miller.[87]

The Court effectively served as the enforcer of part of the federal government's pro-railroad policy. This entailed making local taxpayers face extraordinary hardships and extending recessions so the bond market would continue to function. The Court made a choice along the trilemma with attendant costs and benefits.

3.1.2. Railroad Bonds and Local Government Law

State officials responded to the railroad bond crises by attempting to limit the power of local governments, but not in ways that excessively limited their ability to borrow to build infrastructure. Despite the fact that states amended their constitutions to impose debt limits on municipalities, and judges developed legal doctrines narrowing the powers of cities, municipal investments in infrastructure went up. Why? Federal protections for creditors kept the municipal bond market strong, meaning that this round of state constitutional changes did not destroy the capacity of governments to borrow to build infrastructure.

After the railroad bond defaults, states adopted constitutional reforms to limit the ability of local governments to issue debt.[88] Between 1872 and 1879, 19 states passed constitutional amendments restricting the ability of cities to provide aid to private corporations.[89] Many states passed strict limits on the total amount of debt that municipalities could issue, often tying the amount of debt that could be issued to the assessed value of property in the jurisdiction.[90] Many states also created procedural restrictions on debt issuance, requiring public votes before bonds could be issued or limits on bond maturity.[91]

On top of these debt limits, local governmental authority was cabined more broadly. Iowa Supreme Court judge, famous local government and municipal debt law scholar, and Samuel Miller's close friend, John Forest Dillon, developed a set of legal doctrines that dramatically reduced the powers of city governments.[92]

Dillon's treatise on municipal corporations laid out "Dillon's Rule," the best-known doctrine in local government law. The treatise reflected Dillon's deep distrust of the judgment of local governments, which was surely shaped by the railroad bond crisis.[93] The background rule applied by most state supreme courts for much of the 19th and 20th centuries (and to this day, in some places), Dillon's Rule declares that local governmental authority should be limited to powers explicitly granted by state legislatures, powers incidental to those expressly granted, and powers necessary to achieving the ends of the municipality.[94] Further, Dillon's Rule tells courts to rule against the existence of local authority if there was any ambiguity in the state's enabling laws.

In the 1980s, legal scholar Gerald Frug argued that Dillon's Rule was part of a long effort to remove local governments from their role as participants in economic life, and in so doing, to perfect the divide liberalism demands between state and market.[95] But as I have argued elsewhere, the content of Dillon's Rule can be better explained by state officials' reasonable skepticism toward local subsidies to firms, given the nature of agglomeration economies at the time.[96] Given the high transportation costs of the period, cities had a strong incentive to subsidize firms to come to their cities, as one firm coming would draw others. If all cities did this, though, it would lead to a huge amount of beggar-thy-neighbor competition for firms and a huge amount of waste. This was not an idle concern either; this is exactly what happened with railroads. Dillon's Rule reasonably limited the range of things that cities could do more broadly as a way to limit their ability to subsidize industry indirectly. But it did not stand in the way of their promotion of basic infrastructure and services. Understanding Dillon's Rule in its original context provides a clearer view of what was at stake.

Similarly, the "public purpose" doctrine forbade local governments from using tax dollars to support private purposes like businesses. As articulated by Dillon in his treatise on the powers of municipal governments, the rule served to narrow the role of local government, even as it did not stop cities from providing basic services.[97] The US Supreme Court—with Justice Miller writing—cited Dillon's description of the public purpose doctrine, holding that municipal aid to private industries other than railroads was *ultra vires* and impermissible.[98]

Although local governmental support for private industry fell, local governments continued to borrow in order to fund public investment.[99] This time, unlike in the 1840s, debt limitations did not stand in the way of borrowing.

Local governmental debt as a percentage of GDP rose from 1.6% in 1840 to 6.1% in 1870 to 7.1% in 1880, took a brief decline in 1890 to 6.7%, and then rose thereafter, increasing to over 10% in 1902 (roughly what it is today, despite some ups and downs).[100] The high period of Dillon's Rule was also a growth period of municipal investment in public services and utilities.

Local governments also developed tools to get around debt limitations.[101] Three of the most significant innovations were special assessment bonds, revenue bonds, and special authorities.[102] Special assessment bonds (funded by nontax charges to properties near a public improvement) and revenue bonds (funded by fees or other charges, often from the project itself) are not backed by the "full faith and credit" of the issuing government. If the charges or fees that support them cannot cover the cost of paying back the debt, bondholders are out of luck, theoretically at least.[103] These tools increased borrowing capacity because courts ruled that the debt issued to fund these bonds does not count toward debt limits.[104] Special authorities and districts (new governments created by either local or state governments) are able to issue debt not subject to the debt limits of the governments with which they share territory.[105]

These innovations enabled the huge increases in local borrowing, despite the enactment of debt limits. And because efforts to default on debts were foiled by the Supreme Court, bond markets were still willing to fund new infrastructure investments.

This growth in public services and infrastructure can plausibly be seen as the product of the prior period's strong enforcement. After 1893, the municipal bond market grew tremendously and saw few defaults.[106] The Court's support for the municipal bond markets, at the expense of taxpayers and macroeconomic conditions during several recessions, set the stage for an amazing infrastructure expansion.

3.1.3. America's Urban Civic Infrastructure: "The Achievements of Government . . . Rivaled the Feats of the Old Testament God"

In popular imagination, the city governments of the late 19th century are known for their corruption—Boss Tweed and all that.[107] And while there surely was a great deal of corruption, the second half of the 19th century was also a period in which cities built an amazing amount of public infrastructure. The civic infrastructure in American cities was far more advanced than those of their international peers. This can be credited in large part to local governments' easy access to capital.

Many of greatest pieces of urban infrastructure in the United States date back to this period—New York's Central Park, Brooklyn Bridge, and the Second Croton Aqueduct; Boston's Public Library; Chicago's Chesbrough Sewers; and Baltimore's Gunpowder Water Tunnel.[108] The quality of urban engineering grew tremendously, and cities developed mechanisms for achieving previously unimaginable feats.[109]

Historian Jon Teaford writes that the City of Chicago:

> had ordained that the level of the swampy city be raised ten feet, and it had been done. [It] ordered that the flow of Chicago River be reversed and so it was reversed. The achievements of government in Chicago at times rivaled the feats of the Old Testament God.

Major American cities had far more advanced civic infrastructure than their international peers. As Teaford notes, "prosperous American urban dwellers enjoyed the highest standard of living in the world."[110]

Take water provision. As Teaford shows, in 1889, the 10 largest cities in the United States all had more water mains per capita than any city in Germany; 9 out of 10 had more sewer mains.[111] Per capita water supply in all 10 of the biggest American cities exceeded that available in any British or German city. St Louis had twice as much water available per capita as London; Chicago more than three times; Buffalo more than six times. By 1902, cities like Boston and St. Louis had more total water mains than Berlin, despite having less than one-third the population. The result was that flush toilets and bathtubs were widely available in American cities, but not in Europe. In the 1890s, only about 10% of the population of London had flush toilets, whereas more than half of tenement dwellers in New York City did.

Or streets. The absolute number of paved streets in cities like Boston and Baltimore exceeded the number in Berlin (which had three times the population). And, as Teaford notes, "in the field of street lighting the American municipalities enjoyed an even-more commanding lead."[112] In 1903, Chicago had 10 times as many electric streetlights as Berlin, and more gas lights too. St, Louis and Buffalo both had more electric lights than any city in Germany in 1903. American street cars systems dwarfed European ones. Buffalo and Cleveland had more miles of streetcars than London. Nine out of the 10 largest American cities exceeded the number of streetcar rides per inhabitant available in every German and English city.[113]

Political scientist Alberta Sbargia credits the amazing growth of American civic infrastructure and investment in this period to the fact that growing American cities did not have to ask Washington for permission to borrow and build.[114] They just borrowed and built.

American cities' easy access to affordable capital through the municipal bond market was in large part a result of the federal government's earlier response to the railroad bond crisis. Although avoiding bailouts and enforcing municipalities' debts undoubtedly had significant and painful costs, it also seems likely that the federal government's protection of creditors encouraged continued flows of funds to American cities. Without the availability of these funds, American cities would not have been able to develop such remarkable infrastructure and experience such fast economic growth.

It is clear that whatever leg of the trilemma the federal government chooses comes with both costs and benefits.

3.2. The Other Debt Crisis of the 1870s: Southern State Post-Reconstruction Repudiation and the "Odious Debt" Doctrine

At the same time the Supreme Court developed its aggressive pro-creditor case law in the railroad bond cases, it was developing an aggressive pro-debtor position in response to another debt crisis: the repudiation of Reconstruction Era debts by southern states after the return to power of White-only governments.

At the end of the Civil War, the Fourteenth Amendment forced the repudiation of all Confederate war debts.[115] But many southern states carried pre-Confederate debts.[116] Further, Reconstruction-era mixed-race southern state governments issued debt to build improvements like railroads and increased spending on schools and other social services.[117]

Southern opponents of Reconstruction also became critics of paying back this debt, calling themselves "readjusters" or "coupon killers."[118] In the 1870s, and particularly after 1877, these groups surged into power in southern states, seeking both to end Reconstruction and to repudiate debts issued by Reconstruction state governments. At the close of Reconstruction, eight Southern states—Alabama, Arkansas, Florida, Georgia, Louisiana, Mississippi, North Carolina, and South Carolina—repudiated their debts.[119] By 1890, Southern states had repudiated over $110M in debt.[120] Virginia and Tennessee also scaled down their debt by passing laws making it harder for bondholders to recover, and then in some cases negotiating write-downs.[121]

As Sarah Ludington, Mitu Gulati, and Alfred Brophy argue, this is one of the few instances in the history of sovereign debt where debtors were successful in making what we would now call "odious debt" arguments.[122] In general, it is a standard international law rule that new governments of sovereign states are liable for debts incurred by their predecessors in office. A new head of state cannot come into office and refuse to pay her country's debts because they were incurred under a prior head of state's regime. The "odious debt" doctrine is a proposed exception to this rule, theoretically giving governments the ability to not pay debts if the following three conditions are met: the regime that incurred the debts lacked popular consent; the spending enabled by the debt did not benefit residents; and creditors knew about the likely misuse of the funds they were advancing.[123]

However, the odious debt doctrine has very, very rarely been successfully invoked. But, ironically given how odious their own behavior looks in retrospect, southern states made arguments that sounded a great deal like modern claims of odious debt.[124] They argued in favor of repudiation because Reconstruction Era governments were corrupt and run by newly freed Black citizens and northern "carpetbaggers" and thus were despotic and not for the benefit of (white) residents.[125]

These arguments by Southern states were broadly accepted by a post–Compromise of 1877 political world eager to put Reconstruction behind them. The key audience was the Supreme Court, which would hear suits brought by bondholders.

The Court did not decide cases by invoking a version of the odious debt doctrine. Instead, as legal scholars Jonathan Orth and John Gibbons have shown, the Court instead protected repudiating Southern state by changing the nature of the doctrine of sovereign immunity.[126]

The Eleventh Amendment states that "[t]he Judicial power of the United States shall not be construed to extend to any suit in law or equity, commenced or prosecuted against one of the United States by Citizens of another State, or by Citizens or Subjects of any Foreign State."[127] This means creditors cannot go into federal court and sue states to recover on bonds issued by those states.

But, in *Osborn v. United States*, decided in 1824, the Court made a distinction between suits against states and against officers of states, often allowing the latter to proceed in federal court.[128] As late as 1875, in *Board of Liquidation v. McComb*, the Court ruled that sovereign immunity did not bar federal courts from ordering state officials to engage nondiscretionary duties, including paying funds by issuing a *mandamus* order, just as they had done in railroad bond cases against local governments.[129]

In 1882, the Court reversed course, barring bondholder claims against state officers from federal courts and thus allowing the southern states to successfully repudiate their debts.[130] While there were cases from a number of Southern states, the most important came from Louisiana after the state passed a law requiring its officials not to collect taxes to make payments on its bonds.[131] In *Louisiana v. Jumel*, a case involving a different aspect of the same law that had been at issue in *McComb*, the Court held that it had no jurisdiction to hear a case against Louisiana's state treasurer for failing to enforce the terms of state bonds that Louisiana had repudiated. The Court held that the suit was effectively against the state itself and thus barred by sovereign immunity.[132] The Court distinguished *McComb* on technical grounds, and overcame vigorous dissents that argued that the decision effectively vitiated the Contract Clause.[133] Sovereign immunity does not bar suits between states, but in *New Hampshire v. Louisiana*, the Court barred a suit by New Hampshire on behalf of its residents to collect on Louisiana bonds on the grounds that this was simply a ruse to get around sovereign immunity.[134] This reached its apogee in the famous case of *Hans v. Louisiana*, in which the Court found that sovereign immunity protected states from suits by citizens of their own state.[135]

Hundreds of articles have been written about *Hans* and the broader status of sovereign immunity in our law. But for our purposes, it is more important to consider the context and effects of the Court's decisions. After the Compromise of 1877, federal policy shifted dramatically to allow newly white-dominated southern state governments to repudiate the policies and politics of the Reconstruction era. The Supreme Court played its part, building a doctrine that punished lenders for working with racially mixed Reconstruction era governments. The Court's decisions meant that creditors, rather than taxpayers, bore the cost of paying for southern state debt.[136]

It is hard to square the generous attitude the Court took toward southern state debt with the aggressive, law-making stance it took toward city debt during the same period, except by reference to broad federal rejection of Reconstruction and support for white-dominated "Redeemer" state governments in the post-1877 period.[137] Neither was obvious legally, nor were they ideologically similar. But, in both situations, the Court followed the broad direction of federal policy.

Whatever the reason, though, the Court adopted different legs of the trilemma for municipal and southern state debt. In the railroad bond cases, the Court intervened to aid bondholders, increasing the confidence of municipal bond investors but at major cost to current taxpayers, service recipients, and macroeconomic conditions. The pain the Court's decisions created was immediate and real, but the decisions also encouraged future lending, which led to the development of urban infrastructure and railroads.

In contrast, in the sovereign immunity cases, the Court made bondholders take losses, provide short-run benefits to newly empowered White-dominated "Redeemer" governments. These governments did not have to face as much immediate economic pain as they would have if the Court had rejected their sovereign immunity arguments.

The effects of the Court's choices were felt for decades. In contrast with the ready capital that funded successful investments by northern cities, capital markets punished Southern states, charging repudiating Southern states high interest rates for debt and in many cases refusing to buy debt from them entirely for decades.[138] London and New York exchanges refused to list Southern state bonds for many years.[139] Southern cities and counties also faced huge difficulty borrowing in national capital markets, while local governments in the West as well as in the developed core of the country were able to sell their bonds to investors in New York, Chicago, and Boston.[140]

This had the effect of substantially reducing the capacity of Southern states to invest in the infrastructure needed to build an industrial economy. The availability of railroads, in particular, drove the urbanization of manufacturing and the broader development of the economy.[141] Infrastructural investments were also essential to making urban places capable of housing many workers. To have thick labor markets, cities needed sanitation, parks, and street cars. Without the capacity to invest in infrastructure, southern states had less capacity to build the pre-conditions for an industrial economy.

There is no escaping the trilemma.

3.3. Conclusion

If the first 50 years of the country provided two examples of what happens when the federal government does or does not offer bailouts, the post–Civil War period provides two examples of what happens when the federal actors—in this case the Justices of the Supreme Court—attempt to allocate the cost of state fiscal crises between taxpayers and creditors. In the railroad bond cases, city and county taxpayers were forced by federal courts to raise taxes and cut spending in order to pay off creditors. This created macroeconomic and social costs, but also set the stage for an explosion in municipal infrastructure investment. Post-Reconstruction southern states were allowed to default on their debts by the Supreme Court, making creditors take heavy losses. This reduced the economic pressure on these states, but also meant they couldn't easily borrow going forward, limiting their capacity to build needed infrastructure.

State and Local Debt Crises in the 20th Century

Over the course of the 20th century, at least after the 1930s, there were fewer state and local defaults than there were in the 19th century. For our purposes, there are two notable facts about the crises that did happen.

The 20th century clearly saw a series of massive changes in the relative sizes of the federal, state, and local governments. Further, the ways in which federal and state governments interacted changed dramatically, with far more federally raised money coursing through state and local budgets.

But what's interesting is that the federal responses to acute state and local fiscal crises hardly evolved. The federal government did ease away from the hardline position in favor of creditors of municipalities and against federal bailouts that marked the railroad bond crises. But most of these moves—like the original versions of municipal bankruptcy that Congress enacted in the 1930s or the federal loans offered to New York City in the 1970s—were baby steps in other directions, rather than a very different choice in the trilemma. It was not until the 1990s, with federal response to the Washington, DC, fiscal crisis, that there was a major bailout, a first since the federal government rejected Hamilton's approach in the 1840s.

Second, in a number of these crises, particularly the Arkansas road debt default of 1932 and the New York City fiscal crisis of 1975, the federal government did not adopt all-or-nothing approaches to the trilemma. Instead, it used what one might consider a mixed strategy, combining austerity, defaults, and bailouts. Federal officials also changed their tactics during the middle of these crises, taking one position and then reversing it.

Put together, federal responses to state and local budget crises in the 20th century were more nuanced (or confused—take your pick!) than the responses in the 19th century.

4.1. State and Local Fiscal Crises during the Great Depression

The relationship between municipal debt and the federal government took a decisive turn with the passage of the Sixteenth Amendment in 1913 and with the introduction of the modern version of the income tax.

The first income tax after 1913 exempted income earned from interest on municipal debt. Because buyers of municipal bonds do not have to pay taxes on the interest income, state and local governments do not need to pay as much in interest to attract investment. The exemption effectively made the federal government a partner with state and local governments in building infrastructure.[1] From the time the exemption was enacted, presidents have tried to get rid of it, but it has persisted, for reasons I will return to in Chapter 11.

The federal government's support for municipal bond markets was made concrete by the exemption. And early in the 20th century, the exemption supported fast-growing state and local governments. State and local governments substantially increased their spending and borrowing over the first three decades of the 20th century. Total local government spending increased from 4% to 6% of GDP between 1902 and 1927; total local governmental debt increased from 10.1% of GDP in 1902, to 12.2% of GDP in 1922.[2] State governmental revenue grew from 0.8% of GDP in 1902 to 2.1% of GDP in 1927, with state debt increasing as well.[3] Part of the increase of state spending was due to the rise of the automobile, as state governments often played an important role in inter-city road construction.[4]

When the Great Depression hit, states and localities were overwhelmed by both increasing demands for services and declining revenue.[5] Local governments began defaulting left and right. In 1932, there were 678 local governments in some form of default. By December 1935, there were 3,200 local governments in default, meaning that about 16% of all municipal debt was in default.[6] Cities were forced to cut spending very dramatically.[7] States faced severe challenges too, and at least six states were paying more than 20% of their revenue in debt payments in 1932.[8]

One could talk about the New Deal endlessly (as many, many others have done). But needless to say, the New Deal not only increased the overall size of the American public sector, it changed radically the relative share of spending by the federal, state, and local governments. The federal government grew not only in size but also in its share of public spending substantially. State governments increased in size, as well, as they were regular partners with the federal government in the administration of New Deal programs. Local governments shrunk relative to other levels of government, but not in absolute size.[9]

The New Deal also changed the fiscal relationship of the federal government to states and cities. Radically increasing a trend that started earlier, much New Deal spending took the form of programs that were paid for, in whole or in part, by the federal government but administered by state and local governments. Other purely federal programs took responsibilities off the plates of state and local governments, relieving their budgets by displacing some of their tasks.

The legacy of these "cooperative federalism" programs lives on to today, with large parts of the welfare state, including Medicaid and Temporary Aid for Needy Families, paid for by the federal government but administered by states (which also often bear responsibility for jointly paying for them).[10]

What Congress did not do in the 1930s was directly bail out the most indebted state and local governments. Local governments pleaded with President Franklin Delano Roosevelt for bailouts. But, in the words of *Time Magazine*, they "only got sympathy."[11] The huge amount of overall spending and increased federal programs, however, meant that most jurisdictions were able to muddle through. While there were many local defaults, only one state government—Arkansas—defaulted during the Great Depression.

But even as the whole project of American governance was radically changing, the federal government only took small steps toward changing how it responded to acute state and local fiscal crises.

4.1.1. The Creation of Chapter 9 Municipal Bankruptcy

The first iteration of a municipal bankruptcy law emerged in the aftermath of the Great Depression. Because many local governments were unable to meet their debt burdens, state governments and Congress developed bankruptcy processes to facilitate private workouts of that debt (negotiations between creditors and cities that reduced the amount of debt owed). While these bankruptcy laws facilitated defaults, their authors were very concerned about their effect on future lending and structured them to reduce their potential negative effects.

In the 1930s, efforts by defaulting cities to persuade creditors to agree to reductions in the amount owed in return for a resumption of payments were regularly thwarted by small groups of "hold-out" creditors, seeking payment in full.[12] Unless everyone agreed, such workouts would fail and no one would get paid.[13] And if no one was getting paid back, no one would lend.

Faced with frozen municipal bond markets, state governments sprang into action. In the 1930s, New Jersey passed laws authorizing the state government to take over insolvent cities and allowing cities to adjust their debts if a plan was approved both by a state agency and by 85% of the creditors. Such a policy could help creditors as well as cities, by stopping "hold-out" creditors from standing in the way of reasonable reductions in debt that would get at least some money flowing back to creditors.

Some creditors sued, claiming that the law violated the Contract Clause of the US Constitution. In *Faitoute Iron and Steel v. City of Asbury Park*, the Supreme Court rejected this argument. Arguing that it aided creditors as a class, the Court found that the New Jersey municipal bankruptcy law was both practically necessary and constitutionally permissible:

> How, then, can claims against a financially embarrassed city be enforced? Experience shows that three conditions are essential if the municipality is to be kept going as a political community, and, at the same time, the utmost for the benefit of the creditors is to be realized: impartial, outside control over the finances of the city, concerted action by all the creditors to avoid destructive action by individuals, and ratable distribution. In short, what is needed is a temporary scheme of public receivership over a subdivision of the state. A policy of every man for himself is destructive of the potential resources upon which rests the taxing power which, in actual fact, constitutes the security for unsecured obligations outstanding against a city.... The payment of the creditors was the end to be obtained, but it could be maintained only by saving the resources of the municipality—the goose which lays its golden eggs—namely, the taxes which alone can meet the outstanding claims.[14]

The Court justified New Jersey's municipal bankruptcy law in the same way corporate bankruptcy is often justified, because it serves the interests of creditors as a whole, if not the interests of specific hold-out creditors.[15]

In 1933, when Congress created its own municipal bankruptcy law, it was similarly focused on the issue of hold-out creditors.[16] A plan of adjustment (i.e., a decision about how large the haircuts creditors would have to take) would go into effect if 75% of all creditors approved of it and a court determined it was fair and equitable. Cities were only allowed to file if they were given authorization by state governments. The law did not provide for an "automatic stay" of all claims against local governments upon determining eligibility. Nor did it include a mechanism by which a court could "cram down" losses on creditors without approval by a supermajority of bondholders. (These innovations would not be introduced into municipal bankruptcy until the 1970s.) The original version of municipal bankruptcy was meant to facilitate private workouts and that was it.

Even so, the Supreme Court found the first municipal bankruptcy law unconstitutional in *Ashton v. Cameron County Water Imp. District*.[17] The Court held the law violated the Tenth Amendment because it interfered with the sovereignty of the states. The Court was not persuaded that the rule that a state government must authorize a bankruptcy filing by a municipality mitigated its federalism concerns. The Court also expressed apprehension that the availability of a bankruptcy process would reduce local willingness to raise taxes to cover debts.[18]

Congress responded by passing a virtually identical municipal bankruptcy law a year later, generally referred to as "Chapter 9."[19] A House committee stated without much explanation that it did not believe the new law was contrary to the *Ashton* decision. As part of its famous shift in the mid-1930s from challenging to upholding New Deal policies, the Court upheld the new municipal bankruptcy law in *United States v. Bekins*, finding this time that the law did not impinge on state authority because it relied on state and local consent.[20] The Court noted that the law helped creditors as well as debtors:

> Improvement districts, such as the petitioner, were in distress. Economic disaster had made it impossible for them to meet their obligations. As the owners of property within the boundaries of the district could not pay adequate assessments, the power of taxation was useless. The creditors of the district were helpless.[21]

But what is most notable about municipal bankruptcy is how limited its scope was. Even as the New Deal radically changed how government in America worked, Congress would not enact laws that did more than encourage a better form of negotiations between creditors and municipal debtors.[22] It would not be until the 1970s that Congress reformed municipal bankruptcy to give local governments more power to write down their debts.

The legislative history of Chapter 9, as legal scholar John Patrick Hunt showed, revealed that Members of Congress were concerned that cities would use bankruptcy as a justification not to tax aggressively.[23] This was the same concern the Court had in *Ashton* when it invalidated the first municipal bankruptcy law.

Congress and the Court understood municipal bankruptcy as a fundamentally pro-creditor law, allowing them to overcome collective action problems while still preserving their power to recover. Municipal bankruptcy would encourage future lending by coordinating the behavior of creditors, making it easier to achieve debt workouts that benefit creditors as a whole.

Notably, this is an argument that takes place inside the bounds I describe through the trilemma. Congress created a limited municipal bankruptcy law because it did not want to create too much moral hazard or to disrupt the municipal bond market too much. Even as the Great Depression raged, and the New Deal upended beliefs about the proper role of the federal government, Congress was afraid to force bondholders to bear too much of burden during local fiscal crises.

4.1.2. When a State Goes Broke: Arkansas in the 1930s

Arkansas's 1933 default is the only state government default of the 20th century. At first, the federal government—both the courts and the executive branch— acted to ensure the safety of municipal bondholders by effectively forcing Arkansas to pay its creditors. Several years later, the federal government acted again, this time with investment to ease the terms of the deal Arkansas struck with creditors in 1933.

Arkansas's troubles began with its local governments. Beginning in 1907, Arkansas law gave local governments the power to set up improvement districts that could issue bonds to fund the construction of roads, backed by local taxes and federal funding.[24] Through roughly 1920, local and federal revenue for roads increased, and a construction boom ensued. But a recession in 1920 left districts with unbuilt roads and huge unpaid bills, even after they repeatedly raised pro-perty taxes.[25] In 1923, the state took over most road funding, but local road districts still faced heavy debt loads.[26] In 1927, the state agreed to make payments on $64M of local road district bonds on behalf of local property owners to help them avoid foreclosure (the state did not assume local governments' debt; it just made payments to bondholders on behalf of local taxpayers).[27] The state also continued to borrow to build itself, borrowing $91M, backed by road usage fees and gasoline taxes.

By 1929, the state was first in the nation in per capita indebtedness despite being 46th in per capita income.[28] As B.A. Ratchford noted, "Probably no state ever embarked upon a more ambitious borrowing program, in relation to its re-sources, than did Arkansas in 1927."[29]

Despite the onset of the Depression, the state kept spending, re-electing its governor in 1930 despite a primary challenge from a candidate who claimed that continued borrowing would bankrupt the state.[30] This echoed decisions by states (including Arkansas itself) after the Panic of 1837 to keep borrowing and spending despite a national economic calamity.

In 1931, things took a massive turn for the worse. State and local tax rev-enue dried up along with the broader economy. The state government tried to help the road districts by offering a trade to holders of local bonds. Road dis-trict bondholders could turn in their bonds for new bonds issued by the state. However, these new bonds were revenue bonds not backed by the full faith and credit of the state, only by particular road-based revenues.[31] Investors rejected the deal. They instead demanded that, in return for exchanging their local bonds, the state give them new bonds that came with contractual assurances that road maintenance expenses would not be paid before creditors, and that the state's highway fund would never drop below a level sufficient to pay the interest and principal on its highway and revenue bonds.

The state agreed to those terms, although it insisted that the new bonds did not have the protection of being backed by the state's full faith and credit, only the road-based revenues. Only some investors agreed to take on the new bonds, while most others rejected the offer. To make payments to bondholders who did not take the deal, local road districts were forced to raise property taxes and increase foreclosures even further. The state didn't hold up its side of the bargain with those who did take the deal: it failed to make payments on the replacement debt. This was not technically a state sovereign default, as they were revenue bonds and not a full faith and credit promises. But it was a sign of things to come.[32]

In 1932, despite tax rate increases, state tax revenues continued to fall in the state. Early the next year, Arkansas decided to default on its own bonds, refusing to make payments on any road-related debt. The state legislature also passed a bunch of tax cuts. To add insult to default, the state legislators also took some money out of the highway fund to increase their own pay.[33]

The final thumbing of its nose at creditors was the "Ellis Refunding Act." The state "offered" any holder of any of then-$146M of outstanding debt, no matter which government issued it, a deal where they could trade their bonds for new bonds with 25 years maturity and an unfavorable 3% interest rate.[34] The bonds were not backed by any specific source of revenue and the legislature was clear that payments on them would only come after the state engaged in necessary road maintenance expenditures.

The offer was not technically mandatory, but the state appropriated no money to make payments on the old debt. Effectively, Arkansas told creditors to take these lousy new bonds or get lost.

Bondholders were so displeased by the state's "offer" that they rushed to federal courthouses. Road district bondholders who did not exchange their bonds in 1931 wanted to hold on to their ability to force local districts to increase property taxes. Road district bondholders who had exchanged their bonds in the 1931 bond swap argued that the Ellis Act broke the state's promise to maintain a sufficient balance in the road maintenance account and thus violated the Contract Clause.[35] State bondholders thought their claims were senior to other road bond creditors, and that they should be paid even if others were not. The States of Pennsylvania, Nevada, and Connecticut sued as well, acting on behalf of pension funds and insurance companies headquartered in their states, bringing their case directly to the Supreme Court under its original jurisdiction over disputes between states.[36]

The bondholders' cases seemed to be foreclosed by the Supreme Court's sovereign immunity jurisprudence in cases like *Louisiana v. Jumel* and *New Hampshire v. Louisiana* (which found that sovereign immunity barred suits against government officials and by other states on behalf of their citizens in similar contexts).[37]

Even so, state bondholders won a case in district court, forcing the state to stop using highway fund money for maintenance.[38]

Before any of the cases made it up to the Supreme Court, the federal government—after lobbying by bondholders—got in on the act. The Public Works Administration suspended all loans to the state until the state agreed to negotiate a better deal with bondholders.[39] Between the litigation risk and federal pressure, the state was forced to negotiate with its creditors.

Without much leverage, these negotiations over a new debt exchange did not go well for Arkansas. As part of the deal it was forced to make with creditors, the state agreed not to build any new roads until all of its renegotiated debt was paid off.[40] This was extremely severe, as some of the bonds were not due to be repaid until 1977! The state also lost control over its highway fund, pledging to spend almost every penny in the fund on debt service. The state also agreed to pass a number of large tax increases—including raising its gas tax to a level that is five times higher (in real terms) than it is today—and cut services substantially.

This is the trilemma at work. Because Arkansas defaulted, the bond market refused to lend to Arkansas. Arkansas debt was considered "speculative" until 1939. Banks in Connecticut, Massachusetts, New York, and Pennsylvania were barred from lending to the state into the 1940s and 1950s.[41] Even a brief default meant that the state paid a huge premium on its debt for years. Arkansas's ability to invest in infrastructure was limited because markets would not lend.

The potential harm to the bond market caused other states, federal courts, and eventually the federal executive branch to intervene. Because of federal pressure, Arkansas had to pay much more of its debt than it originally intended, forcing it to raise taxes and cut spending at the height of the Great Depression. This was clearly extraordinarily painful from a macroeconomic perspective. But the federal government's intervention also managed to avoid Arkansas's default spreading to other states. There is no evidence of "contagion," or Arkansas's default making it harder for other states and cities to borrow. And the federal government did not create moral hazard in states by bailing Arkansas out.

Arkansas's story also shows how the federal government can makes states pay their debts despite the fact that formally there are protected by sovereign immunity. In theory, sovereign immunity means that states can default if they so choose and no one can go to court to make them pay. But, in Arkansas's case, federal courts found a way around this, creating substantial risk for the state's strategy. And, most importantly, the executive branch intervened to force the state to negotiate a better deal with bondholders. So while, in theory, sovereign immunity provides a bar to recovery, in practice, states do not have impunity to default if the federal government chooses to force them not to do so.

There is an interesting coda to this story. By 1939, Arkansas wanted to get out from under in terms of the deal it struck in 1933, but could not do so as long as there were outstanding bonds.[42] The federal Reconstruction Finance Corporation stepped in and agreed to purchase new bonds from the state, allowing Arkansas to repay all of its existing debt (letting it out of the terms of the 1933 deal). The RFC then resold the bonds it had bought to private investors.[43]

Other states howled, complaining that Arkansas was getting a special deal. But the RFC's investment helped Arkansas out of the consequences of its debt crisis. This was not a traditional bailout, but federal aid did allow the state to invest more in infrastructure than it otherwise would have been able to, while also creating some of the concerns related to federal aid, particularly complaints from sister states.

4.2. When Big Cities Go Broke

The pro-creditor, anti-bailout federal policies of the 1870s and 1880s during the railroad bond crisis produced substantial economic pain by forcing cities to cut spending and raise taxes during recessions—worsening and prolonging those economic downturns. But they also reduced moral hazard and encouraged municipal bond investors to fund the great flowering of municipal civic infrastructure at the turn of the century. The Great Depression and the New Deal changed almost everything about the way the federal government operates and how it relates to state and local governments. But there was not a radical change in how the federal government responded to specific local fiscal crises. Federal interventions were not quite as bondholder friendly as they were in the 1870s. But when combined with the innovation of the income tax exemption for interest on municipal debt, they did not harm too substantially the municipal bond markets.

By the time of the next great subnational fiscal crisis, New York City's in 1975, the country had again changed radically. Many things were different of course, including the size of the federal government. Between World War II through 2008, federal revenues ranged between 17.9% and 22.3% of GDP, compared with 2.4% to 7% between 1900 to 1940.[44] This increase, though, did not come at the expense of states and localities, although it did shift the relative power of each level of government. State governmental revenue increased over the postwar period, steadily increasing from 4.1% of GDP in 1952 to 11.2% in 2007, while local revenue increased slightly, from 4.0% in 1952 to 7.4% in 2007. State debt increased substantially over this period as well, increasing from 1.9% of GDP in 1952 to 6.7% of GDP in 2007. This increase happened despite a wave of new state constitutional tax and expenditure limits (TELs) passed in tax revolts during 1970s and after.[45] The most famous of these was California's Proposition 13 (1978), which imposes supermajority requirements for tax increases and stops property assessments from increasing by more than 2% a year, among other limitations.[46] Other major TELs, like Colorado's Taxpayer Bill of Rights (1992), which capped government revenue increases at the rate of inflation and population growth, were also approved.[47] Local debt bounced around between 6.5% and just over 10% during the second half of the 20th century, roughly similar to the period before the war.

The increase in federal spending and debt meant that more federal dollars were spent on infrastructure. The federal government funded the interstate highway system, among many other marvels. Despite this, federal spending on most categories of infrastructure spending has always been substantially less than state and local spending.[48] Only at the height of interstate highway construction did federal spending on capital expenditures on transportation exceed state and local spending. When operations and maintenance are included, state and local spending was higher even in that period.

The reason for this remains the same. The federal government faces real challenges in determining the importance of particular projects, relying heavily on submissions by states and localities in making investment decisions. Federal spending on infrastructure remains plagued by pork-barrel spending, being allocated by district or based on the power of individual Members of Congress, rather than being directed at the highest value uses. (The interstate highway system, which naturally was everywhere in the country, is the exception that proves this particular rule.)

Over the course of second half of the 20th century, state and local fiscal crises did not come in waves as we saw in previous periods. But there were more localized crises. Further, the most important crises of the period were in a particular type of place, the declining major metropolis—New York in the 1970s and Washington, DC, in the 1990s.[49]

There are three interesting themes that emerge in this period. The first is how innovations in financial engineering both helped forestall fiscal crises and raised questions about what would happen if these tools failed and default ensued. The second is that states and the federal government latched on to the idea of attaching conditions to crisis-driven bailout, and particularly the creation of institutions like fiscal control boards that reduced or removed local authority, to reduce moral hazard and to ensure that reforms were made. Third, there were efforts to balance across the parts of the trilemma, including policies that involve some subsidies, some defaults, and more than a little austerity.

4.2.1. New York City: Ford to City, Drop Dea... Well, Wait a Minute

The story of New York City's near-bankruptcy has been oft-told, even appearing as a topic of conversation in major films like *Annie Hall*.[50]

New York City almost succumbed to bankruptcy for a number of reasons, some unique to it and others common to other metropolises of the time.[51] New York City had a truly massive government, which provided more services and public employment than any other city in the country by a huge, huge margin.[52] As Carol Bellamy and Donna Shalala noted, relative to its resources, "New York City itself probably tried to do too much for too many."[53] Over the course of the 1960s and 1970s, city spending increased but the city's economy did not prosper. As was the case in many cities, manufacturing plants closed, corporate headquarters moved out, and residents increasingly moved to the suburbs.[54] The City paid its bills by borrowing, not only for capital projects but also to support its structural budget deficits.[55] That is, it was engaging in lots of short-term borrowing to make ends meet.[56]

The key financial innovation that New York State used to address New York City's fiscal crisis was first developed only a few months earlier, during the fiscal crisis of a New York State authority, the Urban Development Corporation (UDC).[57] In 1975, the UDC, which was responsible for building affordable housing, was broke.[58] Banks refused to lend it any money, which brought the construction of some 30,000 new affordable housing units to a screeching halt. The UDC bonds were supposed to be paid back by a combination of federal subsidies and the rents on the as-yet uncompleted units.[59]

Richard Ravitch, brought in to run the UDC board, formulated the idea of creating a new entity that could borrow and finance government activities.[60] Ravitch convinced the federal government to transfer the UDC's federal subsidies to a newly formed Project Finance Authority (PFA), which then issued bonds secured by those subsidies. Investors were interested in the bonds because they would be paid back regardless of whether the UDC as a whole defaulted. UDC bondholders complained vociferously about the federal subsidies that were supposed to pay back their bonds. It was unfair, they argued, that federal subsidies were being taken from them and given to new PFA bondholders, who would be paid even if the UDC was forced to default.

Even so, the PFA gambit ultimately worked. The UDC bondholders did not have a legal right to federal subsidies, only a claim against the UDC backed by a strong expectation that the revenues would be used to support their bonds. When combined with new subsidies and substantial cuts, the money from the PFA bonds ensured that the UDC could finish projects in construction, allowing

Richard Ravitch and Governor Hugh Carey, the men behind the financial instrument that helped save New York City, Bettmann/Getty Images

it to earn rents on the projects. Eventually, all bondholders were paid and many affordable housing units were built.

The same approach was subsequently used in New York City's fiscal crisis. The City was heavily reliant on short-term debt to meet its cash needs—it borrowed to make ends meet. But its fiscal position became so perilous that a number of major banks decided to stop participating in its efforts to issue short-term debt, creating a crisis because the city needed the cash to make payroll.

The solution the state came up with was to create a new public authority to issue bonds and finance city activity.[61] The Municipal Assistance Corporation ("Big MAC" or "MAC") was given the power to issue bonds backed by New York City's sales tax authority, which was handed over to the MAC, along with money from the City's stock transfer tax.[62] The MAC would then pay for city activities in the short term. The idea, taken from the UDC/PFA playbook, was that investors would be willing to buy MAC bonds because, in case of default, their interest in these revenue sources would be secured.[63] That is, the MAC bondholders would be paid back with sales tax revenue even if general obligation bondholders had to take haircuts because the City was bankrupt.

Demand for MAC bonds, however, was limited at first.[64] New York State adopted a number of strategies to generate confidence in the new entity. Most notably, it created an Emergency Financial Control Board (EFCB) with members largely appointed by the governor, to review and control city spending.[65] The EFCB imposed a wage freeze, rejected previously approved municipal contracts, and changed the city's financial plan, leading to layoffs, reduced services, and newly enacted taxes and fees.[66] The state authorized the city to pass new taxes, increasing revenues. The City's labor unions, worried about further layoffs, agreed to buy MAC bonds with their pension funds. To encourage demand for MAC bonds, the state also imposed a moratorium on repayment of short-term City bonds, forcing such bondholders to roll their debt over into longer-term MAC bonds. (The highest court in New York State, the Court of Appeals, later found that this forced rollover violated the state constitution.)[67]

In the popular version of the New York City fiscal crisis, the federal government's response was in keeping with its long-held policy of refusing to bail out struggling states and localities.[68] Initially, this version of the story was true. Governor Hugh Carey and other New York officials repeatedly asked for federal help. After one such entreaty, President Gerald Ford gave a speech at the National Press Club, arguing that the City's fiscal crisis was its own fault and that it should consider filing for municipal bankruptcy. The *New York Daily News* summed up his speech with its most-famous headline: "Ford to City: Drop Dead."[69]

But that was not the end of the story. Originally, Congress favored reforming municipal bankruptcy law over providing aid. But troubles in New York City— one of the biggest subnational governments in the whole country—were creating problems for other borrowers and for the broader national and international banking system. Foreign and domestic officials, prodded by bankers worried about international financial contagion, put substantial pressure on both Ford and Congress to provide aid.[70]

Congress responded by passing a bill authorizing $2B in federal loans to New York City. Just a few months after his National Press Club speech, President Ford signed the bill.[71]

Whatever help the city got from the state and federal government came with severe conditions. The state had already imposed painful governance reforms. The federal loans were only offered after those governance reforms and the state's passage of the law forcing bondholders to roll over their debt into MAC bonds. Further, the terms of the federal loans were not particularly generous, requiring earmarking of city revenues for loan repayment and periodic reporting by the city.[72]

But the federal government did provide loans. There were several reasons for this, of course, but the most important were concerns about contagion. Among officials in Albany and Washington, there was widespread fear that a default in New York City would cause investors to abandon New York State and even beyond, destabilizing national and even global bond markets.[73] The fear that not offering aid might harm the broader municipal bond market pushed the federal government to adopt a policy quite different from its post-1843 "no bailout" position.

When looked at as a whole, the federal government's final position mixed elements of the trilemma. It provided aid, but only after the state had imposed severe conditions on the city's fiscal authority. The city was forced to cut its budget severely, fundamentally transforming the structure and even the ambitions of its government. The state also effectively sanctioned a modest default in the form of the forced rollover of local debt.

But the federal government did not adopt one position from the outset. Rather than make one choice, the president and Congress bounced back and forth between options. This mix of reactions captured how difficult the tradeoffs facing the federal government are. Upon seeing the downsides of one choice— in particular, the reaction market actors gave when President Ford seemed committed to not providing any aid—the federal government doubled back on its decisions.

The downsides were all there as well. Austerity was not as bad as it might have been absent state and federal actions, but it was very substantial, creating social and economic costs during the 1970s. New York's credit rating was hurt, and its investments in infrastructure dried up. And the limited federal aid created public concerns about moral hazard, although the grudging nature of Ford's decision to offer aid and the limited form it took substantially reduced this worry. All of that said, the mixed strategy set the stage for the city's glorious revival in the years to come.

There is an interesting post script as well. New York City did not file for bankruptcy, although it did come close when the city's teachers' union briefly balked at using pension funds to buy MAC bonds.[74] When teachers' union leader Albert Shanker debated whether to use teacher pension funds to buy the MAC bonds, famous lawyer and former Judge Simon Rifkind reassured him that if a default came, the MAC bonds had a security interest in the revenues. Investments in MAC bonds would be safe in bankruptcy, Rifkind argued, even if general obligation bonds faced substantial losses.[75] The City did not file for bankruptcy, so we don't know if Rifkind was right. But this exact question would re-emerge during Puerto Rico's fiscal crisis and may be a key issue in future state and local fiscal crises.[76]

Although New York City did not file for bankruptcy, the effort to make municipal bankruptcy a possibility for the City led to a dramatic transformation in the law. Congress was not yet ready by the time New York's crisis hit its nadir, but, soon after, it did make Chapter 9 bankruptcy a much more attractive tool for jurisdictions.[77] The revision of Chapter 9 introduced an automatic stay, a rule that, upon a determination of eligibility, means that all claims against a city are unenforceable until the resolution of the case. Further, Congress allowed filings without majority credit support, and "cramdowns," or adjustments of debts even without approval from a majority of creditors, under certain conditions and with judicial approval.

Despite these changes, Chapter 9 remained a pretty marginal policy, used by very few municipalities until the mid-2000s.[78] After the Great Recession, though, these innovations led to the greater use of Chapter 9.

4.2.2. Bailouts without Moral Hazard: The Case of Washington, DC

After the rejection of the Johnson Report in 1843, Congress avoided giving bailouts to states and cities facing fiscal crises because doing so would create moral hazard. It did provide types of aid during the Arkansas and New York fiscal crises, but nothing like Alexander Hamilton's assumption of state debts. This led important scholars like Robert Inman to note that subnational governments mostly do face "hard budget constraints."[79]

There was one major exception: the federal government's 1997 intervention in Washington, DC. It was a bailout by almost any definition. But there is no evidence it created much moral hazard. There are surely many reasons for this. Perhaps the conditions tied to the money were severe enough that no government thought it would want to go through something like DC. did. Or maybe it was the uniqueness of the relationship of governments with their capitals.[80]

After many years of direct governance by the federal government, DC was given a substantial degree of home rule in 1973.[81] But, as Alice Rivlin and others argued, the conditions Congress set on home rule left DC without a number of important fiscal powers.[82] First, although it is not a state, DC was required to perform all functions of a state as well as those of a city. In particular, the District had to bear the cost of its Medicaid program, which was a major drain on the local budget. Second, although states have the power to tax the incomes of nonresidents, the federal Home Rule Act bars DC from taxing nonresident income.[83] In DC, roughly two-thirds of all income is earned by people living in other states, so taxing this income could raise a lot of revenue in theory. Relatedly, despite having the responsibilities of a state, DC is geographically quite small, and the city's rich inner-ring suburbs in Virginia and Maryland are outside of the scope of its taxing powers. Finally, like many state capitals and university towns, much of the property in DC is not taxable. The federal government, international organizations, and universities own huge amounts of property in downtown DC but cannot be taxed.[84] Also, the City was saddled with the pension obligations and debt that were accrued before Congress granted the city home rule, an unfunded amount that had mushroomed to $5B in 1997.[85]

DC simply did not have enough fiscal resources to fund an adequate quasi-state government. Until 1997, the federal government's response was to provide an annual cash payment. But the amounts were small potatoes next to the costs of running the District.

In 1995, DC's budget deficit reached a crisis level of $722M. Moody's downgraded its bonds to "junk" or non-investment-grade status.[86] People left the city at very high rate; 75K people moved out of DC between 1990 and 1997, around 12% of the City's population (and its 1990 population was already about 20% lower than its 1970 population.).[87] Crime was a major problem. There were 474 murders in 1990 (compared with 114 in 2017).[88]

The fiscal crisis of 1995 pushed the federal government into action. Congress created a fiscal control board for DC, modeled on New York's from the 1970s. The body had the power to reject the local budget and review local contracts.[89] Then, in 1997, Congress passed the Revitalization Act.[90] It ended the federal government's annual payment to the District, but removed from the District a whole host of costs. The federal government assumed the District's preexisting pension liabilities, increased its Medicaid payment, took over the local jail system, and agreed to pay for the local court system. Congress left the Control Board in place for several years and substantially strengthened it, giving it the power to directly hire and fire the heads of city agencies.

Critics called it a bailout, which actually understates what the Revitalization Act did.[91] The federal government not only assumed some of the District's debt; it fundamentally changed the nature of the DC government's cost structure. Despite not removing all of DC's fiscal problems, the Revitalization Act was a massive success. Due to improved governance, growth in the regional economy, and increased demand for city living, DC has been an economic success since, seeing substantial increases in employment, population, and property values.[92]

While the Revitalization Act was understood as a bailout, no one has provided any evidence that it created much moral hazard. DC has not been particularly profligate since, and there is no evidence that markets interpreted the Revitalization Act as evidence the federal government would intervene in other cities or states.

There are a few reasons why this might be the case.

The conditions imposed were quite severe, particularly the power over the City delegated to the Control Board. This suggests that substantial conditions on aid to state or local governments—whether they take the form of policy conditions or suspensions of local democracy—might blunt concerns about moral hazard while also ensuring reforms take place.[93]

Further, the federal government clearly has more authority with respect to, and a different relationship with, the nation's capital than it does with other jurisdictions. The failures of DC in the 1980s and 1990s created substantial costs of the federal government, both real (administration officials and Members of Congress have to work there) and in terms of public relations. It is not clear that officials in Baltimore, Maryland, or Cincinnati, Ohio (or the purchasers of those cities' bonds) should have changed their beliefs about the likelihood of bailout because the federal government bailed out DC.

Other jurisdictions have offered bailouts to capital cities. Take Hartford, the capital of Connecticut. Like DC, Hartford has a huge amount of tax-exempt property, is a geographically small jurisdiction inside a larger region, and lacks any capacity to tax outsiders.[94] Hartford also suffered from population outflows, high crime, and huge budget problems. In 2018, after years of fiscal problems, the state government in Connecticut agreed to take over responsibility for making payments on Hartford's debt.[95] Connecticut demanded some control over Hartford's local governance, but did so in form that was far short of the severe conditions presented to DC or New York City.[96]

The state of Connecticut, like the federal government, clearly had a strong interest in bailing out its capital. Notably, because the nature of the interest was sufficiently distinct, few commentators believe that these bailouts created much moral hazard in other jurisdictions. Politicians from both parties in Connecticut scoffed at the idea of bailing out other fiscally troubled cities in the state—New Haven, Bridgeport, and Waterbury.[97] And there's not much evidence that either local politicians or bond-rating agencies expect those cities to receive similar bailouts.

To the extent federal (or state) officials can convince local officials and bond market investors that the jurisdiction getting a bailout is somehow different from other jurisdictions, the downsides of bailouts become much lower.

The Great Recession and State and Local Fiscal Crises

Recessions lead to state and local fiscal problems, which, in turn, worsen recessions. When the economy is bad, incomes, sales, and property values fall. As a result, state and local revenue from income, sales, and property taxes goes down. At the same time, expenses go up, as demand for government services increases. This forces state and local governments to make spending cuts, lay off employees, and/or increase tax rates to balance their budgets.[1] This takes money out of the economy just when it needs stimulus the most. Because states and cities cannot easily run deficits, for both legal and practical reasons, their budgets are painfully pro-cyclical.

The Great Recession created genuinely great fiscal problems for states and cities which worsened and prolonged the severe economic effects of the recession. The scale of the Great Recession in 2008–2009 meant state tax revenues fell dramatically.[2] By the second quarter of 2009, across the states, sales tax revenue was down by 17% and income tax revenue was down by 27%.[3] On top of this, demand for social welfare services financed by these same governments went up substantially.[4]

State and local deficits grew considerably, becoming as large as 20% of the size of overall budgets in 2009.[5] Because of substantial (albeit short-lived) federal aid, state and local payrolls did not crash at the beginning of the Great Recession.[6] But they contracted substantially several years later, falling by more than 560,000 jobs between August 2008 and September 2012.[7]

These job losses had the effect of slowing the recovery from the Great Recession. Even as private sector employment returned to pre-Recession levels, the huge decline in public sector employment meant that the economy did not recover in full.[8] As Patrice Hill noted in 2013, "The biggest downsizing of state and local government in modern history has proved to be . . . a primary reason the four-year-long recovery is more sluggish than other recoveries since World War II."[9]

However, despite the depth of the fiscal problems faced by states and cities, there were only a handful of local defaults and no state government defaults (unless one counts the Commonwealth of Puerto Rico, as will be discussed below).[10] Federal aid was sufficient to get states and cities over the immediate crisis period and then a long period of retrenchment allowed states and cities to avoid defaults.

But state budgets were battered by the Great Recession. And they bear the marks of it to this day, with smaller workforces relative to population and heavy debt loads in some jurisdictions. Importantly, much of this debt took the form of underfunded public employee pension liabilities. Further, investment in infrastructure declined, as jurisdictions hoarded cash rather than make investments in the future.

And there were some defaults and bankruptcies. Federal bankruptcy judges in Chapter 9 municipal bankruptcy cases had to contend with the trilemma, deciding how and whether to allow tradeoffs between austerity and the size of defaults. Further, the combined federal approach to the Great Recession and state and local finance—some federal aid, a lot of state austerity, and increasing debt loads in the form of pension underfunding—can be understood as a way of splitting the difference across legs of the trilemma.

5.1. The American Recovery and
Reinvestment Act

Often called the "stimulus," the American Recovery and Reinvestment Act (ARRA) was President Barack Obama's administration's main fiscal policy response to the Great Recession.[11] ARRA included both tax cuts and new spending measures, intended to revive the economy. But a very substantial part of the legislation—two-thirds of its spending and 25% of its total stimulus—took the form of aid to states and localities.

ARRA aided state and local budgets in a number of ways. The most important was a $87B increase in federal spending on the jointly administered Medicaid program through an increase in the federal "match" of state spending by 6.2%, plus an additional increase in the match that depended on a state's unemployment rate.[12] There was also a $48B state fiscal stabilization fund, administered by the Department of Education, most of which was directed to school districts and universities to make up for falling state spending.[13] ARRA also included a variety of block grants on specific issues, and funds not directly aimed at providing fiscal relief, but that provided indirect benefits to state budgets, including transportation spending, "Race to the Top" education reform money, and increases in federal support for unemployment insurance.[14]

In total, aid to states in ARRA covered 20%–40% of the holes in their budgets.[15] The money went to *all* states. While there were some efforts to target aid at areas with more need (like the part of the Medicaid match increase that considered a state's unemployment rate), most of the bill spread money across the states in ways that were not closely tied to the extent of their fiscal distress.[16] This meant that ARRA was not sufficient to forestall severe fiscal cuts in the most heavily affected states and cities. But it also meant that it likely did not create substantial moral hazard concerns. The money was available regardless of what shape state budgets were in coming into the recession, and therefore likely did not do much to increase anyone's desire to run deficits going forward.

Aid to states had a *huge* effect on employment. Gabriel Chodorow-Reich, Laura Feiveson, Zachary Liscow, and William Gui Woolston show that $100K in marginal Medicaid aid to states resulted in 3.8 "job-years," 3.2 of which were outside of the government and healthcare sectors.[17] Bailouts reduce the macroeconomic harm caused by state budget cuts.

Support for state governments is usually seen as one of the most effective parts of what in retrospect has been understood as an effective-but-too-small response to the Great Recession.[18]

5.2. Build America Bonds

One part of ARRA deserves a bit more discussion. In 2007–2008, the municipal bond market was a mess.[19] A number of bond insurers, companies that improve the credit ratings of bonds by promising to pay when an issuer cannot in return for a fee, were downgraded by rating agencies, making their insurance less useful.[20] The market for auction-rate municipal securities and other variable-rate debt obligation securities—long-term bonds that, through regular auctions that reset their interest rates, are able to have borrowing costs that approach those of short-term bonds— also ran into trouble.[21] In February 2008, the auctions that make that market work began failing, as there were fewer and fewer buyers for the securities. On top of all of this, spreads between the interest rates on municipal bonds and Treasury bonds widened substantially, increasing the price cities and states paid to borrow.

The problems of the municipal bond industry, along with state and local fiscal problems, threatened the ability of states and cities to be able to build new infrastructure. The Obama administration, looking for "shovel-ready" infrastructure projects that would get Americans back to work, built into ARRA a fix for a municipal bond market in turmoil: Build American Bonds (BABs).[22]

The interest on traditional municipal bonds is exempt from federal income taxes, providing states and local governments with the ability to sell these bonds with lower interest rates. Investors buy municipal bonds with lower interest rates than comparable corporate bonds because they do not have to pay taxes on the interest.[23] The BAB program allowed states and cities to issue municipal bonds with a different and more direct form of federal aid. The interest on BABs was taxable, but instead of providing a tax exemption, the federal government just provided a direct cash subsidy to the issuing government.

BABs came in two flavors. The first and most important were "direct payment bonds."[24] The Treasury paid issuers of direct payment BABs—i.e., state and local governments—a subsidy equal to 35% of the interest payments. That is, they replaced the implicit subsidy to bond issuers that comes with the tax exemption on interest with a direct subsidy in the form of cash payments. The other type were "tax credit bonds," which entitled the purchaser to a federal tax credit worth 35% of the interest.[25]

The central goal of the BAB program was to broaden the market for municipal bonds in order to spur investment.[26] Tax-exempt securities are most attractive to people who pay taxes; foreigners and tax-exempt investors, like pension funds, traditionally avoid them.[27] This means that the market for municipal bonds can be somewhat illiquid, particularly for bonds with long durations used to fund major capital investments.[28]

In contrast, direct payment BABs were equally attractive to all purchasers, domestic or foreign, tax-exempt or not. This was intended to increase the number of potential buyers, thereby increasing liquidity and investment in the market. ARRA only allowed states and cities to issue BABs to fund the building of capital investment projects.

BABs provided other benefits. The tax exemption for municipal bonds is inefficient in an important way. The value of the tax exemption depends on purchasers' tax rates. After all, the reason investors want to buy them is to avoid paying taxes on the interest, making them most attractive to buyers who pay the top marginal tax rate. The subsidy the federal government provides is the foregone tax revenue. But unless all purchasers are in the top marginal income tax band, jurisdictions have to price their bonds (i.e., pay an interest rate) to attract investment from buyers who pay lower tax rates and thus receive a lower effective subsidy than top tax-rate payers.[29] This means there is a windfall for high-income purchasers, who get a tax subsidy based on their high marginal income tax rate, while the interest is priced to make it attractive to someone with a lower marginal income tax rate.[30]

BABs do not have this problem. They provide the same subsidy no matter who the purchaser is. Studies have found that BABs provided a greater subsidy to issuers than the tax-exempt bonds did.[31] The program only lasted two years, but many have called for reviving it today.

There is a powerful argument that traditional tax-exempt municipal bonds are better than BABs, because they are less subject to capital flight and "contagion" risk (an argument I will make in Chapter 11). But BABs proved popular among issuers, constituting a third of newly issued long-term municipal bonds in 2009–10.[32] They also broadened the market, with investments flowing in from nontraditional municipal bond investors.[33] Build American Bonds re-emerged as an idea during the Biden administration, with Congress considering and then rejecting reviving the program as part of an infrastructure push in 2022.[34]

5.3. The End of Stimulus and the Rise of the Pension Crisis

The stimulus ended long before Great Recession did, with Republicans in Congress opposing new rounds of stimulus and pushing for fiscal retrenchment. State and local governments, having received aid during the 2009–10 period, began having to make severe cuts as it aid wound down. These cuts were substantial and lasting.[35] This can be seen clearly in public employment data. Total public employment fell so far that it took years for it to recover. State government only returned to their pre-2008 levels of staffing in 2016. For local governments it was not until 2019.[36] On top of this, states and cities were forced to shift money away from investments in things like roads and K-12 education to pay for two things: healthcare and debt service, particularly on underfunded public pensions.[37]

Healthcare spending takes up an increasingly large share of both private and public expenditures. States, which jointly fund Medicaid programs, were responsible for paying for some of these exploding costs (and Medicaid spending grew faster than ordinary healthcare spending).[38] As a result, healthcare captured an increasingly large share of state budgets.

One major way jurisdictions survived the Great Recession's aftermath was by hiding their fiscal problems by underfunding their public employee pension funds. Despite a long bull stock market, state and local public employee pensions were less well-funded in 2019 than they were in 2009.[39] And underfunded "other public employee benefits" (OPEBs) plans, mostly healthcare benefits for retired public workers, represent a huge and growing pension-like challenge for a number of states and cities.[40] That is, states and cities avoided cutting their budgets by simply not saving money that they would need to provide promised retirement benefits to their workers.

In order to understand the challenges created by pension underfunding, it is important to see that pension underfunding is just a form of debt. And it is a form of debt that states are encouraged to rely on by state constitutional law.

Most state and local public employee pensions are "defined benefit" programs, paid for through a combination of employee and public employer contributions (although the mix and even the presence of public employee contributions varies widely).[41] Money is put into a fund and invested, and then used to pay benefits upon retirement for the rest of the public sector worker's life. Accountants have developed rules for determining how much governments need to save today in order to make sure there is money available when today's public workers retire. What underfunding pensions means is that a government has saved less than accountants believe they need to pay benefits in the future, either because the government has not put enough money away or because investments in funds did not perform to the expected level (more on this below).

Retirement benefits make up a much larger share of total compensation in the public sector than in the private sector.[42] That is, pensions are bigger relative to salaries in the public sector than they are in private sector. This is partially a product of politics. Politicians facing fiscal challenges frequently back-load compensation for public employees, paying for services today with promises of future benefits rather than with present-day wage increases.[43] Public workers are extremely reliant on pension income. Not only do they exchange wage increases for retirement benefits, but many public employees are not eligible for Social Security.[44]

If governments are going to use pensions as a major way to compensate public sector workers, public workers are going to try, both through negotiations and through lobbying, to make sure those benefits cannot be taken away from them. And because pensions are so central to how public employees get paid, their argument that their pensions should be protected against future policy changes is very powerful.

Traditionally, public employee pensions were treated by courts as a gratuity, unprotected by law. But, in response to arguments from public workers, states placed into their constitutions strong legal protections for public employee pensions, either through formal constitutional amendments or judicial interpretations.[45] The exact legal basis for the protections varies by state—in most places, pensions are understood as binding contracts, but in others they are understood as a type of property that the government cannot take without providing just compensation—but almost all states have provided some kind of constitutional protection for pensions.

The scope of this protection varies substantially by state. In some states, these legal protections apply only to the "vested" parts of pension, the benefits the worker has earned and locked in by working for a period of time.[46] But a number of other states have adopted something called the "California Rule," which means that the rules governing pensions cannot be changed for the worse during the life of a worker's public employment. California Rule jurisdictions—including California, New York, and Illinois—cannot change the terms of pensions for existing workers, even for the yet-unearned parts of their pensions. From a teacher or cop's first day on the job to her retirement, the terms of the policy governing pensions must not be diminished. Governments can change other aspects of employment, like salaries, but not pensions.[47] Governments can also give fewer benefits to newly hired workers, but their hands are tied for the entire existing public workforce.

While states like Rhode Island with weaker (or rather, less clearly strong) legal protections have been able to reform and reduce their pension obligations when their debts reached dangerous levels, the California Rule has stood in the way of many efforts to reduce pension obligations.[48] Concerns about under-funding became so severe that state courts in a few California Rule states allowed governments to make changes to things like cost of living adjustments or rules governing the use of vacation time to increase a worker's final salary (which determines the value of a pension).[49] But broadly speaking, the California Rule means pension reform can only affect future workers, not current ones.

However, state constitutional requirements to fulfill pension obligations do not come with a corresponding constitutional duty that states and cities save money in advance so they can actually pay for them.[50]

In theory, pensions are just part of worker compensation. The state, enjoying the services those workers provide today, should put enough money away today to pay for those benefits tomorrow. Not doing so is effectively borrowing money to fund a deficit today.

But this is not how state constitutional law works. A failure to save for pensions due tomorrow is not considered debt for the purpose of state debt limits.[51] A failure to save actually makes it easier for a state to balance its budget. Putting money in a pension fund is generally considered "spending," so not put-ting money away allows for other spending or tax cuts.

On top of this, it is very hard to see what exactly is happening in pension funds. Pension accounting is notoriously complex, and politicians can use this complexity to hide debt.[52] The simplest (but far from the only) mechanism for doing this is by manipulating discount rates. Because pensions must be paid as a legal matter, economists generally believe that states and cities should save enough in their pension funds to pay pensions if the fund were invested at a "risk-free" rate. Because they absolutely have to pay, governments should only count on returns from investments they are absolutely sure will not go down. As a result, the "discount rate"—that is, how you determine much how much you will have tomorrow based on how much you have today—should be equal to the returns on US treasury debt, the classic "riskless" asset.[53]

Pension funds generally do not do this. They frequently make aggressive assumptions about investment returns to set their discount rate.[54] This makes sense under some principles of accounting, but is not considered prudent by economists given the guaranteed nature of the obligation.[55] A government that assumes that it will get a 8% return (perhaps because it has gotten 8% in the past when the market was good) will have to save a lot less than one that assumes it will get 4% return, because it is assuming that the money it puts in today will grow quickly. But to get an 8% expected return, a fund has to bear some risk that its investments will go down. If the market goes down (or the fund does badly for other reasons), the government will still have to pay retired workers, as their pensions are constitutionally guaranteed.

If a state were to adopt more conservative assumptions about future returns, it would have to raise taxes or cut spending today. Doing that would make voters unhappy. Imagine running a political campaign in which you tried to explain that the reason you supported tax increases was because of your deep commitment to prudent accounting assumptions!

Put together, there is a mismatch between state constitutional rules about debt and deficits broadly and the logic of pension accounting and politics. States must pay pensions when they come due, but do not have to save for them. Their failure to save for them does not count as debt. This combination turned public pensions into the ultimate workaround for debt limits and balanced budget rules.

Because states and cities could underfund their pensions as a way of avoiding short-term fiscal pressures, they did so. Pension underfunding in 2019 was worse than it was before the Great Recession, despite a long bull market that should have buoyed pension funds.

Importantly, the level of underfunding has no mechanistic relationship to how much money pensioners receive. A state willing to tax and save for it can provide workers with rich pensions without underfunding. A jurisdiction with cheap pensions can still underfund them. Pension underfunding is just using a form of debt to fund annual budget deficits. States are limited in their capacity to do this in other ways, so they use pension underfunding to help them run deficits.

OPEB liabilities are a bit different. Although rarely tested in the courts, most analysts believe they do not have the same legal protections as pensions.[56] In order to reduce reliance interests in them (which might cause courts to give them legal protections), states and cities often do not save for OPEB liabilities in advance. As healthcare costs have exploded, OPEB liabilities have exploded with them. Not all states and cities have substantial OPEB liabilities, but in some states and localities, they have become a very large part of future liabilities. Even without the strong legal protections pensions have, it is politically hard for jurisdictions to cut OPEB liabilities and thus they are effectively another kind of debt.

Pension underfunding is just like debt in that it creates liabilities that a jurisdiction is legally required to pay in the future. And in many jurisdictions, it is *by far* the largest type of debt. Illinois's had an "adjusted net pension liability" of $241B in 2018, according to Moody's, representing 505% of annual own-source state revenue and 27.8% of state GDP.[57] States differ, of course, but many of them—like Kentucky (308% of own source revenue), Connecticut (286%) and New Jersey (274%)—developed huge and problematic pension underfunding problems.[58]

But pensions are not like bonded debt in an important respect. Debt is supposed to be used to support capital expenditures—things like buildings and roads. The duration of the debt is supposed to be linked to the useful life of the piece of infrastructure.[59] The idea is that each generation that uses a piece of infrastructure should pay for it.[60] If a state borrows to build a bridge, all the users of the bridge pay for their use in the form of payments on the bond.

But pension and OPEB underfunding is not like that. "Pension debt" is money owed to workers for services they have already rendered. There is no building, no road, that current residents enjoy.[61] Instead, taxpayers in jurisdictions with underfunded pension systems are paying taxes not only for the services they enjoy today, but for services yesterday's residents enjoyed. Pension underfunding is an obligation that is not backed by a specific asset. Heavily underfunded pensions mean today's taxpayers are paying for two school systems—today's and yesterday's—as well as two police forces, two set of firefighters, and so on.

There is currently a very lively scholarly debate over whether it makes sense for jurisdictions with underfunded pensions to even try to reach fully funded status. Most scholarship about pensions tries to analyze how hard it would be for states to save enough to "fully fund" their pensions, or to have enough money in their pension funds to be sure they will be able to make payments on pensions for current workers.[62]

Jamie Lenney, Byron Lutz, and Louise Sheiner argue that, instead of focusing on fully funding pensions, states should aim to make paying pensions fiscally sustainable.[63] Pension debt is just debt, they argue, and there is no reason to make today's taxpayers (as opposed to tomorrow's) fully liable for yesterday's decisions not to fund pensions. Stabilizing the cost of pension benefits as a percentage of Gross State Product—effectively making tomorrow's taxpayers pay the same amount for yesterday's pension promises as today's taxpayers do—requires far fewer sacrifices than trying to move toward full funding. They argue that modest changes can lead to stabilization.[64]

This is a powerful argument. But Robert Costrell and Josh McGee disagree. They show that pension underfunding leaves state budgets brittle against shifts in investment returns in pension funds, suggesting an effort to stabilize outflows will frequently leave a state facing challenges.[65] There is some agreement, however. Both sides of this debate agree that at least some jurisdictions need to change their budgets radically even to achieve the more modest goal of stabilizing fiscal outlays.

But the Lenney et al. approach also ignores something else, which is the opportunity cost of pension debt. Ordinary municipal debt is retired as assets age—a city borrows to build a road and pays money back over the life of the road. When a city or state borrows against an asset that has already depreciated, it is called "scoop and toss," one bond replacing another, now unmoored from the goal of spreading out the cost of paying for infrastructure over its useful life. In municipal finance, "scoop and toss" is considered a major no-no, as it reduces the jurisdiction's ability to use borrowed money to invest in new infrastructure.

Lenney et al. effectively propose "scoop and toss" for pensions. Seeing dark clouds ahead, state and local governments in the mid-2010s did not increase their levels of bonded debt much in recent years despite record low interest rates.[66] Just when one would have expected state and local governments to borrow to rebuild roads and bridges, relieve overcrowding in school buildings and fix aging water systems, they cut back.[67] Pension debt has clear effects on bond ratings and borrowing costs.[68] Because states and cities owe so much in pension debt, they are doing less to invest to help their economies grow.

Even though pension debt does not count toward state debt limits, there are both market and political limits on how much debt states can or are willing to bear. And pension debt limits the ability of states and cities to invest in the future. You can see the cost of pension underfunding in crumbling roads, leaking water pipes, and too-crowded school classrooms.

* * *

A combination of disparate actions, undertaken by a politically divided Congress and president, resulted in the federal government effectively splitting the difference between choices along the trilemma. The federal government provided some aid in ARRA but did not renew it even as the recession continued. The federal government also did not provide specific aid to particularly heavily indebted jurisdictions, lest there be too much moral hazard. The reduction in support and the lack of targeting meant that many states and cities had to cut back on spending on services and public employment sharply, extending the recession.

In most cases, there were no defaults or losses for investors. The financial costs to states and cities, however, forced many of them to reduce their investment in new infrastructure, instead building huge portfolios of pension debt. While pension underfunding was a problem before the Great Recession, the combination of the huge fiscal pressures created by the recession and the way state constitutional law encourages pension underfunding turned it into a massive crisis.

But not all jurisdictions were able to avoid default.

5.4. Municipal Bankruptcy in the Great Recession and the Puerto Rico Crisis

After its re-passage in 1938, and even after its reinvigoration in 1975, Chapter 9 municipal bankruptcy was not used frequently. From 1938 to 2015, there were fewer than 700 Chapter 9 bankruptcy filings.[69] And among those, there were only 49 cases involving general-purpose local governments.[70] Other tools were more frequently used in cases of local fiscal crises—most notably, state takeovers and state aid. With a few exceptions, Chapter 9 was not used by big cities or counties.

Local governments need to be "specific[ally] authorized" by the state in order to file.[71] States are loathe to authorize bankruptcy filings because they are worried that allowing one jurisdiction to file will lead lenders to be less willing to lend to local governments generally.[72] That is, they are afraid of "contagion," or the possibility that a default in one jurisdiction leads investors to pull their money from other jurisdictions.[73] Further, because there were so few cases, it was not at all clear how well Chapter 9 functioned at addressing the problems facing heavily indebted general-purpose municipalities.

But the period after the Great Recession was different, with several large municipalities filing for bankruptcy. Court decisions in these cases reshaped how Chapter 9 works, making it a more (if not entirely) functional regime for addressing debt overhangs in general-purpose municipal governments.

For our purposes, what is notable about the decisions in these cases is how openly courts wrestled with the trilemma. Judges debated how far services had to be cut before creditors could be asked to take write-downs as part of bankruptcy. They openly considered whether "plans of adjustment" that favored one class of unsecured creditor over another could be justified on the ground that doing so would reduce future harms to borrowing or hiring. And states offered aid after cases were underway, calibrating their aid to reduce but not eliminate losses by creditors and service recipients.

The result was that the combined set of policies adopted by courts and other governments mixed elements of the trilemma. Rather than choosing to fully burden federal or state taxpayers (through bailouts), local taxpayers (through making debt payments) or creditors (though writing down debt), they burdened all three groups in smaller amounts.

5.4.1. Chapter 9: A Quick Primer

Before discussing the post-2008 cases, it is necessary to explain how Chapter 9 works.[74]

Chapter 9 is built on the form of corporate bankruptcy, but it is conceptually quite different.[75] Unlike a corporation that can't pay its debts, creditors cannot take ownership of a municipality or sell it off for parts. And constitutional concerns stand in the way of a federal court ordering a state government or a municipality from engaging in certain actions. As a result, only a municipality— not its creditors—may initiate a bankruptcy filing. And only a municipality may propose a plan for exiting bankruptcy. Further, it is also, for cities, the only game in town for reducing their debts through a legal process. Federal law now bars states from creating their own municipal bankruptcy systems.[76]

A municipality is only "eligible" to file for bankruptcy under certain limited conditions.[77] First, the municipality must receive "specific authorization" from the state to do so.[78] Second, it must be "insolvent" or unable to pay its debts, a determination that turns out to be quite complex in some cases. Third, the municipality must "have a desire to effect a plan to adjust its debts." And finally, it must have received agreement to file from a majority of different classes of creditors, made an attempt to negotiate in "good faith," or have been "unable to negotiate with creditors because such negotiation is impracticable."[79]

If a municipality is eligible to file, the court will issue an "automatic stay," blocking collection actions by creditors against the city.[80] The municipality generally can then break executory contracts and collectively bargained labor deals.[81] But the court cannot order a city to do much. Under sections 903 and 904 of the bankruptcy code, the court may not direct municipalities to raise taxes or to spend (or not spend) money or to sell property.[82] Whether courts can use discretion in other parts of Chapter 9 to encourage bankrupt cities do to these things has been much debated in the scholarly literature.[83]

To get out of bankruptcy, the municipality must propose "a plan for the adjustment" of its debts—that is, a plan on how debts should be revised by the court, if at all, and about its future fiscal plans.[84] The plan must be "feasible" to implement, that is, it must provide a realistic, not "visionary" path for the municipality to pay what debts remain and provide adequate public services.[85] And the plan must be "in [the] best interest of creditors."[86] However, because unlike in a corporate bankruptcy, a city cannot be liquidated, this has been interpreted to mean that a plan of adjustment need only be better for creditors than the alternatives to bankruptcy, which, given the free-for-all that would follow a dismissal of a Chapter 9 case, is not a high hurdle.[87]

The plan must specify the treatment of the claims of each class of creditor. If the plan of adjustment is accepted by a majority of each class of creditors that is impaired, and by two-thirds by value, a bankruptcy court can confirm it.[88] But if a plan of adjustment is not accepted by some groups of creditors, the bankruptcy court can still confirm the plan and "cram down" the debts owned by dissenters, that is, reduce the amount owed without the creditors' consent.[89] For a cramdown, the plan must be accepted by at least one impaired class of creditors and meet all of the other confirmation requirements (including the feasibility and best interest of creditors tests). Further, the municipality must prove that the plan is "fair and equitable" and does not discriminate unfairly among creditors.[90] This "fairness" inquiry has turned out to be one of the most important parts of Chapter 9.

Until 2010, Chapter 9 was not a major part of our law. And then, after the Great Recession, it was.

5.4.2. Chapter 9 in the Great Recession

The most important Chapter 9 case from the Great Recession was from the city of Detroit. But there were several cases that preceded it and developed the legal framework that would be fully established in the *Detroit* case.

Jefferson County, Alabama

The Jefferson County, Alabama, case was the most sui generis of the post-2008 Chapter 9 cases. Jefferson County had acquired a huge number of underperforming sewer systems from nearby local governments, and, after being sued by the EPA, entered into a consent decree to improve the systems.[91] The County issued bonds to fund repairs, but the cost of these projects was huge, in part because of a corruption scandal.

Trying to save itself, Jefferson County engaged in a complex series of transactions involving auction-rate bonds and interest rate swaps.[92] The transactions also involved an intricate web of payoffs and bribes, which eventually meant the County overpaid by nearly $100M. The main banker, JP Morgan, eventually had to pay penalties to both the County and the SEC.[93]

These contracts blew up in 2008, as part of the broader crisis in the municipal bond market. The collapse of these contracts and swaps crushed Jefferson County's balance sheet: its debt load ballooned from $53 million to $636 million between 2008 and 2009.[94] To make matters worse, in 2009, the Alabama Supreme Court struck down a state law giving the County the power to enact a business license and occupation tax, and, in 2010, struck down a follow-up law passed in 2009 to re-empower the County to pass a similar tax due to some procedural failings.[95] After that, the state refused to reenact the measure, depriving the County of a crucial source of revenue.

After cutting services and expenses and negotiating with creditors, the situation became untenable, and the County filed under Chapter 9.[96]

For our purposes, the most interesting thing about *Jefferson County* case is nothing internal to it, but rather how the State of Alabama responded. Alabama made no effort to bail out Jefferson County. Further, after it made one effort to re-empower the County to raise occupation and business license taxes, it did not make another.[97]

This forced the County to file for bankruptcy. In theory, the state might have been worried about contagion, but it clearly wasn't *that* worried. And there does not seem to have been much to worry about, as there is no evidence that borrowing costs increased for other local governments in the state.

Why wasn't there contagion? One possibility is the weird features of the story of Jefferson County's indebtedness led to a lack of contagion. Jefferson County's crisis was very different from what was going on in other jurisdictions, making its bankruptcy filing potentially less damaging to the broader municipal bond market.

Central Falls, Rhode Island

Central Falls is the smallest, but most densely populated city in Rhode Island. It is also very poor.[98] In an effort to give its economy a shot in the arm, the city borrowed substantially to build (and then rebuild) a prison to house federal detainees.[99] Central Falls also had a massively underfunded pension system.[100] The result was a debt crisis and eventually a Chapter 9 filing.

Two notable things happened in the Central Falls case:

First, the state government in Rhode Island appointed a receiver to govern Central Falls as it navigated Chapter 9, fully displacing the power of the municipal government.[101] We saw types of displacement of local authority in both the New York and Washington, DC, cases, but state laws that entirely removed the power of local officials became more prominent during the post–Great Recession crises.

Second, the state legislature intervened to help bondholders, rather aggressively. It passed a law declaring that bondholders had a statutory lien on property taxes and general fund revenues.[102] In general, debtors cannot create priorities among otherwise equal classes of unsecured debt.[103] But, giving general obligation bondholders a security interest in property taxes—effectively saying these creditors owned the tax revenue in part—moved them ahead in line of other creditors, notably pensioners.[104]

In Central Falls, pensioners ended up taking a 55% haircut and cost of living adjustments were removed (although this was later reduced to about 25% due to increased state aid).[105] This is very different from other Chapter 9 cases in this period, in which pensioners did substantially better than bondholders. The public payroll was reduced by a third.[106] But bondholders were protected.

Rhode Island argued that its bondholder protections were necessary to prevent contagion.[107] Were bondholders asked to face severe haircuts, the broader bond market would be less willing to lend to other jurisdictions, including the state. The state's revenue director was clear: "We wanted to make sure access to credit markets was protected for all the communities in Rhode Island."[108] The state, facing fiscal challenges of its own, was not going to offer a bailout. Instead, it ensured that pensioners, rather than bondholders, saw losses in order to reduce contagion risk, despite the political and social risks of such a move.

San Bernardino, Stockton, and Vallejo, California

Between 2010 and 2012, three California municipalities filed for Chapter 9: San Bernardino, Stockton, and Vallejo.[109] The cities faced similar problems, a decline in revenues due to the post-2008 foreclosure crisis and substantial legacy costs, both in terms of bonded debt and underfunded public employee pension liabilities. In each case, it took courts a lot of time to determine whether they were eligible for bankruptcy, as the courts wrestled with questions about how to determine whether the cities were "insolvent."[110]

For our purposes, the most important developments happened in the *Stockton* case. In order to determine whether Stockton was insolvent, the bankruptcy court needed to wrestle extremely directly with the questions posed by the trilemma.

To be insolvent, and thus eligible to file under Chapter 9, a municipality must either be "generally not paying its debts as they become due" or be "unable to pay its debts as they become due."[111] For a decently sized general-purpose municipality, it is extremely difficult to determine whether a jurisdiction is "unable to pay its debts." After all, a city that sold all of its assets—all of its fire trucks and garbage cans—could get *some* money to make the next payment on its debts. But forcing a city to sell everything that isn't nailed down before it can file for bankruptcy hardly seems wise or even in bondholders' collective interests.

Stockton certainly was in bad shape. It had a 22% unemployment rate. Property values had fallen by 50%, and it had one of the highest foreclosure rates in the country.[112] Further, municipal revenues had collapsed, particularly when compared to the city's large stock of bonded debt and underfunded public employee pensions. Before filing, Stockton cut its spending harshly, reducing spending on departments like police (by 20%) and recreation (56%). Unsurprisingly, service quality declined dramatically. Even so, the city claimed it could not pay its enormous debts with its existing revenue.

But was it insolvent as a legal matter? Creditors argued that government services could be cut even further and that taxes could be increased. The *Stockton* court rejected these arguments, and, in so doing, changed how Chapter 9 works.

The *Stockton* court broke the question of insolvency into three categories— "cash insolvency, budget insolvency and service delivery insolvency."[113] While it was clear that cash insolvency meant not having money on hand, the latter two categories were creations of the court to attempt to fill out what "insolvency" means in the context of a large general-purpose local government.

The *Stockton* court looked into the quality of local services to make sure the city government's cash insolvency was not a "chimera."[114] That is, the city might not have cash on hand to pay its debts, but only because it was spending lavishly on services. The court defined "service delivery insolvency" as a situation in which a city no longer has "the ability to pay for all the costs of providing services at the level and quality that are required for the health, safety, and welfare of the community."[115] Stockton was service delivery insolvent, as "the police department has been decimated. The crime rate has soared. Homicides are at record levels. The City has among the ten highest rates in the nation of aggravated assaults with a firearm. Police often respond only to crimes-in-progress."[116]

However, it is unclear from the court's opinion exactly how one would determine that services are so bad that a jurisdiction faces "service delivery insolvency."[117] There is no federal or state constitutional right to a particular level of local public services.[118] As a result, there is no clear baseline for what level of services are required for health, safety, and welfare.[119] Services inside municipalities like Stockton are likely better than they are in rural areas outside of any municipality.[120]

The most intuitive definition of service delivery insolvency is that a jurisdiction is insolvent when further cuts would reduce revenues by inducing exit or loss of business activity. But this has very little to do with what the court actually did in *Stockton* (or later, in the *Detroit* case). Such a view of the doctrine would require a city to stop providing all or most services to residents who do not pay much in taxes before it becomes eligible for bankruptcy.[121] That is, access to Chapter 9 could only come after city to cut off services to the poor. Needless to say, this would be a crazy rule. And, as the courts in these cases paid close attention to the quality of services for all residents, including those provided to residents not paying much in taxes, it is clear that this is not a rule they applied.

But it is not clear what rule they did apply. That said, the *Stockton* court is surely right that is impossible as a practical matter to determine whether general purpose municipality is insolvent without some concept like service delivery insolvency. Cities can usually make their next payment—by selling off City Hall, perhaps—but a bankruptcy regime that required this would not serve residents, creditors as a whole, or the goals of the statute well.

Scholars have sought to provide their own legal standards to explain service delivery insolvency, but they have not settled on any clear way to make this determination.[122]

The reason is that "service delivery insolvency" requires a fundamentally political decision about the trilemma, rather than a technical or formal one. That is, to make a determination about service delivery insolvency, and thus about insolvency more broadly, the court must decide whether municipalities have made enough cuts that the court will allow them to force creditors to take some losses as well. This is a political determination—it is choosing between two legs of the trilemma—but it also one required by the nature of Chapter 9.

The *Stockton* court also had to address the question of whether the city should be forced to raise taxes before it filed for Chapter 9, that is whether it is "budget insolvent."[123] A tax increase would have needed voter approval and the court held that it did not think voters would approve such an increase without reductions to its bonded debt. Again, the question of how much to ask of voters was not resolvable without making a political judgment.

The other major issue in the *Stockton* case dealt with the status of public employee pensions.[124] The court held that pensions could be reduced in a bankruptcy, as they were a form of debt. But Stockton's eventual plan of adjustment did not call for any cuts to its public employee pensions, despite those pensions constituting the largest part of its debts. A bondholder who saw substantial losses claimed that treating groups of unsecured creditors—bondholders and pensioners—differently constituted unfair treatment and a lack of good faith. The court rejected the bondholders' argument, claiming that city employees had agreed to substantial cuts when negotiating a new collective bargaining agreement and retirees saw their city-provided healthcare cut. Put together, this treatment was fair enough.

Detroit, Michigan

Commentators have compared Detroit's bankruptcy to the way Mike Campbell went broke in Ernest Hemingway's *The Sun Also Rises*: Detroit went bankrupt gradually and then suddenly.[125] The gradual decline was a product of both broader economic trends and local policy decisions that led to the city losing both residents and tax revenue. Total property values fell by 77% in real terms from 1962 to 2012.[126] The city invested in all sorts of projects, from the infamous and rarely used "People Mover" to subsidies for General Motors.[127] But none of this could stem the city's economic decline. The state gave the city a number of new taxing powers over the course of the 20th century, but economic decline ate away at the actual revenues these tools generated. On top of this, the State of Michigan also reduced aid to the city, further worsening the city's budget.

The city's population declined from 1.85M in 1950 to 777K in 2010.[128] This meant it had way too many buildings for its now-smaller population. By 2010, photographers regularly prowled the city for "ruin porn," or pictures of once grand buildings now reduced to rubble.[129] The city's government did not shrink alongside its reduced population and economy. Particularly in the 1990s and 2000s, the city built up huge amounts of debt, both in unfunded pension obligations and bonded debt.[130]

In the final few years before Detroit filed for Chapter 9, it engaged in increasingly desperate tactics. Complex financial engineering made a bad situation worse in the Jefferson County case; it did the same in Detroit.

In 2005, the city was at its debt limit, but needed to put money into its pension fund.[131] With the help of a number of investment bankers, Detroit came up with a bizarre scheme that combined one unwise financial move after another. The city entered into contracts with several newly created nonprofit "service corporations," controlled by city officials, agreeing to pay them money over time in return for money today for the pension fund. These vehicles then created trusts which sold certificates of participation (COPs). The COPs were, for all intents and purposes, pension obligation bonds, or bonds issued to put money into a pension account.[132] Experts are generally skeptical of pension obligation bonds, even when they are not part of a weird transaction, as there's no guarantee that the pension fund will make a return high enough to cover the interest on the bond—it is like borrowing money from the bank to put money into your brokerage account. But the city could not acknowledge that it borrowed money to do this, as it was at its debt limit. Instead, it claimed the contracts with the nonprofits were future-oriented service contracts, as if what it was doing was hiring a janitor but paying him at the end of the month.[133] Further, the city used interest rate swaps, or bets on the future path of interest rates, to protect against interest rate increases (rates ended up declining dramatically, costing the city a pretty penny). The deal, which in retrospect seems totally ridiculous, was so loved by the financial community that it won an award from *The Bond Buyer*, the trade paper covering the municipal bond industry: Midwest Regional Deal of the Year.[134]

The city's decline reached a breaking point in 2012. The state declared a financial emergency and appointed an emergency manager, a prominent bankruptcy lawyer named Kevyn Orr, to take over all governing authority from the mayor and city council.[135] This decision was highly controversial, particularly given the differences in the racial and partisan makeup of the electorates that choose city officials and state ones. After the state gave its authorization, the city filed for bankruptcy under Chapter 9.[136]

The bankruptcy court determined that Detroit was indeed eligible to file for bankruptcy. The decision hit several of the same notes as the *Stockton* case. There

Protestor Outside the Courthouse during the Detroit Bankruptcy Case, Photo by Bill Pugliano/Getty Images

were many legal challenges to the city's eligibility to file, but the three most important were a broad challenge to the constitutionality of Chapter 9, a claim that the state constitution's pension clause rendered the authorization invalid, and an argument that the city was not insolvent.

The court rejected each of these arguments. The broad constitutional challenge to Chapter 9 was that the law was invalid under the 10th Amendment and several "new federalism" cases decided by the Supreme Court in the 1990s and early 2000s.[137] The court rejected these arguments, finding that Chapter 9 did not conflict with constitutionally protected aspects of federalism, as it requires state governments to specifically authorize a bankruptcy filing.[138] We will see this issue come up again in debates over whether Chapter 9 could be extended to state governments.

The court rejected the state constitutional challenge as well.[139] Claimants argued that the pension clause in the Michigan Constitution, which protected pensions against being "impaired or diminished," meant that the state legislative act providing Detroit with its authority to file was unconstitutional. The court rejected this, arguing the pension clause gave pensions the same kind of protection received by other contracts (the federal and Michigan constitutions' Contract Clause provisions bar legislatures from "impairing" contracts), not immunity from bankruptcy.[140] Bankruptcy by its very nature involved reducing the value of contracts. Pensions, like bonds, can take haircuts in bankruptcy.

The final argument involved the nature of insolvency. The court held that Detroit was "service delivery insolvent" and thus had no ability to pay its debts. Without providing a clear standard, the court discussed at length how bad a number of different types of public services in Detroit had gotten to prove that the city government was in fact insolvent.

One crucial issue in the case was how to think about the city's assets, particularly the art in the city-owned Detroit Museum of Art, which included pieces by artists like Vincent Van Gogh, worth hundreds of millions of dollars.[141] The existence of the art did not stop the court from declaring the city eligible for bankruptcy, with the court noting that one-time infusions of cash would not solve Detroit's problems: "When the expenses of an enterprise exceed its revenue, a one-time infusion of cash, whether from an asset sale or a borrowing, only delays the inevitable failure, unless in the meantime the enterprise sufficiently reduces its expenses and enhances its income. The City of Detroit has proven this reality many times."[142]

With eligibility secured, the case could proceed. The bankruptcy court appointed Gerry Rosen, the chief bankruptcy judge of the circuit, as a mediator.[143] Working with Orr, Rosen convinced a number of major philanthropic organizations with ties to Detroit to donate more than $300M to help preserve the value of public employee pensions in return for the museum's art being put under the control of a nonprofit. Rosen and Orr then convinced Michigan's governor Rick Snyder and the state legislature to appropriate money that matched the philanthropic donations.[144] This was a bailout, but it came after a bankruptcy filing rather than before; it also was funded by the state government and private philanthropists rather than the federal government.

With this "Grand Bargain" made, the terms of the plans of adjustment could be reached.[145] Under it, public employee pensioners took much smaller haircuts than other unsecured creditors. Bondholders themselves were divided up, and took losses based on the extent of their legal protections.[146]

The court then had to make another decision, whether to affirm the plan of adjustment.[147] It did so. Like the *Stockton* court, the *Detroit* court's decision affirming the plan accepted the smaller haircuts for pensioners than bondholders. The plan, the court held, was "fair and equitable" for all classes and, while it did discriminate against bondholders, such discrimination was not "unfair."

The court argued that the proper standard for determining unfair discrimination was quite open-ended, interpreting Chapter 9's open-ended language as an invitation for it to "rely[] upon the judgment of conscience."[148] The court then provided several reasons for why in good conscience it could not find that there was unfair discrimination against bondholders.

The state constitution, the court argued, provided a justification for special treatment for pensioners, as its requirement that the state not "impair or diminish" language is a bit stronger the contract clauses requirement that contracts shall not be "impaired."[149] This was in some conflict with the prior holding at the eligibility stage that pensions were contracts just like bonds. The court read the constitutional language to provide a justification for the city treating these different types of unsecured claims differently, even though all could be impaired in a bankruptcy.

The court also argued it was a reasonable to believe that cutting pensions would have a greater impact on the local economy than cutting money for bondholders. And cutting pensions would make it harder to hire public workers in the future, particularly given the harsh cuts to public services the city had made already. The city and state clearly thought this concern was more important than potential effect on the bond market and its future willingness to lend to the city.

The court then accepted the feasibility of the plan going forward. The plan of adjustment had reserved a substantial amount of money for improving services after the crisis, which creditors wanted to recover.[150] But the court found that the plan, and particularly the money for services, put the city on a path to recovery.

The Detroit Chapter 9 case is perhaps the clearest example of a court and a state government wrestling with the trilemma. The court's "service delivery insolvency" decision was all about how much services needed to be cut before it would allow the city to use bankruptcy to reduce claims made by creditors. The State and philanthropists had to decide how and whether to provide aid, despite concerns that it would create moral hazard or come at the expense of other municipalities or interests. In turn, the bankruptcy court had to decide whether the city's decision to favor of one class of unsecured creditors over another was acceptable, eventually determining that the plan would do less to harm the capacity of the city to provide services going forward than other options and would create less short-run economic harm.

Looked at from 10,000 feet, the combined federal and state response to the Detroit bankruptcy split the difference along the trilemma. There were very substantial service cuts leading up to the bankruptcy filing, but some money was saved as part of the plan of adjustment to allow for service improvements. Bondholders and, to a lesser degree, pensioners took losses, although smaller losses than they would have if the state did not offer aid. And the state offered aid, but only after creditors took a hit and after the state had effectively displaced local democracy through the appointment of an emergency manager, reducing moral hazard.[151]

Unlike its response to the New York City fiscal crisis, the federal government did not offer much substantial aid, despite efforts by President Obama to convince Congress to do so.[152] This made the recovery efforts by the city harder, but also seems to have burnished the federal government's reputation for not providing bailouts. This had real effects, reducing market willingness to lend to bad credit risks like Puerto Rico.[153]

Although there are still many critics and the decision to remove authority from city officials remains very controversial, the Detroit Chapter 9 case is commonly seen as a success.[154] The city—at least its downtown and business district, if not all of its neighborhoods—has seen a pretty substantial economic recovery, including large inflows of investment.[155] There are still substantial worries that the city carried too much debt even after bankruptcy and that it still cannot provide sufficient services, particularly to its poorest residents. But, even so, taken as a whole, the response by the federal government and the state of Michigan was balanced.

One final note. As Detroit was going bankrupt, the Detroit school district—an independent government with the same geographic boundaries as the city—was also in fiscal crisis.[156] The state provided enough aid that the school district did not have to file for bankruptcy. This was a pure bailout. Further, it meant that people who lent to the school district and teacher pensions saw no losses, while people who lent to the city and firefighter pensions took substantial losses.

5.5. Puerto Rico and PROMESA

The fiscal and humanitarian crisis of Puerto Rico in recent years and the federal response to it is complicated enough to deserve several books of its own. But despite its wild story, involving several natural disasters, multiple Supreme Court cases,[157] and a truly unique federal response,[158] some lessons can be derived from it.

The very short version of the story of Puerto Rican debt crisis starts with two parts of federal tax laws that aided the Commonwealth for many years. The first was Section 936 of the Internal Revenue Code, which granted US corporations a tax exemption from income originating in US territories.[159] This gave companies an incentive to locate in Puerto Rico. It was very successful, bringing large pharmaceutical producers to the island. Second, Congress provided special tax incentives to holders of Puerto Rican bonds.[160] Municipal bonds are generally exempt from state income taxes for holders who live in the state in which they are issued. By federal law, the interest earned on Puerto Rican bonds is exempt from federal tax and taxation by all states and all municipalities, making Puerto Rican debt "triple tax exempt" in all jurisdictions.[161] This allows Puerto Rico to borrow at a much lower rate than other jurisdictions with its level of risk.

Starting in 1996, Congress began a 10-year phase out of Section 936's corporate tax breaks, landing a hammer blow to Puerto Rico's economy.[162] It did not remove the other tax break, meaning that Puerto Rico's government could still borrow at favorable rates. And borrow it did.

The end of the corporate tax break and the 2008 recession sent Puerto Rico's economy into a tailspin. By 2015, over 45% of the population was in poverty, and less than half of eligible workers were participating in the formal economy.[163] Puerto Rico has lost over half a million inhabitants.[164] This left a much smaller economy and population, though, to support a very large amount of public debt.[165] Puerto Rico had fifteen times as much debt per capita as the median US state and slightly less than three times as much per capita as the most indebted state.[166]

And, although Puerto Ricans benefit from the Commonwealth's non-state status, avoiding federal income taxes, the Puerto Rican government also does not receive direct funding at the level of actual states, including, crucially, substantially less Medicaid funding.[167] On top of this, Puerto Rico's government was, to say the very least, not a model of efficiency. The government continued to grow, even as the population, and the island's revenues, continued to shrink.

Puerto Rico's debt was spread across a number of public entities and authorities.[168] This was made more complicated still in 2006, when the Commonwealth created a new public finance corporation known as COFINA.[169] The idea was similar to what New York City did during its fiscal crisis. COFINA was given the power to issue bonds backed by the Commonwealth's sales tax revenue and transfer the proceeds to the government.[170] General obligation (GO) bondholders had expected sales tax revenue to be part of how they'd get paid back themselves, particularly because a clause in the Commonwealth's Constitution seemed to require GOs to be paid first in case of default.[171] But, because COFINA's bonds provided purchasers with an interest in a specific revenue source, COFINA purchasers arguably were in a stronger position in the case of a default. The structure encouraged investors to purchase bonds they might not otherwise have, even as it caused consternation among the holders of GOs bonds.

Puerto Rico continued to issue debt right until the bitter end. Its last issuance of GO debt in 2014—arguably issued in violation of the Commonwealth's constitutional debt limit—paid yields above 8%, which, for tax-exempt bonds in a generally low-interest rate era, was incredibly high.[172] Several scholars have shown that one reason lenders kept lending to Puerto Rico was that they expected the Commonwealth to be bailed out.[173] Once Detroit did not get federal aid, however, interest rates on Puerto Rican debt spiked.

But after a series of downgrades from credit-rating agencies, the Puerto Rican government was forced to acknowledge that "the debt was not payable."[174] The Commonwealth asked famed economist Anne Krueger to study its finances. She found that the government had almost no available money to pay its debts.[175] Puerto Rico tried to plunge several of its instrumentalities into a bankruptcy system of its own creation.[176] The Supreme Court stopped this, holding that, despite the fact that Puerto Rico municipalities were specifically barred from using Chapter 9 municipal bankruptcy by statute, the federal law that stops states from creating their own municipal bankruptcy systems still applied to Puerto Rico.

In the summer of 2016, after a complex negotiation between President Obama's administration and the Republican-controlled Congress, Congress passed the Puerto Rico Oversight, Management and Economic Stability Act (PROMESA).[177] PROMESA created a federally appointed Oversight Board, with the power to either accept a fiscal plan proposed by the governor or, alternatively, to propose its own. Future budgets would have to match that plan (and the Board had the power to reject spending inconsistent with the plan).[178] The Board did not have direct control over the Commonwealth's government, however, or control over a number of key policy areas.[179]

Further, under Title III of PROMESA, the Board could declare that Puerto Rico and any of its instrumentalities had no ability to pay their debts and file for something that was much like Chapter 9 bankruptcy.[180] Although technically the decision of whether to file under Title III was up to the Board, it was clear beforehand that PROMESA was an effort to make creditors share in the cost of the fiscal crisis, while also ensuring that Puerto Rico reduced the size and scope of its government spending. Like Detroit, this involved a balance between two legs of the trilemma without federal bailout money. But, unlike Detroit, there was no state government or nonprofit sector money to help out. The Board and the Puerto Rican government agreed on a fiscal plan, and put the Commonwealth and many government instrumentalities into Title III.[181]

But the situation all changed when (more) tragedy struck. Hurricanes Irma and Maria hit the island, killing thousands of residents and doing more than $100B in damage.[182] Many more people fled the island. Federal disaster aid helped the government out, but also reduced the power of the Oversight Board, as the Puerto Rico's government no longer needed the board's permission to spend money.[183] While the island struggled to get back on its feet economically, policy reforms favored by the Oversight Board stalled.[184] (This was true even when the governor at the time, Ricardo Rosselló, was enmeshed in a corruption scandal and had to resign.)[185]

The Title III case continued, with the Board engaging in negotiations with creditors over the course of several years. These negotiations went on despite the lack of a clear picture about the future of Puerto Rico's economy and fiscal outlook once disaster relief ended.[186]

After striking a number of deals with creditors, the Board proposed a final plan of adjustment just before the COVID pandemic hit.[187] The plan included some cuts to pensions, and very substantial haircuts for a number of bondholders, including recoveries that were contingent on increased economic activity on the island.[188] The haircuts, however, were smaller than many critics wanted, leaving substantial doubts as to the long-term health of the Commonwealth's fiscal situation.[189] The Board proposed a revised plan in November 2021 that reduced the cuts to pensions due to pressure from Puerto Rico's governor, and the judge in the Title III case approved the plan of adjustment in January 2022.[190]

So much about the Puerto Rico case is unusual that it is hard to draw lessons from it. Still three important elements are worth highlighting. The first is the federal government's effort to differentiate this case from all others. For instance, Congress explicitly did not call Title III "bankruptcy." This was an effort to differentiate Puerto Rico's situation from that of fiscally challenged states.[191] The goal was to avoid one of the long-term downsides of Puerto Rican default by claiming that Puerto Rico is an exceptional case, so investors need not worry about losing money when lending to state governments. And Puerto Rico really is very differently situated than US states. Because Puerto Rico is an oversees territory and not a state, it lacks direct Congressional representation. The owners of Puerto Rican debt were different as well. Because Puerto Rican debt is triple-tax exempt, bondholders came from all over the country, not just one state. Eventually, a substantial amount of Puerto Rican debt was held by "vulture" funds, investors who scooped it up when its value was very low, making a bailout very difficult politically (the same issue that bedeviled Alexander Hamilton before he succeeded in pushing through his assumption of state debts.)[192]

Even so, the municipal debt market for state governments responded directly to a series of legal decisions in Puerto Rico, suggesting that the market sees Puerto Rico as a relevant precedent for future state defaults.[193]

Second, the COFINA bonds used the same basic technology as New York City's "Big MAC" bonds. That is, they took a major revenue stream that GO bondholders had expected to be used to support their debt and assigned it to a new set of bondholders in return for new capital. The COFINA bonds, however, differed from "Big MAC" bonds in a few key respects. The COFINA bonds were legally weaker, as the Puerto Rican constitution requires that all available revenues first be dedicated to paying back GOs.[194] Further, they were issued by the same level of government—the Commonwealth—that issued the GOs, unlike "Big MAC," which the state set up the new entity and removed the taxing authority from the city. The COFINA bonds were also a more abusive structure. The "Big MAC "bonds were used to bridge a short-term liquidity problem as part of a broader restructuring of New York City government. The COFINA bonds predated any real effort at reform and were just an effort to prolong the solvency of the Commonwealth.[195] Even so, COFINA bondholders were able to strike a deal with GO holders on substantially favorable terms, suggesting that insiders thought such tax-assignment strategies would hold up in court. As a result, these tax-assignment strategies will likely remain a viable tool for struggling governments.[196]

Third, while Title III was modeled on Chapter 9, it contained two major innovations. Title III did not require a court to certify the insolvency of any entity. That the Board decided to file was sufficient for determining eligibility.[197] Further, all PROMESA cases, across the variety of heavily indebted government entities in Puerto Rico, were heard by a single judge.[198] This is in stark contrast with how Chapter 9 operates, where there is no mechanism for having a single judge hear cases of overlapping local governments (like counties, cities, and school districts).

5.6. Conclusion

The Great Recession of 2008 ushered in a variety of innovations in how the federal government addressed state and local budget crises. The most important of these—the Puerto Rico Title III case and the *Detroit* and *Stockton* decisions— put courts and state officials in position to wrestle with the question of how much austerity is required before creditors can be asked to take losses.

COVID-19, the CARES Act, the MLF, and the ARP

At the end of 2019, states and cities were finally beginning to pull out of the fiscal problems they faced during the Great Recession. The number of state public employees had surpassed their 2008 total in 2016, but the number of local governmental employees only returned to July 2008 levels in 2019.[1] State "rainy day funds," or the savings accounts states hold in case of budget downturns, were at record highs in 2019.[2]

However, danger lurked. Pension funds were less well-funded than they were in 2008, despite a long bull market.[3] And states had foregone investment in infrastructure and education for many years, instead devoting resources to healthcare and pension payments (and not raising taxes).[4] Across the board, aggregate data obscured a great deal of variation, as some states—notably Illinois, but also Connecticut, New Jersey, Kentucky, and a few others—and a number of large cities, counties, and school districts had accumulated very severe loads of bonded and pension debt, while others were relatively healthy.[5]

Then the COVID-19 pandemic hit in March 2020. States had to shut down most of their economies in response. State and local budgets experts projected a complete collapse in tax revenues.[6] The threat of vast revenue declines loomed over states as unemployment spiked to record highs.[7] Certain taxes—like gas, hotel, and restaurant taxes—took a particular beating (although the capacity to tax online sales, made much easier by Supreme Court in 2018, cushioned the blow for many states and cities).[8] Revenues from road tolls, transit fares, and elective surgeries at public hospitals collapsed.[9]

On top of this, expenses exploded. In recessions, demand for redistributive services always expands, from Medicaid to aid for the homeless. As this was a massive recession, demand increased for services dramatically in early 2020.[10] And the fact that it was a pandemic meant that expenses for things like cleaning up buildings, opening schools, operating public hospitals, and providing homeless shelters and services for populations facing very high risks from the pandemic went up substantially. Running buses and trains remained expensive, but they were less full, due not only to reduced consumer spending but also to public health concerns.

Then the municipal bond market seized up, making borrowing difficult.[11] State officials, like the president of the Illinois State Senate, sought massive bailouts from the federal government.[12] Newspapers began covering the fiscal travails of particularly hard hit types of local governments—authorities governing shuttered convention centers, public hospitals unable to conduct elective surgeries, transit agencies suddenly lacking passengers and farebox revenue.[13] To many observers, it seemed as if a wave of state and local fiscal crises was in the offing.

States and cities around the country started furloughing and laying off workers almost immediately at the beginning of the crisis, with nearly 5% of public sector workers nationwide losing their jobs due to layoffs and furloughs.[14] Even as employment numbers increased in the late spring and early summer of 2020, public sector job numbers continued to decline. By the year's end, more than 1.2M public workers had lost their jobs since the beginning of the crisis.[15] Jurisdictions also started not making payments into their pension systems, a form of debt financing for operating expenses.[16] States and cities were battening down the hatches for a major crisis.

But state and local governmental budgets recovered far more quickly than experts predicted. The central reason is that wages and investment income did not decline as much as expected. This was in part a technological story. More of the economy could run online, both sales and higher-end service work, than many expected. But it was also a product of a series of remarkable federal policy interventions.

While it will not be the major focus of this section, the most important interventions were made along dimensions other than direct aid to states and cities. The federal government's (and state government's) public health response to the pandemic will be studied for a very long time, and certainly contained many failures. The extent of the pandemic, the testing regime, and so forth, created the conditions for economic and social distress of 2020 and 2021. The vaccine rollout created the conditions for an economic recovery in 2021 and 2022, although the rise of the Delta variants of COVID-19 and vaccine hesitancy slowed the recovery down at first.

But while the public health response was tepid relative to what was seen in other countries, the federal government's emergency response to the economic recession was genuinely enormous, substantially larger than what was seen across Europe and much of the rest of the developed world.[17] The Federal Reserve's interventions to calm markets, both domestically and internationally, and provide stimulus were momentous. And across a series of bills, both during the last year of President Donald Trump's time in office and the beginning of President Joe Biden's term in office, Congress provided a huge amount of fiscal support to individuals and businesses—from "stimmys" (individual checks to most Americans) to federal programs that lent to businesses to enhanced unemployment insurance to a hugely expanded child tax credit.

These interventions aided the economy substantially and thus indirectly helped state and local coffers (although also kicked off a rise in inflation, a subject for a different book). State tax revenues did not fall as much as expected, and indeed rose as the economy took off.[18] Individual incomes were surprisingly stable, and the stock market boomed, buoying individual income and thus state tax receipts.[19] Property tax revenue, on which local governments are heavily reliant, is backward-looking and did not decline immediately at the beginning of the pandemic. Then, during the recovery, residential housing prices climbed substantially, which should lead to revenue increases in the future.[20] (The long-run effect on downtown office and retail real estate values, in contrast, likely will be quite negative, given the increase in working from home, which will have a substantial effect on local tax revenue.[21])

But the policy responses by both Congress and the Fed also acted directly on state and local budgets. The federal government's policy during this period represented a massive change in how it addresses state and local fiscal distress.

What the federal government did was provide money, and lots of it. Fiscal aid to states and cities across several pandemic response bills more than filled the state and local fiscal gaps created by the pandemic and recession.[22] In March 2020, Congress passed the CARES Act, which provided $150B in general aid to states and cities, and more to schools and transit agencies. This aid, however, did not fully address state and local budget shortfalls, leading to the continuation of furloughs and layoffs through 2020. The CARES Act also backstopped a Federal Reserve program, the Municipal Liquidity Facility (MLF), designed to fix problems in the municipal bond market by lending directly to states and cities.

In December 2020, after much political wrangling and following the November elections, Congress passed a bill that provided $82B in education aid, most of which went to school districts and public universities, and around $30B to transit agencies, roads, and other state infrastructure projects.[23] Then, after Joe Biden replaced Donald Trump as president, Congress passed the American Rescue Plan (ARP) in March 2021.[24] It provided $195B to state governments and $130B to local governments, as well as $122B in aid to schools and $30B more in aid to transit agencies, as well as some other forms of aid. A large infrastructure bill, which devoted a large amount of money to state infrastructure funds, passed later in 2021 further supplemented state budgets.[25]

This was an enormous amount of aid. Many states saw full coffers for the first time in decades. One commentator said of the perpetually strapped New York State budget: "I picture the governor's budget office as being like a drug dealer's kitchen, with bricks of $100 bills hidden in the microwave, under the sink, in the back of the freezer."[26] California's budget was so flush it just started sending tax rebates to residents.[27] Even budget basket cases like New Jersey and Illinois had "surprising cash windfalls," and "swelling tax revenues."[28] The *Wall Street Journal* ran a story in early 2022 with the headline: "States Are Swimming in Cash Thanks to Booming Tax Revenue and Federal Aid."[29]

Without the benefit of hindsight, it is hard to determine the full effect of Congress's state and local aid package, never mind the full suite of stimulus and recovery efforts enacted by Congress in this period.

But the early indications are that the basic structure of the trilemma applied. That Congress did not provide overwhelming state aid early in the pandemic and recession led to a huge number of state and local layoffs and furloughs, deepening the unemployment crisis. The later tranches, though, provided effective stimulus, protecting state budgets and spurring lots of economic activity.

The CARES Act was designed to reduce moral hazard by being provided to all states, with no consideration for budgetary need. Further, it came with substantial conditions that made it hard for states to spend the money, particularly that the money was not supposed to be used to fill in for revenue losses. The MLF was also designed to avoid excessive moral hazard by providing funds only at relatively high interest rates. While it steadied bond markets, the Federal Reserve used to the program to buy bonds from just two jurisdictions.

The later tranches, particularly the ARP, were more generous, although they also went to all jurisdictions. But while Congress now allowed states and cities to use the money to fill in for lost revenue, it still included substantial conditions as to what the money could spent on, limiting states and localities from using federal aid to support tax cuts or pension funds.[30]

The contents of the ARP state aid provisions support Jonathan Rodden's claim that federal aid to subnational government usually comes with conditions that reduce their fiscal independence. A federal government that provides aid but remains worried about moral hazard will seek control over state and local finances, lest state take advantage of the aid to spend without consequence. While this aid was responsive to a particular type of recession, set off by a (hopefully) once-in-a-hundred years pandemic, Rodden's argument was borne out.

Further, even though both the CARES Act and the ARP included many provisions designed to reduce moral hazard, the municipal bond market responded to those acts by making credit very freely available to states and cities, even to jurisdictions that have been seen as posing substantial credit risks. Whether this was a response to their improved fiscal condition because they received federal aid, or whether it was based on expectations of future aid—that is, an expectation of bailouts—is not yet clear. But it seems likely that at least some of the reduced rates available to states and cities are premised on expectations of future aid. That is, it seems likely that federal aid created some moral hazard through its effect on the bond market.

How states write their budgets over the next few years is still up in the air. Some, like Connecticut, seem to be approaching the future conservatively. But many others are aggressively using their federal aid to set up new programs or to cut taxes, rather than putting the money toward their long-term obligations. This story is still unfinished.

6.1. Who CARES about States and Cities?

In March 2020, the COVID-19 pandemic swept across the country, forcing individuals and then governments to shut down much of society and the economy. Congress responded quickly and aggressively. The first stimulus packages were largely aimed at goals other than aiding states and cities, with most of the money going to individuals through personal checks and increased unemployment insurance and to support businesses. That aid, however, indirectly helped states, however, as it meant that, despite increasing unemployment, personal incomes actually increased during Summer 2020. These benefits and on the broader economy they supported meant that state and local tax revenue fell by far less than expected.

Congress approved three economic relief packages at the outset of the COVID-19 pandemic recession, and then another one in December 2020. In the first two bills, there were a few provisions that helped states, the biggest of which was an increase in the "match" rate for state Medicaid spending for the regular Medicaid population (i.e., not those added under the Affordable Care Act's Medicaid expansion).[31] This provided states with about $40B.[32]

The biggest of the three initial stimulus bills was the third one, the CARES Act.[33] While it included many different elements, a substantial piece of the bill was devoted to providing aid to states and cities. The CARES Act included $150B in aid to states, allocated on the basis of population, with a minimum of $1.25B per state.[34] Local governments with populations over 500K were allowed to apply for direct aid, which would be deducted from the allocations of the state in which they sit.

There were conditions on the money, however. The money could only be used for expenditures necessitated by COVID-19 and that were not accounted for in the last budget the state had passed. Further, the money had to be spent on expenses incurred between March 2020 and the end of the year.

The Treasury Department noted that it would interpret the "necessitated" language broadly, but, even so, the funds could not be used to make up for shortfalls in revenue created by the recession.[35] The effect of the conditions was to substantially limit what states could do with the money, stopping them from using it to plug budget holes and slowing the rate at which states actually used the aid.[36]

The CARES Act also included a whole variety of other spending that mostly aided state and local budgets: $8B for tribal governments, $30B for schools and universities, $25B for mass transit systems, $5B for community development block grants, $3.5B for childcare, and $400M for election preparation.[37]

The CARES Act shows how worries about moral hazard and the makeup of the US Senate constrains and shapes state aid. The underlying logic of the aid seemed to be that the federal government, rather than state or local governments, should be the entity that tries to ensure against the risk of global pandemics. But Congress chose to make aid general, based on population, with a minimum per state that aided smaller states, rather than aiming at specific jurisdictions that either had particularly bad COVID-19 outbreaks or were suffering economically. As discussed in Chapter 1, the political structure of Congress makes direct infrastructure spending hard. For the same reason, providing aid to the limited number of states most affected by a crisis is challenging for Congress, as every Senator and representative wants a piece of this aid for her city or state. (That states with small populations got much more money per capita than big ones also reflects the influence of the Senate, which provides representation by state rather than by population.)

Further, providing aid to every state meant that it created less moral hazard. States could access the money regardless of whether they overspent in the past, meaning that the aid produced less of incentive an to overspend in the future. The conditions Congress put on the aid limited federal spending to pandemic relief, rather than bailing out governments for past promises.

However, this combination of (not) targeting and conditions made state and local aid less effective than it might have been at stimulating the economy and improving services. The money went out slowly and was not available for the uses states most wanted to preserve. And the total amount was insufficient to avoid very substantial state and local job losses.

Congress also considered but rejected other approaches. At one point, Senate Majority Leader Mitch McConnell (R-KY) suggested Congress should consider expanding municipal bankruptcy law to allow state governments to file for bankruptcy, as an alternative to providing more state aid.[38] This led to widespread criticism and did not go anywhere. (In Chapter 9, I will respond to these criticisms and lay out the case for Congress passing a state bankruptcy law.)

The state aid in the CARES Act had a real, but limited effect on state and local budgets. Of more importance were the other parts of the CARES Act, which increased personal incomes and generally helped the economy, and thus aided state budgets indirectly. This highlights that state aid is only one way to stimulate a depressed economy and, that, if Congress can actually pass massive stimulus packages, the need to aid states directly is reduced.

In addition to direct aid, the CARES Act also included a genuinely innovative policy of using Congressionally appropriated money to "backstop" programs run by the Federal Reserve to directly lend money to ordinary businesses and other market participants. One of those programs was directly targeted at states and cities.

6.2. The Municipal Liquidity Facility

The other major intervention into state and local fiscal affairs in the Spring of 2020 was the creation of the Municipal Liquidity Facility (MLF). As happened in many markets, municipal bond markets seized up in March 2020, as investors sold securities or refused to buy them, seeking cash as the pandemic first hit.[39] Municipal bond funds are the biggest purchaser by far of municipal securities. When investors fled these funds seeking cash, pulling out more than $19B a week for two consecutive weeks, the funds were forced to sell their underlying securities at a loss.[40] Spreads (the difference in interest rates) between municipal bonds and treasury bonds increased rapidly.[41] States and cities that went to market in this period tried to sell $16B bonds but were able to find buyers for only $6B of them.

The Federal Reserve acted quickly. On March 20, 2020, it began accepting short-term municipal bonds purchased from mutual funds as collateral for lending to banks as part of its Money Market Mutual Fund Facility, thereby backstopping "money market municipal funds" that had seen huge outflows.[42] Three days later, the Fed expanded this program to accept variable rate demand notes (VRDNs)—a market that had suffered particular problems and was causing problems for banks—as eligible collateral for Fed loans.[43] These early interventions had some effect on municipal bond yields.[44]

The scope of Federal Reserve interventions into the municipal bond market increased dramatically after the CARES Act. Congress allocated money to create a reserve for Federal Reserve programs to intervene in financial markets, including $35B to support a Federal Reserve program to buy municipal bonds.[45] The Federal Reserve has always had the power to buy very short-term municipal debt pursuant to its authority under Sec.14(2) of the Federal Reserve Act.[46] However, the MLF was different, since it was created under the aegis of Sec. 13(3) of the Federal Reserve Act, which is not subject to the limits on purchases imposed under Section 14(2).[47] In Sec. 13(3) programs, the Fed can buy other types of debt, but is not permitted to take on too much risk. This made the injection of Treasury money important, as it allowed the Fed to engage in riskier investments, as the Treasury's money could protect against losses.[48]

Under the MLF, the Federal Reserve agreed to buy municipal bonds directly from issuers (i.e., states, cities, and districts).[49] The Fed started off only allowing states and large cities to borrow from the MLF, but later expanded access to the facility to include smaller cities (with populations as low as 250,000 or even lower if they were designated by the state government) and some designated non-general-purpose local governments (like transit authorities).[50]

But even as the number of eligible governments expanded, the goals of the program were limited to the goals of classic central banking. The MLF offered to lend to credit-worthy governments based on their credit rating, plus a penalty term, a classic lender-of-last-resort function.[51] That is, when setting the interest rate it would buy bonds at, it set rates using issuers' credit rating, and then added a bonus, making the interest rates on MLF loans quite high. This was done to ensure that its money was being used to address short-term liquidity crises—an inability to borrow because the market was spooked—not general budget problems. The Fed reduced the penalty in August 2020, bringing down the prices it charged, but not by as much as many critics wanted.[52] Further, the loans were limited to short-term debt, originally one year and then extended to three years.[53] The goal was to ensure there was liquidity in the municipal bond market, that states and cities could borrow if they absolutely had to, not to alleviate the problems of jurisdictions suffering from long-run fiscal problems.[54]

The MLF succeeded in reviving the municipal bond market.[55] In an empirical study, economists Huixin Bi and W. Blake Marsh found strong evidence that "the announcement of a dedicated credit facility for the municipal market with a Treasury backstop led to sizeable declines in municipal bond yields."[56] Much of the municipal bond market had effectively shut down in March, but, by fall, spreads between highly rated municipal securities and Treasuries narrowed very substantially, saving states and localities huge sums of money.[57] The MLF did this without actually buying many securities. In fact, the MLF only made one deal by July 2020, buying some debt from the state of Illinois.[58] In August, New York's beleaguered Metropolitan Transportation Authority, which saw a huge decline in farebox revenue, sold bonds to the MLF.[59] No other government asked to access the MLF. But the existence of the MLF seemed to calm the market.

It is unclear why so few issuers sought to use the MLF. States and cities might have not done so because of constitutional debt limits and state restrictions on using debt to fund operating expenses. Also, because the municipal bond market revived, states and cities were able to sell their bonds without relying on the Fed and the penalty rates it demanded. For instance, New Jersey's plan to borrow (potentially from the MLF) to cover operating expenses became enmeshed in litigation before the state's supreme court finally blessed it.[60] By the time the litigation was done, New Jersey's fiscal condition and the health of the municipal bond market had improved, so it did not need to borrow from the Fed.

Regardless, the existence of the facility had the effect of convincing market actors that state and local governments would not face a liquidity crisis, creating confidence among investors.[61] Federal Reserve economists Andrew Haughwout, Benjamin Hyman, and Or Shachar found "overall secondary market yields and primary issuance for the most part returned to normal market functioning as a result of the totality of Federal interventions that were introduced between mid-March and the end of April 2020."[62] The MLF also convinced investors that governments that needed debt in this period would not default on account of lack of access to credit, making buying their bonds a surer bet. Haughwout and his coauthors also show that direct access to the MLF was particularly valuable for lower-grade issuers, having a large effect on borrowing costs for those issuers in particularly bad fiscal positions.[63]

However, a number of Senators and commentators wanted the MLF to do more, both expanding it to include more issuers and lending at lower rates, in order to provide more aid to states and cities.[64] While the Fed did expand the program to apply to more issuers, it did not do so in a way that has made it attractive to many states and cities.[65] Other critics sought to convince the Fed to extend the program past December 2020. But after President Trump lost the election in November 2020, his outgoing treasury secretary, Steve Mnuchin, asked the Federal Reserve to return the money used in the MLF, and the Fed complied.[66] The December 2020 stimulus bill (see below) explicitly ended Treasury support for the MLF and barred the Fed from using a particular source of money, the Exchange Stability Fund, for facilities it created using CARES Act money.[67]

The reason for the Fed's reluctance to expand the program was likely a concern over moral hazard. Making loans directly to states and cities more closely resembles a bailout than the general aid in the rest of the CARES Act. Unless the Fed bought all new bond issuances from all municipal bonds issuers (i.e., all new state and local government debt), it would need to target its efforts somehow. This would likely mean buying bonds from the most indebted and fiscally perilous states and cities. Even without purchasing many bonds, the MLF had its biggest effects on issuers with low credit-ratings, as the potential for loans from the Fed reassured other lenders that jurisdictions that faced fiscal challenges would not default.[68] A broader MLF would have provided subsidized loans to the most fiscally at-risk jurisdictions, a classic form of bailout.

Using the Fed to provide extensive bailouts would have been very unpopular with many Members of Congress. Further, it would have created pressure to make the loans conditional on recipients making policy changes. Conditionality would have minimized the credit risk the Fed opened itself up to—the conditions would presumably be aimed at improving a state's fiscal position—and would limit moral hazard among issuers.[69] But imposing conditionality would have threatened the independence of the Fed, enmeshing it in state and local politics.

Instead, the Fed built a program that was automatic, short-term, and expensive to access.[70] Doing so successfully addressed the liquidity problem in the municipal bond market and avoided concerns about creating moral hazard. But it did not fundamentally change the fiscal picture for states and cities hit hard by COVID-19 and the recession that followed, meaning that states and cities needed to fire many workers and cut back spending, harming the economy during the recession.[71]

6.3. The December 2020 Stimulus and the ARP

During the election of 2020, there was a substantial debate about state aid. President Donald Trump and Republicans in Congress characterized Democratic proposals for new state and local aid as a "blue state bailout," despite the fact that some of the hardest hit states were controlled by Republicans. Republicans offered arguments rooted in moral hazard, that aid would support underfunded pension systems and government waste rather than stimulate the economy or provide direct services to people who needed it. Democrats countered with macroeconomic arguments about state and local governments firing workers and the particular need for services during the pandemic and recession. Congress debated new stimulus packages through the fall of 2020, but was unable to come to an agreement.

However, once Joe Biden defeated Trump in the Presidential election, Congress was able to come to an agreement. In December 2020, Congress agreed on a new aid package. Again, most of the focus was not on states and cities, with direct aid checks or "stimmys" of $600 and enhanced unemployment insurance benefits, receiving most of the money and media attention. It also explicitly removed funding and legal support for the Fed's credit programs, including the MLF.

Despite Democrats pushing for it, the December 2020 bill did not include general state and local aid.[72] It did, however, include substantial other forms of aid to state and local governments. There was $82 billion in education, including $54 billion for K-12 schools and $20B in higher education grants, most of which went to public universities. It also included a great deal of transportation money, including $14B for transit systems and $10B for highway systems. There was also money allocated to states for vaccine distribution and other COVID-19 response costs, and money for all sorts of things the states might otherwise spend money on, like rental tenant assistance.

Joe Biden, signing the American Rescue Plan, WhiteHouse.Gov

But this was outdone by what Congress passed in March 2020 once President Biden was in office. With control over both houses of Congress and the White House, and relying on the budget reconciliation process to avoid the filibuster, Democrats were able to pass the American Rescue Plan (ARP), a $1.9T package that included everything they sought over the course of 2020 and more.[73] The ARP topped up the $600 individual "stimmys" from the December bill to $2000 by including $1400 individual checks; expanded and made fully refundable the Child Tax Credit, further expanded unemployment insurance, and provided increased paid leave for workers among other elements.

The ARP also provided a *huge* amount of state and local aid. By the time the bill passed, most state budgets were not in particularly rough shape, for the reasons discussed above. But several still had some substantial revenue losses, including large states like Florida, Texas, and New York. In addition, many local governments faced substantial fiscal problems.[74]

Although it was only part of a larger package, much of the criticism of the ARP was focused on the state and local aid package. Even many supporters of the bill argued that the Democrats were excessively locked in on a large state and local aid package that would have made sense given what was known early in the pandemic, but made less sense given the improving state fiscal picture.[75]

The total amount of general aid $350B to states and local governments, plus over $170B for both public and private K-12 schools and universities (and even more for a number of specific state and local programs) was far, far larger than the revenue losses state and local governments faced in total.

Of that $350B, $220B went in direct aid to states, tribal governments, and territories. The money was allocated, though, in a different way from what we saw in the CARES Act. Rather than using population alone with a minimum per state, the ARP state aid was allocated using two formulae. First, $500M was allocated to each state, and then $169B was allocated on the basis of a state's share of overall unemployed workers between October 2020 and January 2021.[76] The rest was directly allocated to tribal governments and territories. The use of unemployment numbers meant that big states that had engaged in more aggressive shutdowns over the course of the pandemic received more than they did in the CARES Act. While small states still did the best per capita, the very largest coastal states like New York and California, who had received the least per capita under the CARES Act, did relatively well per capita under the ARP. On top of this, there was aid to states, territories, and tribal governments for a variety of specific ends: $21.6B for emergency rental assistance, $10B for capital spending on infrastructure, $10B for homeowner assistance, $10B for small business credit expansion, and $1B for emergency financial aid to poorer residents. There was added incentives for states that accepted the Affordable Care Act's Medicaid expansion. And $40B went to higher education, a substantial share of which went to state universities.

There was also $130B for cities and counties. This time, rather than the CARES Act aid policy of letting some cities and counties apply for money that would then be deducted from their state's total, aid was directly allocated to local governments. Counties were allocated $65B, with the money divided entirely based on population. Bigger cities got $45.5B, allocated using a modified version of the system used for Community Development Block Grants, with more money going to poorer jurisdictions and those with high population density. $19.5B went to cities with less than 50K residents, based on each jurisdiction's percentage of state population. In addition, the ARP provided $123B to school districts, $32B for transit agencies, and a whole variety of other grants.

This was just an overwhelming amount of aid. While it will take years to figure out all of the effects of this spending, the theoretical framework of the book suggests several likely outcomes. Providing aid to states should be an effective method of macroeconomic stimulus. Given both its leverage and concerns about moral hazard, Congress should have attached substantial conditions on the aid, reducing state fiscal independence as Jonathan Rodden argued. And the aid should create some moral hazard, causing both aggressive state budgeting practices and lax lending practices by the bond market, as both officials and investors begin to believe that future state and local fiscal problems will be solved by federal aid.

Early indications are that all of these are true. The ARP provided a huge shot in the arm to the economy, leaving macroeconomic analysts more concerned about its effect on inflation than they were about economic output. Although it is hard to separate the effect of state and local aid from the rest of the fiscal package, the economy grew 5.7% in 2021, the fastest pace since 1984.[77] Municipalities borrowed record amounts in 2020 and 2021.[78] The upsides of state aid were easily apparent.

As discussed in Chapter 2, Jonathan Rodden argued that federal aid to provinces almost always includes substantial conditions on how the money can be used. And indeed that was true in the ARP.

Unlike the CARES Act, the ARP specifically allowed funds to be spent to close budget gaps created by the recession and pandemic. It also allowed funds to be used to address and remedy social problems created by the recession and pandemic, or on water, sewer, or broadband infrastructure, and to be transferred to special purpose local governments.[79]

But the ARP also included its own limitations on how the money might be spent.[80] Specifically, it barred states from using federal aid to:

> either directly or indirectly offset a reduction in the net tax revenue of such State or territory resulting from a change in law, regulation, or administrative interpretation during the covered period that reduces any tax (by providing for a reduction in a rate, a rebate, a deduction, a credit, or otherwise) or delays the imposition of any tax or tax increase.[81]

The Treasury Department issued regulations to explain exactly what this meant. According to the regulation, states that accepted ARP dollars were allowed to pass tax cuts if their total tax revenue was higher than their 2019 prepandemic totals (adjusted for inflation) or to the extent the tax cuts were offset by spending cuts, other tax increase or economic growth.[82] If tax cuts resulted in a substantial loss in net revenue that was not offset, the Treasury would determine that ARP was being used for tax cuts and could, in theory, recoup the money.

The attorney general of Ohio, David Yost, immediately filed a law suit after the law was passed, claiming that the tax cut ban was sufficiently unclear in what it required that it impinged on the sovereignty of states (and that agency regulations could not replace Congress's responsibility to be clear in setting out conditions).[83] Yost also argued that the conditions were unconstitutionally severe, as well. "The Tax Mandate thus gives the States a choice: they can have either the badly needed federal funds or their sovereign authority to set state tax policy. But they cannot have both. In our current economic crisis, that is no choice at all."[84] The trial court sided with Yost.[85]

Yost's claim captured the essence of Rodden's argument about federal aid. Federal bailout funds will usually come with strings that reduce the sovereign authority of states. Congress was worried that states would use the aid to create long-term fiscal problems for themselves through permanent tax cuts. Further, Democrats thought tax cuts, which they suspected would be enacted by states with Republican legislatures, would be less stimulative than spending on current needs.

The point of the trilemma is that the upside of something like the ARP—its macroeconomic effect and the way it encourages future investment by states and cities—comes with a downside, an increase in moral hazard. Conditions are a way of limiting the downsides of aid. Attorney General Yost's lawsuit implicitly assumes that the federal government would have offered aid without conditions if it could not offer aid with conditions. But it is equally, or even more, plausible that any ruling that limits the ability of Congress to attach conditions to aid will mean that Congress will not offer aid at all going forward.

By definition, moral hazard occurs over time, making it hard to assess right after an aid package. But early indications are that the ARP did induce at least some moral hazard. As we saw following Hamilton's plan to assume state debts (discussed in Chapter 3), one of the main conduits for moral hazard is its effect on lenders, who are encouraged by federal aid to offer money to even risky state and local governments. Following the passage of the ARP, Moody's upgraded its outlook on state and local debt as a whole from negative to stable, finding that the new aid will help "stabilize state finances" and "allow them to avoid downstream funding cuts for local governments, colleges, universities and other programs."[86]

This increase in confidence wasn't just general, though. High-yield (i.e., risky) municipal bonds performed extremely well in the first quarter of 2021, with spreads between risky and top rated municipal bonds falling substantially.[87] S&P upgraded Chicago Public Schools, one of the worst performing credits in the country, to the level just below investment grade on the basis of federal aid.[88] Illinois has long been the state with the worst credit rating, but Moody's, the credit-rating agency that has viewed Illinois with the most suspicion, gave the state its first rating upgrade in years.[89] The spreads between Illinois debt and top-rated municipal bonds fell in April 2021 below where they had been between 2014 and 2019.[90]

The strong relative performance of risky high-yield municipal bonds is suggestive of moral hazard. All jurisdictions received aid, so all budgets were buoyed. Interest rates on all municipal bonds declined as a result. But for low-rated municipal bonds, the ARP aid provided an extra benefit: evidence that there would be bailouts in the future.

Further, from the moment aid began to seem likely, jurisdictions faced problems making sure they spent the temporary money in ways that would not persist, rather than creating programs that will outlast the aid.[91] Some jurisdictions have been very conservative with their large budget surpluses. For instance, Connecticut plowed extra money into its rainy day and pension funds.[92] That said, there is every reason to believe that the existence of easy federal money will encourage profligacy in at least some jurisdictions.

But the ARP was not the end of the story either. In late 2021, Congress passed the Infrastructure Investment and Jobs Act, a huge infrastructure package.[93] Although larger, this "Bipartisan Infrastructure Framework" largely followed the structure of previous infrastructure packages, with large amounts of money given directly to states through a formula to support infrastructure projects.[94] A larger-than-normal amount of money was also held out for competitive grants to states and localities under the Department of Transportation.[95] Most of the money from the bill is running through states, and although in many cases it will require matching funds, the size of the aid may allow states to save money they might have otherwise spent. The result will be to provide support to state and local governmental budgets, with all of the benefits and costs that come with that.

We will have to watch what happens over the next few years. But it seems that the trilemma continues to explain the difficult choices facing federal officials when addressing state and local fiscal problems.

6.4. Conclusion: The Second Draft of History

If journalism is the first draft of history, a book chapter written soon after an event happens is more like a second, still rough draft than it is a fully considered look back. But Congress's response to the pandemic and the recession that followed was very different from what came before. As it did during the outset of the Great Recession, Congress provided a substantial amount of stimulus, including state and local aid. But unlike the Great Recession, Congress then acted twice more to stimulate the economy, including providing far more in aid than state and local governments lost in revenue.

Although few jurisdictions even approached default, this can be understood as a choice along the trilemma, favoring bailouts over defaults or state and local austerity. Congress's approach provided substantial benefits, a rapid economic bounce back, the continued availability of redistributive services, a robust municipal bond market and state and local investment in infrastructure. But it also seems to have come with costs, moral hazard in state capitols and a bond market that does less to differentiate between good and bad credit risks.

PART III

TOOLS FOR GETTING OUT OF A BAD STATE

An Introduction to the Principles for Responding to State and Local Fiscal Crises

So that's what we've done. How can we do it better? What should the federal government do if a state or major city is on the verge of default?

There are some limits to the types of answers a book of this sort can give to those questions. As I argue throughout the book, there are tradeoffs involved with any type of response. The federal government cannot achieve all three goals of avoiding moral hazard, supporting future investment by states and cities, and reducing austerity during recessions. It's a trilemma. At best, the federal government can achieve two of these goals, but not three.

Providing a convincing answer about how to weigh those three goals in all situations would require providing a convincing set of answers to some of the biggest debates in policy and political philosophy. A few chapters at the end of a book focused on a particular policy area cannot achieve that. As a result, the book will not attempt to convince a Hayekian macroeconomist suddenly to believe in the claims of John Maynard Keynes (or vice versa).[1] It will not try to sell someone convinced that politicians or bond markets are too short-sighted to care about future bailouts on the proposition that moral hazard is more important than other concerns. And it certainly will not try to move people on questions like the merits of redistribution or how to discount benefits felt far in the future, both of which are essential to deciding which choice to make along the trilemma.

Beliefs of this sort are deeply ideological. That is not a criticism. People who care about policy and politics have thought about questions like these before and answer them based on a strongly held set of interlinked normative beliefs and assumptions. You, dear reader, likely have strong feelings about questions like these. A few chapters at the end of a book are unlikely to shake them, nor should they.

Further, this is not a book about a specific crisis. As a result, it does not make much sense to offer general advice about "what to do." State and local fiscal crises in, say, 2008 were different in many ways from those in the 1870s. The availability of alternative methods of spurring the economy, the state of the municipal bond market, the value of different streams of state spending, and a million other factors specific to a given state or city and moment will matter greatly in developing optimal policy responses. The questions one should ask are pretty similar across crises, as the previous chapters argued, but the right answers are going to be different.

This book hopefully explains where to look for the potential drawbacks and benefits of different federal policy responses to state and local fiscal crises. But it can't provide the "right" answer to how the federal government should respond to a specific crisis, particularly well in advance of that crisis occurring.

This does not mean that the book does not have general advice to give. But that advice is not at the level of recommending bailouts, austerity, or defaults as the best choice in all state and local fiscal crises. Rather than focus on *what* the federal government should do in a crisis, this section will focus on *how* it should go about designing whatever policy it chooses. That is, it will argue that bailouts, austerity, and defaults can each be done in better or worse ways and offer some ideas about each of them. Further, it will argue for a few structural solutions that will make the country more resilient if (or rather when) it faces the next round of state and local budget crises. Doing so, I hope, will make it useful no matter what type of crisis emerges. Further, I hope this approach will make the recommendations useful for decision-makers and observers of a variety of ideological stripes, if by no means all.

The four principles should go into designing responses to state and local fiscal crises.

Prudence: One thing that should stand out from the history in the earlier chapters is that state and local default crises are very unfortunate.[2] They are unfortunate in different ways, but each one involves a loss of livelihoods and future government capacity that are much worse than we see during ordinary cycles of policy change. If the federal government can adopt policies during state and local fiscal crises (or before) that help prevent future ones, it will be generally good. Making bailouts or general state aid conditional on the adoption of clearer accounting standards would push state and local governments to budget with more foresight. Bankruptcy rules that restrain more aggressive types of financial engineering by state and local governments would also be wise.

Balance: One of the innovations of federal policy during 20th- and 21st-century default crises was the development of responses that are not all or nothing choices in the trilemma. That is, some federal policy responses involved bailouts, austerity, *and* debt write-downs, rather just one or another. Doing so, though, required more than splitting the difference. It required the creation of institutions and rules to help make decisions in specific cases.

Developing tools that allow federal policymakers to develop balanced policies would have benefits. There are increasing marginal harms to all three downsides in the trilemma. Austerity gets worse as it gets more extreme. The hundredth spending reduction will cut something more socially important than the first. Similarly, it is textbook public finance that increasing taxes from 10% to 11% on income or sales is more economically painful than increasing rates from 1% to 2% because as tax rates get higher they deter more and more valuable activity.[3] Research similarly shows that bigger defaults have substantially larger effects on future borrowing costs than smaller ones.[4] And a small bailout is unlikely to create much moral hazard, particularly given the regular flows of money between the federal government and states and cities. But bigger and bigger bailouts will create moral hazard among politicians and beliefs in the bond market about the likelihood of future bailouts to an increasing degree. The existence of tools that allow policy makers to moderate the amount of austerity, defaults or bailouts, while allowing all three to some extent, will be beneficial for all national level figures other than those who take extreme ideological stances on the trilemma.

Municipal bankruptcy already has some "balancing" tools; extending bankruptcy law to state governmental defaults would be attractive. Similarly, providing federal aid after modest defaults rather than before can encourage balancing, reducing the size of defaults rather than attempting to avoid them entirely. And ex ante state constitutional pension reforms that allow pensions to be modified as part of a broader package of reforms would allow for a balanced approach between a kind of default and austerity.

Spreading: Most Americans are represented by many overlapping subnational governments—states, counties, cities, school districts, and other types of special districts too. When there is a local economic downturn or political failures, there are often crises in a number of overlapping governments at the same time. After all, common economic changes affect all overlapping governments, and the same voters elect the officials for each overlapping government. For example, today, Illinois is one of the most indebted states relative to revenues; Cook County is one of the most indebted counties; Chicago is one the most indebted major cities; and the Chicago school district is one of the most indebted school districts.[5] (And there are other heavily indebted special districts in Chicagoland as well).

As a formal and legal matter, each overlapping government is an independent legal entity. One government's inability to pay its debts has no automatic or legal effect on others. But as a matter of practice, all overlapping governments are dependent on one another. States, cities, counties, and school districts tax the same incomes, properties, and/or sales. They all provide services to the same people.

In fiscal crises, higher-level governments may try to save one government while letting another default. For example, when Detroit was allowed to file for bankruptcy, Detroit's independent public school system was bailed out by the state government (see Chapter 5 for more). Letting one government default while saving others has the effect of making one set of policy stakeholders and creditors bear very severe harms while others are held harmless. Police may see their pensions cut while teachers do not; recipients of firefighting services may see huge cuts while county prosecutors' offices continue to get full funding.

Instead of trying to save some overlapping governments, the federal government should build tools into bankruptcy law and the structure of bailouts that encourage many stricken governments to make sacrifices all at once. Doing so will avoid harmful infighting among overlapping governments. It will also mean smaller cuts and write-downs to a larger group of interests. Because the marginal harm of cuts and defaults is likely increasing (that is, bigger cuts to any one government service or for any one set of creditors are much worse than smaller cuts for many services and creditors), bringing more entities into whatever crisis response is chosen would be attractive.

Resilience: Beyond the specifics of designing crisis responses, the problem of state and local fiscal crises brings into relief broader problems with our federal system. We ought to try and make our federal system more resilient against inevitable localized economic shocks. At points in American history, we developed tools for making the broader federal system sturdier in the face of inevitable shocks to particular regions or cities. Some of these have atrophied. Historically, one of the most important tools in the United States for responding to local economic shocks was that it was relatively easy for people to leave places with bad economies, moving to greater opportunity. That even people with lower incomes could leave bad economies meant that the costs of local economic (or fiscal) crises were felt by fewer people. But inter-state mobility has declined, and public policy has made moving to opportunity harder through limits on construction of housing and regulations on entering specific labor markets. These regulations have a particularly negative effect on mobility among poorer and working-class people, as richer ones can pay the higher housing costs and navigate regulatory thickets necessary to move to stronger labor markets.

Other tools of resilience have come under criticism in recent years. The municipal bond market, which we use to fund infrastructure construction, is currently structured in a way to create state-specific groups of investors, reducing the extent of "contagion," or the extent to which fiscal crises in one place make it hard for other places to borrow. But, in recent years, the central policy that explains why municipal bond market works this way—the tax exemption for interest on state and local bonds—has come under substantial criticism. More broadly, we rely on cooperative federalism arrangements to fund too many parts of the federal welfare state, even though doing so makes us less resilient. In crises or before, we should attempt to structure our federal system to make it more resilient against localized economic and fiscal shocks.

These principles can be included in any type of response to state and local fiscal crises—in bailouts, defaults, or austerity. This section will devote a chapter each to each type of response, and then a separate chapter on to how to promote resilience. That is, it will provide a roadmap for making whatever choice along the trilemma policymakers land on a bit better.

Building Better Bailouts

When there is a state and local fiscal crisis, and the federal government chooses to spend money to help alleviate that crisis, it has a seemingly infinite number of mechanisms for doing so. Because federal and state budgets are so interlinked, the federal government can improve a state's fiscal position in any number of ways. It can tweak the terms of a cooperative federalism arrangement to provide cash to states, as it did through changing Medicaid reimbursement rates in 2008 and 2020. It can provide loans, as it did for New York City in the 1970s, and for Illinois and New York's Metropolitan Transportation Authority through the Municipal Liquidity Facility (MLF) in 2020. Federal investment can be used to remove onerous conditions imposed by lenders, as the Reconstruction Finance Corporation did in Arkansas in the 1930s. The federal government can assume responsibility for certain services, as it did for Washington, DC, in the 1990s. Or it can assume state debts, as it did regularly during from the post-Revolutionary period until the 1830s and in Washington, DC, in the 1990s.

How can we do it better? When choosing among these options, policymakers can build bailouts that incorporate prudence, balance, and spreading strategies. In order to see how, however, it is important to explore the different ways bailouts are structured.

8.1. Traditional Considerations When Building Bailouts

The three traditional questions to ask about government bailouts are whether they are (1) *general or specific*, that is, available to all states and cities regardless of the state or city's fiscal position or specifically targeted at jurisdictions in crisis; (2) *conditional or unconditional*, requiring states and cities to make policy changes in return for bailout funds or not; (3) *loans or grants*, money that is meant to be paid back or not. Each of these can be thought of as a way of turning up or down the dial between providing more (or fewer) benefits to crisis-stricken states and creating more (or less) moral hazard. Specific, unconditional grants are likely to be more effective at alleviating fiscal stress and are more likely to create moral hazard than generally available, conditional loans.

8.1.1. General or Specific?

When providing aid, the federal government must decide whether to give money to all states or whether instead to target aid at states facing a risk of default. The CARES Act in 2020, for instance, was a clear example of general aid. It provided federal money to states on the basis of their populations, not their fiscal condition. The ARP of 2021 was only very slightly targeted, with more aid given to states with higher unemployment rates. A more targeted version of aid are general assumptions of debt, like those that followed the Revolutionary War and the War of 1812. These policies aid all states but do so differently based on their debt levels. Finally, the most specific are bailouts aimed at individual jurisdictions, like federal aid to Washington, DC, or state aid given in response to fiscal crises in Detroit, MI and Hartford, CT.

The more general federal aid is, the fewer questions it raises about moral hazard. If every state gets money regardless of its fiscal position coming into a recession, then federal money does not provide strong incentives to spend too much beforehand. After all, a state comes into a recession in good shape and money is given generally, the state can use the federal money for new projects or tax cuts or any other initiative it chooses.

That said, general federal aid will not avoid creating moral hazard entirely. A state may spend excessively if it expects general aid in a crisis because it can be confident that the worst possible results—default or savage budget cuts—will be avoided. But because the aid will be provided generally and states get the aid regardless, the moral hazard effect is more limited.

General aid, though, is also expensive for the federal government. On the other hand, specific aid—i.e., a bailout of a single highly-indebted state or city—can more easily solve the fiscal problems faced by its recipient. However, such a bailout creates greater risk of moral hazard. Moreover, it can create political blowback in other jurisdictions which do not want to see their tax dollars supporting profligate spending in other states.

8.1.2. Conditional or Unconditional?

A second question to ask about state and local aid is whether it comes with conditions or not. For instance, the federal assumption of state debt after the

Revolutionary War did not have important forward-looking conditions. The CARES Act and the ARP state aid provisions in 2020 and 2021 included a variety of conditions on the use of federal funds, including a prohibition on states using the federal aid to pay for tax cuts or to support their pension funds, but did not encourage policy changes going foward. New York State's response to the New York City fiscal crisis included many conditions, both short-term and long-term, and a displacement of local political authority.

When aid is given to a specific jurisdiction, it very commonly comes with conditions to reduce moral hazard concerns and to encourage repayment. When international organizations like the IMF or the World Bank provide loans to countries facing fiscal or currency crises, they usually impose policy conditions. These conditions are often justified not (mostly) on moral hazard grounds, but because the reforms make it more likely that loans will be repaid.[1]

General aid can come with conditions too. Placing onerous conditions can backfire, though, as they can slow the spending of money and can keep the money from being used efficiently. For instance, the CARES Act required state and local aid to be spent on demands created by the pandemic. This meant that states and cities could not use the money to maintain ordinary government services. As a result, many jurisdictions were forced to lay off or furlough large parts of their workforce, while money sat unspent for many months.[2]

That said, conditions should be thought of as a rather inevitable aspect of state and local aid. As Rodden argues, it is rare for national governments to provide aid to crisis-stricken subnational jurisdiction without any conditions, as doing so creates the risk of too much moral hazard. Further, the existence of aid is likely to give whoever is in power at the national level a tool to impose their policy goals on states and cities. The ARP's rule that states and cities cannot use federal money to support tax cuts married these two effects—it was designed to make sure states and cities didn't use one-time aid to create long-run fiscal problems by cutting taxes, and it furthered the goal of Democratic politicians, in power in Washington, to encourage greater government spending rather than reductions in taxes.[3]

There are important questions about the constitutionality of conditions on federal aid. In *NFIB v. Sebelius*, the Supreme Court adopted a tighter rule governing conditions on federal spending, finding that tying all federal Medicaid money to state decisions to expand eligibility for Medicaid under the Patient Protection and Affordable Care Act (also known as Obamacare) was unconstitutionally coercive, even as it upheld other parts of the law.[4] However, since *Sebelius*, there have not been many decisions finding conditions on federal spending to be unconstitutional coercive.[5]

Conditions on a bailout would come under searching review after *Sebelius*. Bailouts would not be leveraging participation in an old program to coerce participation in a new one, a key factor in *Sebelius*.[6] But bailouts are given when a state or city is under substantial economic distress, creating a possibility that the court would view the federal government's condition as an effort to "dragoon" the state into compliance.[7] However, the justification for conditions on state emergency fiscal aid are pretty powerful as well. Without conditions, aid could create too much moral hazard, as politicians grow to expect bailouts without any cost to them. Further, if the conditions are aimed at encouraging greater fiscal rectitude, the claim that they are justified is stronger. In that case, the federal government is simply using conditions on aid today to make it less likely that it will have to provide aid in the future.

Conditions on state aid might also face procedural limits. Under the Supreme Court's holding in *Pennhurst State School & Hospital v. Halderman,* Congress must state conditions on federal aid "unambiguously," something that can be hard to achieve in the fog of responding to a fiscal crisis.[8] As we saw in Chapter 6, the conditions on state aid in the ARP were challenged on both of these grounds.

The federal government can avoid these challenges by not making aid conditional in a formal sense. Instead, the federal government can wait to see what reforms the state/city had already made before offering aid. Such aid would be unconditional in a formal sense but would be conditional in reality. For instance, the federal aid to New York City in 1975 came after the state imposed severe conditions on the city and made city bondholders take losses. President Ford changed his mind about the propriety of aid after he determined that investors had taken sufficient losses and the state and city had engaged in necessary reforms. State aid to Detroit during its bankruptcy was also not conditional, but only came after the state had imposed an emergency manager and the city had filed for bankruptcy.

8.1.3. Loans or Grants?

A final question about bailouts is whether they come in the form of loans or grants. The federal government has lent money to jurisdictions in fiscal crisis a number of times, notably the loans to New York City in the 1970s and the Federal Reserve's MLF program in 2020. In contrast, the state aid provisions in the CARES Act and the ARP, and Hamilton's assumption of state debts, were outright grants.

The cases for and against grants are straightforward. If a jurisdiction is in fiscal trouble, making it go further into debt by loaning it money can seem counterproductive. Grants, unlike loans, do not create more debt. But grants are also obviously more expensive to the federal governments than a similar amount of aid in loans. To the extent that one is worried about moral hazard, grants also exacerbate that concern.

Loans, on other hand, create a set of complex problems. If a jurisdiction faces a short-term crisis, a loan may be more appropriate, as it will not let the jurisdiction off the hook when the economy recovers. But providing loans can enmesh the federal government in an ongoing relationship with a fiscally troubled state. If the federal government provides loans, the federal government may be forced to decide whether to roll those loans over if the state is still in fiscal trouble when it is time to make payments. If the state defaults on federal loans, federal officials will have to decide how hard to press to be repaid. The federal government surely can get paid back by subnational borrowers, if only by withholding future federal aid. But whether it can do so as a legal matter and whether it can do so practically and politically are different questions. The desire to avoid entanglements of this sort is one of the factors that likely drove the Federal Reserve to limit the scope of the MLF in 2020.

Loans may also create complicated problems in state law. States, since the 1840s, have had a variety of limitations on issuing debt, both in terms of process and substantive limits. While these rules differ by state, debt limits can get in the way of a state borrowing to meet short-term budget problems.[9] To the extent that federal programs are designed to provide short-term aid to fight recessions, aid offered through loans may not draw takers because of these state law limits.

8.2. Building Better Bailouts: Advancing Prudence, Mixing, and Spreading in Bailout Design

The choices above largely replicate the problems of the trilemma. Some structures create more (or less) moral hazard but also avoid more (or less) austerity or impairment of debts.

But bailouts also can be designed to reduce the starkness of the tradeoffs in the trilemma and to improve state and local balance sheets going forward. That is, bailouts can promote the values of prudence, balance, and spreading.

8.2.1. Conditions on General State and Local Crisis Aid

Conditions on general aid (or other forms of spending) can encourage states and cities to adopt safer budgeting practices going forward and to spread the costs of fiscal crises across many levels of government and types of creditors and service recipients.

For instance, the ARP's requirement that recipients of federal aid were not to spend the money on tax cuts should be understood as an effort to encourage future fiscal prudence. It was designed, in part, to stop state officials from using short-term aid to create long-run fiscal problems for themselves by passing tax cuts that were unlikely to be repealed once aid stopped flowing.

Longer-run concerns can be built into bailouts as well. If the goal of a general state aid package in a recession is to fight a recession, pre-existing state indebtedness makes that state aid less efficacious. Heavily indebted states will often need to use federal aid to pay back their debts, rather than to maintain state employment or redistributive services. As such, it makes sense to attach conditions to general aid that encourage states not to be too indebted before the next recession.

One major cause of excessive state indebtedness is bad state accounting practices. As we saw during the discussion of pensions in Chapter 5, the efficacy of state balanced budget and debt limit rules turn very heavily on what is counted as debt. Failing to adequately save for pensions often does not violate debt limit or balanced budget rules and thus becomes an attractive place to hide deficit spending.

The deeper reason is that state and local budgeting is done on what is effectively a "cash" basis.[10] That is, state governments generally seek to balance dollars coming in and going out in a given year. Experts generally prefer "accrual" budgeting, where the costs of obligations incurred today are spread across budget years during which they are enjoyed.[11] Whatever costs this year's receipt of services creates for future obligations (including the pensions earned by workers this year) should count against this year's budget. If a government agrees to pay for five-years' worth of office products after five years, it should budget each year for roughly one fifth of that cost, rather than acting as if nothing happened until the money comes due in the fifth year.[12] Similarly, the fact that pensions are paid after an employee retires should not matter; the government should understand the money needed for her pension as a present-day cost. (This elides a lot of details about both how state budgeting works now and how accrual accounting would work in practice but captures the basic problem.)

Governments take advantage of the "cash" nature of budget accounting in many ways. For instance, after the Great Recession, Arizona sold its state house building to a private investor, but then executed what was effectively a rent-to-own plan, keeping its offices in the building and eventually reclaiming the building at the end of the deal. This gave the state cash immediately to address a budget deficit, but effectively guaranteed the purchaser a stream of income.[13] This arrangement helped the state balance its budget, as it increased cash this year, even though it created a long-term obligation. While these all too common "sale and lease back" arrangements are much like loans, they generally do not count as debt for the purpose of state debt limits because formally they are simply agreements to rent with an option to buy.[14] (This particular deal, though, was so ridiculous that Comedy

Central's *The Daily Show with Jon Stewart* devoted a whole segment to it.[15]) A few courts have limited the use of the most abusive of these arrangements, but many more have found them not to count as debt, allowing states and cities to take out effectively take out loans to finance deficits through subterfuge.[16]

If the federal government offers state aid, it could set as a condition of aid changing state budgeting rules from cash to an accrual method. New York State required New York City to budget in accordance with generally accepted accounting principles (GAAP) after its fiscal crisis.[17]

Tying general state aid to the adoption of new budgeting standards would face legal challenges from states claiming it was unconstitutional condition. Further, state budgets are passed each year, while crisis-relief aid is a one-time infusion, meaning that the federal government would need to have some method of monitoring state budget practice and some enforcement mechanism.

However, Congress could—in the same act as it passed emergency aid—make another stream of federal aid contingent on states changing their budget practices. The most promising would be to condition the income tax exemption for municipal debt on the adoption and use of some set of best budgeting practices. This would be constitutionally permissible, as the link between the federal tax expenditure, designed to encourage states to use debt to fund investments, and the condition, which would limit states' ability to use debt-substitutes to fund deficits, is very tight.[18] In theory, Congress could authorize federal agencies to challenge state budgeting decisions, but it would be wiser to decentralize enforcement. The federal government could require states and municipalities to put covenants into their general obligation bonds that they will use accrual accounting when budgeting as a condition for the bonds being tax exempt. This would allow and encourage bondholders to sue to punish deviations from accrual budgeting standards on the grounds that doing so violates their contract or even the Contract Clause of the Constitution.

This idea is very different from conditions that appeared in the CARES Act, which limited the use of federal money to new problems occasioned by the pandemic. That type of condition slowed spending and limited the ability of states to direct money to their highest priorities. It did not require prudent budgeting going forward, nor did it maximize the utility of the aid in fighting a recession.

There are other reforms Congress could undertake to encourage greater prudence.[19] For instance, states and cities are exempt from securities law provisions that require issuers to submit information to them prior to the sale of securities. Under the "Tower Amendment," neither the Securities and Exchange Commission nor the Municipal Securities Rulemaking Board can issue regulations forcing states or cities to disclose information in advance of selling bonds.[20] States and cities argue that disclosure is unnecessary to protect investors, as the default rate on municipal bonds is low, and that disclosure requirements are costly to comply with.

But, as Christine Sgarlata Chung argues, disclosure requirements for states and cities would serve ends beyond investor protection.[21] Making states and cities publish honest accounts when they issue bonds would improve the information available to the public about state and local budgets. Issuers could be forced to disclose their use of complex financial instruments or budget chicanery. Disclosure would make it easier for the bond market to enforce fiscal discipline on states and cities by making risky behavior more salient.[22] And the argument that defaults are low and thus regulation is not necessary is much less powerful in a world where the reason defaults are low is that federal government is providing emergency aid.

General state and local aid in a crisis can also help spread the costs of crises. Federal aid can be given to a state government with an expectation that some of it will be shared with local governments, or the federal government can give aid directly to local governments. For instance, the CARES Act provided aid to states and larger cities, with the amount to going to the larger cities in a state removed from that state's allocation.[23] But states were free (and in fact many did) take some of their allocation and give it to local governments.[24] The MLF was empowered to buy bonds from states, large cities and several designated authorities per state. But for smaller cities, the Federal Reserve allowed states to borrow on their behalf, rather than directly buying their bonds.[25] In sharp contrast, the ARP just directly provided money to local governments, both big and small, and gave lots of aid for school districts and transit agencies, separately from giving aid to state governments.

When federal government only provides aid to states, it assumes states will share with local governments, relying on state politicians acting reasonably. In a crisis, though, a state can and very well might use federal aid to save itself from having to make cuts, while abandoning creditors and service recipients in stricken cities.

Direct aid to cities and counties can avoid this problem, spreading money across governments in a state, reducing the size of cuts any government needs to make. States could in theory reduce other forms of aid to cities and local government, as state aid to local governments far outweighs federal spending in most cases. But the federal government should not encourage them to do so.

8.2.2. Conditions on Aid to Specific Jurisdictions in Fiscal Crisis

When international organizations offer crisis aid to countries, they often attach conditions, requirements that the recipient change certain policies in return for receiving the emergency funds. Such conditions make the most sense in the context of loans, as one of their explicit purposes of conditions is to make it more likely the jurisdiction can pay back debt. In the domestic context, however, as we recently saw with Federal Reserve's MLF program, policy conditions tied to loans from the federal government to states are uncommon and politically difficult.

Any effort to impose policy conditions would require the federal government to closely monitor state budgets going forward, as a policy adopted one day could be reversed or undermined the next. Putting policy conditions on specific aid would also raise constitutional questions.

At the state level, state governments do not generally respond to crises with conditional loans either. Rather than imposing policy conditions on local governments, we have mostly seen state governments (and in the case of Washington, DC, and Puerto Rico, the federal governments) imposing oversight boards or emergency managers on local governments in fiscal crisis. Control boards are appointed entities with the power to veto local budget decisions and in some cases, directly make governance decisions. Michigan and Rhode Island went even further, appointing emergency managers or receivers, officials that entirely displaced local governments and directly governed cities.[26] That is, rather than imposing policy conditions, state (or federal) interventions often impose oversight and/or remove power from local governments.

This is a direct response to the problem of monitoring. It is hard for states to impose particular policies on cities, as the city may seek to avoid restrictions, forcing the state to react. Allowing state or federal appointees to look over local books, or even directly govern cities, addresses this problem.

There are more and less strict versions of this. Some states have agencies that review all local budgets and provide advice or direct oversight.[27] Other states condition the receipt of state aid on review of local budgets or limit local capacity to issue bonds.[28] And then there are interventions like control boards and emergency managers for truly crisis-stricken jurisdictions.

Removing local authority by imposing a control board in return for state aid is a very severe condition. As a result, it should reduce the extent to which aid creates moral hazard. Many critics argue that control boards are antidemocratic, as they displace local elected officials. As a theoretical matter, this objection is less powerful than it might seem at first. Having higher levels of government make policy decisions—here the state rather than the city—is not inherently antidemocratic. There is no legal right to live inside the boundaries of a general-purpose municipal government, and indeed many Americans do not (people who live in "county land.") Further, as Clayton Gillette argues, it is unclear whether a city government that has managed its budget so badly that it is on the edge of default is actually representing the preferences of local voters.[29] In the context of a bailout, taxpayers from other jurisdictions ought to have some say, as their taxes are being spent to resolve the fiscal crisis. Even outside the context of crises, state governments directly govern all sorts of issues without putting them up for local referenda without anyone thinking their decisions are antidemocratic. While there are valid concerns arising from the fact that control boards displace elected officials, the strength of these concerns turns very much on the specifics of the type of control board and on how representative the government in question actually is.

Imposing control boards has sometimes, even often, worked well, but there are also a number of failures. There is an active debate over whether control boards and emergency managers outperform elected officials in crisis periods. Locally elected officials often know much more about their cities than state officials, even during rough fiscal periods, and can ensure important values are protected. Many credit New York City's Emergency Financial Control Board with helping it survive the fiscal crisis and grow in the next several decades.[30] The Board in Washington, DC, was similarly lauded.[31] Kevyn Orr, the emergency manager of Detroit, has received many plaudits for his work during the Chapter 9 case.[32] But Puerto Rico's Oversight Board, according to its own members, faced serious challenges because of a lack of authority and changing conditions.[33] The emergency manager in Flint, MI bears substantial responsibility for the city's water crisis.[34] The very qualities that make control boards useful—their independence from local politics—can make them ineffective or unresponsive. A control board or emergency manager is no guarantee of good policy results, even if one is often necessary. The devil is in the details.

Outside of special circumstances like Washington, DC, and Puerto Rico, though, the federal government cannot create or operate control boards for states or cities. Doing so certainly would run afoul of constitutional limitations on federal power. However, the federal government does not need to set formal conditions, nor does it need to assess state responses to local fiscal crises in theory. The federal government can wait until a state has adopted a specific set of governance reforms until it provides aid, allowing Congress to assess specific reforms rather than having to ponder questions of democratic theory.

Waiting to provide aid until after reforms are passed would encourage state or local governments to produce governance reforms and encourage fiscal prudence. Similarly, the federal government can wait until a state has made sacrifices in the name of promoting a balanced response to a crisis. They can also wait and see who gets appointed as an emergency manager.

Traditionally, bailouts are posed as an alternative to defaults or austerity. Hamilton's assumption of state debts was intended to remove fiscal pressure from states. The debt assumption ideas in the Johnson Report, rejected in 1843, were seen as an alternative to defaults. The Washington, DC bailout in 1997 avoided a default.

But bailouts can be used alongside defaults and austerity as well. For instance, the federal government only offered aid to New York City in 1975 in the form of the Seasonal Financing Act after the state imposed the Emergency Financial Control Board on the city, leading to substantial budget cuts. President Ford also considered the suspension of repayments on city debts that were not rolled over into Municipal Assistance Corporation bonds (eventually found unconstitutional by the New York Court of Appeals) an impairment of the city debt, justifying a bailout. The result was a balanced solution, a policy that involved some of all three possible responses to the trilemma—bailouts, austerity, and defaults—rather than only one.

Similarly, Michigan's state legislature provided aid to Detroit in 2014. It did not do so instead of having the city file for bankruptcy, but rather did so as part of the city's plan of adjustment for getting out of bankruptcy. The aid the state offered—matching aid from nonprofit groups as part of the "Grand Bargain"—reduced haircuts for pensioners but did not eliminate them entirely. Nor did the aid eliminate the larger haircuts faced by other creditors (or, for that matter, cuts to services). This was a balanced response, one that included a small state bailout, real losses for creditors and substantial service cuts, rather than all of any one policy.

As a result, in both the case of Detroit and New York, bailouts of a sort were provided, but the moral hazard effect was likely very limited. Similarly, while lenders saw losses, the contagion effect was not large or long-lasting. And while budgets were cut, bankruptcy proceedings allowed the city some funds to continue (and even improve) necessary services. Waiting until other sacrifices had been made before providing federal aid allowed for this mixed strategy.

Building Better Defaults

If the federal government chooses not to bail out a state or local government in default, it faces another choice: Should it intervene to aid creditors at the expense of current taxpayers? Or should it create mechanisms that make it easier for states to force creditors to take losses? The former strategy promises more intense and longer-lasting recessions. But the latter strategy risks roiling the municipal bond market, harming not only the defaulting jurisdiction and its future capacity to borrow but also the ability of other jurisdictions to sell bonds due to the risk of contagion.

Over the course of American history, the federal government has intervened in some situations on behalf of creditors. During the railroad bond crisis, the Supreme Court made up a whole body of law to protect creditors. In 1932, the federal government threatened to take federal loans away from Arkansas if the state went through with a massive default.

In other situations, the federal government intervened in ways that helped states *avoid* creditors. For instance, the Supreme Court, over several prominent dissents, built out the doctrine of sovereign immunity doctrine in 1880s and 1890s in a way that protected Southern states from having to pay debts incurred by Reconstruction-era governments.

In recent years, federal interventions have been channeled through the mechanism of municipal bankruptcy, often called "Chapter 9." Notably, Chapter 9 provides tools that the international community has spent years debating about whether to create for sovereign debt (debt taken out by countries). Many maintain that international institutions should be given the power to create a legal regime for sovereign country to file for bankruptcy in order to make defaults by countries more manageable and to reduce conflict among creditors.[1] Chapter 9 is a sovereign bankruptcy regime for municipalities. But only for municipalities—Chapter 9 only applies to local governments, not state governments. No state has defaulted since the 1930s, so this limitation has not mattered much. When a real crisis emerged for a state-like entity, the federal government created a municipal bankruptcy-like system for Puerto Rico in 2016.

Chapter 9 is now the exclusive legal mechanism for cities seeking to readjust their debts (other than voluntary reductions by creditors). Federal law bars states from passing their own municipal bankruptcy laws.[2] But for many years it was not widely used. In the 1970s, prodded by the New York City fiscal crisis, Congress reformed Chapter 9 substantially. This still did not lead to Chapter 9's widespread use. After 2008, however, several large cities used Chapter 9 to restructure their debts following the severe fiscal impact of the Great Recession.

Particularly after judge-made doctrinal developments in the post-2008 period, Chapter 9 is itself a move away from the stark choices that the trilemma posits and toward more balanced policy results. Doctrines internal to Chapter 9, including the requirement of "service delivery insolvency" for eligibility and the "feasibility" requirement for plans of adjustment, effectively require a bankruptcy judge to decide the question of how much services must be cut before creditors can be impaired.

Congress and bankruptcy courts should lean into this understanding of the statute. In reforming and interpreting the law, judges should think of themselves as balancing the downsides of austerity and defaults. Municipal bankruptcy law effectively requires judges to consider these issues; courts should acknowledge and openly wrestle with the task assigned to them by Congress. That is, by passing Chapter 9, Congress left bankruptcy courts in charge of making certain decisions about which leg of the trilemma to adopt. Given the gravity of the choice (and the lack of constraints put on them), bankruptcy courts should openly acknowledge the policy stakes of their decisions.

Moreover, elements should be added to Chapter 9 to further the goal of spreading harms among many governments, following legal innovations developed as part of the response to Puerto Rico's fiscal collapse. Courts, state legislatures, and Congress should each act to make it possible for single Chapter 9 case to address multiple insolvent local governments at once—one case with a city, a county and a school district in it. This will ensure that similarly situated creditors are treated equally and that services are cut across all areas. The result will be smaller losses for all creditors and smaller cuts in each type of service.

Finally, Chapter 9 should be extended to state governments, as David Skeel has argued.[3] Bringing states into Chapter 9 would allow the federal government to respond their fiscal crises with mixed and spreading strategies.

These steps would build the values of prudence, balancing and spreading into our domestic system of sovereign bankruptcy law.

9.1. Building Better Defaults: Reforms to Chapter 9

In reforming Chapter 9, the courts and Congress should attempt to build rules that encourage balanced solutions, help avoid future crises, and allow losses to be spread across several overlapping insolvent governments. Here's how.

9.1.1. Insolvency

A city must be insolvent before it can file for bankruptcy. Figuring out whether a large, general-purpose local government is insolvent, though, is an almost impossible inquiry. A city can often make one more payment to creditors by selling off key assets like city hall or the city's fire trucks. But forcing a city to do so before allowing it to be eligible for bankruptcy is not in the interest of creditors as a whole or the city's residents. Paying creditors today may leave the city unable to pay creditors with claims that come due in the future, and city residents will be worse off if city assets are liquidated before a global settlement is reached.

But this makes it hard to determine exactly what insolvency means in the context of a large municipality. The best approach would be to acknowledge determinations of insolvency are fundamentally about balancing austerity and default, allowing the judge to openly wrestle with the costs and benefits of different options.

To decide whether cities are insolvent, courts have developed the "service delivery insolvency" test, which asks whether a city's lack of cash is a "chimera," a product of a refusal to cut spending, or instead whether it is real, because local services are so underfunded that they cannot be cut further.

Unfortunately, there is little content to this test. Residents do not have a legal right to a particular level of local services, so courts have no way of determining whether services have been cut enough. As applied in cases like *Stockton* and *Detroit*, the "service delivery insolvency" test provides no clear standard for determining when a municipality has cut its services to such an extent that it should not be asked to do more in order to pay creditors. Judges just know it when they see it.

A number of scholars have argued that the insolvency requirement should just be abandoned, or at least substantially reformed and weakened.[4] The requirement that state governments must specifically authorize any municipality's Chapter 9 filing addresses any worry that cities will opportunistically file for bankruptcy to impair creditors, they claim. States generally do not want to cities to file for bankruptcy due to worries about "contagion," or the fear that a city filing for bankruptcy will make it harder for other cities or even the state itself to borrow. City officials do not want the reputational stain of being the leaders who put their city into bankruptcy. So, they argue, why further restrict access by requiring insolvency? The insolvency requirement, they argue, does little useful work and makes the process longer and more complicated, holding up needed filings.

Others scholars respond that, despite its lack of clarity, the insolvency requirement is a useful tool for policing abuse of Chapter 9, giving judges greater authority to ensure cities raise taxes and cut spending before filing.[5] The exact content of the rule is less important than the fact that it gives a judge a moment of discretion to make sure a city has actually tried to cut services, raise taxes, and reform government before it seeks relief under Chapter 9.

The criticisms of the insolvency test are powerful and important. Insolvency determinations are indeed long and costly. But these critics ignore the long history states have had helping cities avoid creditors. Recall the "corporate suicide" cases discussed in Chapter 3 or Arkansas's actions in the road debt crisis discussed in Chapter 4. Simply because some states have been unwilling to allow bankruptcy filings recently does not mean that this attitude will last.

More importantly, the insolvency requirement makes Chapter 9 possible as a *political* matter. Without the requirement that a judge determine that a city is actually broke, the political pressure on state governments not to authorize bankruptcy would be intense. Creditors would have solid political arguments that the city should just buckle down because no neutral arbiter has said that doing so is practically impossible. But because the question is referred to a judge, critics of bankruptcy are channeled (at least somewhat) into making their arguments in court, rather than in the legislature or to the Governor.

Further, without a judicial determination of insolvency, the contagion effects of a bankruptcy filing would be worse. Without a judge explaining that the filing city is in unusually deep fiscal trouble, the bond market may infer that the state legislature is likely to plunge other cities into bankruptcy. Absent a judge providing what amounts to permission for the state and city to go forward, it is hard to imagine any state actually invoking Chapter 9 on behalf of a city.

But if insolvency is going to remain a part of Chapter 9, judges are going to have to decide what it actually means. What the post-2008 Chapter 9 cases reveal is how unavoidably political these insolvency determinations are. Courts are asked to decide how much services need to be cut before bonds or pensions can be impaired. That is, they are using doctrine to wrestle with the fundamental tradeoffs posed by the trilemma.

The best approach to the question of insolvency is transparency about the substantive determination the court is making. Chapter 9 puts a bankruptcy judge in position to decide how to balance costs along the trilemma.

Legal scholar Clayton Gillette has recently argued that the service delivery insolvency doctrine should be understood to allow access to bankruptcy only when excessive debt leads to the breakup of valuable agglomeration economies in cities. That is, courts should find a city insolvent when its debt load is sufficiently large to cause real economic dislocation from an urban area.[6] Rather than looking at some abstract idea of service quality, courts should look at whether business firms are moving out of the city. If firms leave en masse, it could trigger a "death spiral" in which firm departures beget further firm and individual out-migration, cratering any possibility of recovery.

Gillette's approach is the first to try to answer the right question. He argues courts should look at the real economic harms (and not just the harms to services) created by excessive debt and the resulting dislocation of urban activity.[7] That is, he suggests a cost-benefit analysis about whether the harm to the bond market that a bankruptcy filing would cause can be justified by looking at the benefits writing down debt would have for the city's (and the broader) economy.

Applying the doctrine this way would be challenging, to be sure. Any amount of local debt is certain to cause some dislocation—debt implies higher taxes or fewer services in the future. Some people who would have chosen to live in a place will choose to move due to the future tax increases presaged by local debt. Gillette acknowledges that there would still need to be a difficult line-drawing exercise in determining how much dislocation is too much.[8]

Further, to do a full cost-benefit analysis, the economic harms associated with debt loads are only one side of the coin. The other question is how much harm granting a given city access to Chapter 9 would do to the broader bond market, future investment, and the risk of contagion. Courts should consider this as well in shaping service delivery insolvency doctrine.

Even so, Gillette is pushing us down the right path. Bankruptcy judges have been delegated the role of assessing the costs and benefits of allowing a city to file for bankruptcy. Gillette provides a way for judges to start to think about that question.

9.1.2. Preferences

During the fight over the Detroit bankruptcy, there was a scholarly dispute about whether cities in Chapter 9 could prioritize paying pensioners before bondholders, as bankruptcy law generally requires equal distribution among similarly situated unsecured creditors.[9] Legal scholar David Skeel (later chairman of Puerto Rico's Financial Oversight and Management Board) argued they could; other bankruptcy law experts, Richard Hynes and Stephen Walt, argued that they could not.[10] Hynes and Walt argued that none of the traditional exceptions to the general bankruptcy rule of equal distribution applied, and that a city could only favor one class of creditors if those creditors had a security interest in the city's property.[11]

There has been no clear theoretical resolution to this dispute and Hynes and Walt's argument has a lot of force. But, in practice, Skeel's view has won out. In a number of the cases discussed in Chapter 5, bankruptcy courts approved plans of adjustment that allowed pensioners to take smaller (and in some cases no) haircuts, while bondholders took more substantial losses. Those courts provided varied justifications for *why* they accepted this unequal treatment, including the importance of pensions to future hiring, the normative force of state constitutional pension clauses, and losses born by public employees in other areas. But they allowed plans of adjustment to favor pensioners over bondholders.

A few states have responded to pro-pension Chapter 9 decisions by providing general obligation bondholders with a "statutory lien" in local taxes, a protection that puts them ahead of unsecured creditors.[12] In Central Falls, Rhode Island, this type of provision meant that pensioners took a very substantial haircut while bondholders did not. However, whether assignments of security interests will work to protect bondholders in all cases is not entirely certain.

Congress could act to clear this up, perhaps, by changing the law to make a clearer order of priority among creditors. Doing so would require detailing which creditors are more important *ex ante*, at least as a default matter. A clearer set of priorities would speed up Chapter 9 cases, which are very long and expensive, and thus make the system easier to use.

However, there are reasons to think that such proposals would do more harm than good to the Chapter 9 process. It does not make much sense to provide a single set of rules governing priorities among debtors in Chapter 9. First, the central rule of Chapter 9 is state authority.[13] Creditors cannot push cities into bankruptcy; courts cannot order tax increases or spending cuts; cities and cities alone can design plans of adjustment. State authority is important to the constitutionality of the regime. Giving cities some power to treat different creditors differently fits with the broader state authority embedded in Chapter 9.

But more relevantly, strictly requiring equal distribution among unsecured creditors would force Chapter 9 to be more like corporate bankruptcy than it actually is.[14] Courts in Chapter 9 cases provide a forum, procedure and some legal limits for political figures to make what are irreducibly political judgments about where to land on the trilemma and how to write down debt with as little effect on future investment as possible. It is tempting to reduce this to a strict rule that can be set ex ante, but the best policies may be very different across place and time, and thus a loose standard is preferable.

9.1.3. Financial Engineering

A number of recent municipal default (and near default) stories involve complex financial engineering. Courts have struggled with figuring out how to deal with some of these transactions, increasing the incentives for jurisdictions to use financial tools in abusive ways. Reforms to Chapter 9 should address this problem, making it a more functional tool for addressing excessive municipal indebtedness in a balanced way.

The basic story is similar in all cases, even if the specifics are always different. Faced with legal limitations on issuing more debt and/or market limitations on borrowing, cities work with investment banks to design ever more clever ways to borrow. Sometimes bells and whistles are added that provide some benefits to the city, but also expose the jurisdiction to risk, like the use of interest rate swaps. Versions of this story can be told about New York City; Jefferson County, Alabama; Detroit, Michigan; and Puerto Rico.

Some of the cases involve truly unique financial instruments. But one legal technology has been used several times.

First devised for New York State's Urban Development Corporation (UDC) by Richard Ravitch, a heavily indebted political jurisdiction takes a stream of revenue (like sales tax revenue) and pledges it to new bondholders. The jurisdiction's existing general obligation bondholders expected that stream of revenue to be used to repay them, but this type of deal takes it away from them. The new bonds are then sold with the promise that they will be safe in bankruptcy, or at least safer, because they are backed by the specific revenue stream. That is, the new bondholders and not the old bondholders, will get the money from the revenue stream in case of a default. In return, the government gets an infusion of cash, at interest rates lower than it could have gotten otherwise (if ordinary financing was available at all).

New York City used the basic structure developed by the UDC to help address its fiscal crisis. The state assigned the city's sales tax and a few other revenue sources to support bonds issued by the newly created Municipal Assistance Corporation (MAC). The point of the MAC bonds was to provide short-term liquidity to New York City while it got its act together. Banks had refused to support any short-term financing for the city, leaving it on the brink of bankruptcy. The MAC bonds provided money in the short term while other reforms helped the city better match its spending to its revenue. Importantly, the assignment of the revenues was not done by the indebted entity, New York City, but instead by the state government. And states always have the power to reassign taxing authority as they see fit.

Puerto Rico's "COFINA" bonds were a more abusive version of the same basic technology. The Commonwealth hived off its own sales tax revenue to support COFINA bonds. But they did not do so to provide short-term liquidity to support a broader set of reforms. Instead, they were just used to push off insolvency for a number of years. Further, COFINA bonds were not created by an outside entity, but instead by the Commonwealth itself. Recently, Illinois gave municipalities the power to issue sales tax securitization bonds that share many traits with both MAC and COFINA bonds.[15]

There are two big legal questions about this type of creative financing. The first is whether the Contract Clause of the US Constitution imposes any roadblock to their use. I will address that question in an appendix to this chapter, but the answer is probably not.

A separate question is whether the assignment of revenues to new bondholders would survive in bankruptcy. In theory, a bankruptcy court could determine that the assignment of the revenues to the new bonds was a "fraudulent transfer" and void the transaction. But fraudulent transfer rules generally apply to interests in property or in an asset, and the power to tax is not really an interest in property.[16]

Beyond whether current law is best interpreted to limit "Big MAC"–style financial engineering is the question of what federal law *should* be.

Ideally, courts or state legislatures would differentiate between socially useful and abusive financial engineering. To the extent that the "MAC" technology is used to create liquidity in response to a short-term financing crunch, it can help everyone. Because they were paired with structural reforms, the actual "MAC" bonds were helpful for all parties. The city remained solvent and was able to improve its financial position over time.[17] If a state tried to replicate New York State's response to New York City's fiscal crisis, but it did not work out (and the city the state sought to save went bankrupt), there would be little reason for a court to unwind it.

However, it would be wise to encourage cities and states not to use the MAC technology just to aid one group of bondholders over another or as a stopgap measure. When jurisdictions use this type of financial engineering without also engaging in a broad plan to reform their budgets, they just extend and worsen fiscal crises. In those situations, the "MAC" technology enables one group of politicians to pass a fiscal crisis on to another, exacerbating these untreated, underlying problems.

Congress should include in Chapter 9 rules that treat tax-stripping bonds as voidable transactions if they are used in situations other than a government that is facing a short-term liquidity problem and is engaging in substantial structural reforms with the goal of avoiding bankruptcy. Specific determinations would be challenging, so Congress would do well to be provide examples which existing uses fall into which camp. Even if the rule is not clear, the threat of such bonds being invalidated would hopefully encourage states that chose to use the "MAC" technology to pair them with structural reforms and treat them as a short-term liquidity tool rather than a means by which to pass the buck to a future set of political leaders.

9.1.4. Chapter 9 and Overlapping Local Governments

With some reforms, Chapter 9 could do a great deal to spread the harms of defaults across multiple governments, reducing the harms to any one set of creditors or service recipients.

In addition to being residents of a state, most Americans are governed by *many* local governments: a city, a county, a school district, and often several other special-purpose districts, like transit, parks, or mosquito control districts.[18] While legally separate, overlapping local governments are deeply integrated practically and politically. Each government taxes the same people and property; their leaders are elected by the same voters. When a place faces an economic shock, all overlapping local governments are likely to face substantial fiscal challenges.

But in an insolvency crisis, Chapter 9 operates on one government entity at a time, pretending that each government is independent of all of the other entities that raise money from the same tax base. States sometimes plunge one local government into bankruptcy while bailing out others. For instance, when Detroit went bankrupt, Detroit's public school system received a bailout and its promises were kept. Neither school district pensioners nor bondholders took any haircut at all.[19]

As Aurelia Chaudhury, Adam Levitin, and I have argued, courts and Congress should reform Chapter 9 to allow and encourage states to put multiple overlapping local governments into a single bankruptcy case.[20] This would not be an entirely unprecedented reform. In 2016, Congress assigned one judge to hear all of the insolvency cases arising out of Puerto Rico's default.

Having multiple local governments in one case would provide substantial benefits. Treating overlapping local governments as entirely separate entities can create unfairness, as the Detroit case makes clear. Creditors of one entity that governs a group of taxpayers get paid in full, while creditors of another government that represent the same taxpayers take massive haircuts. Services in some policy areas decline massively, while other areas remain untouched.

Further, an inability or refusal to join cases together creates the potential for costly strategic or bad-faith interactions. One government may delay filing for bankruptcy because a filing by another would open up capacity to raise taxes. If there are strong political links between the entities (e.g., the mayor of a city appoints the head of the school board, despite it being a legally separate entity), officials could in theory strategically dump assets in one entity or another ahead of a bankruptcy filing.

New rules could facilitate the consideration of multiple cases from overlapping local governments at the same time, providing a solution to these problems. Courts can do a lot of the necessary work through interpretations of the vaguely worded Chapter 9 statute. When judging the feasibility of a plan of adjustment for leaving bankruptcy, courts should consider the effects of one jurisdiction's plan on other overlapping governments. Courts should also take into account the ability of a tax base to support all of its various debts and services when judging insolvency, not focusing myopically on the jurisdiction that files.

But some new legislation might be necessary as well. State legislatures should give overlapping jurisdictions the capacity to veto each other's plans of adjustment, forcing them to develop common plans (ideally with some kind of majority rule requirement, so that one recalcitrant entity can't stand in the way of a broader solution). And Congress should amend the Chapter 9 statute to make clear that one court can hear cases involving multiple local governments.

Put together, these reforms would allow Chapter 9 cases to mimic rules that already exist in corporate bankruptcy cases involving conglomerates. "Joint administration" allows courts to hear cases involving all subsidiaries inside a single conglomerate. "Substantive consolidation" allows a court to act as if a conglomerate were a single entity for the purpose of bankruptcy.

The reforms proposed here are less dramatic than the ones used in the corporate context. But they would allow states to plunge a set of overlapping local governments into bankruptcy at the same time.

Doing so would serve to spread out the harms of the bankruptcy across multiple sets of creditors and service recipients, reducing the harm to one group by making everyone take losses. More importantly, it would allow a court to review holistically how a set of jurisdictions is addressing the trilemma, providing a venue for more rational and even balancing of creditor losses, austerity, and bailouts.

9.2. Building Bigger Defaults: State Governments and Chapter 9

Municipal bankruptcy provides a forum for competing interests to negotiate, and an adjudicator—a judge—who can promote values like prudence, balance, and spreading. But municipal bankruptcy only applies to municipalities, not to state governments. Extending it to states would promote the same values.

Following the Great Recession, there were a number of proposals—from scholars like David Skeel and from politicians like former Speaker of the

House Newt Gingrich and then-Florida-governor Jeb Bush—to allow state governments to file for bankruptcy under Chapter 9.[21] Senate Majority Leader Mitch McConnell brought the idea up again at the outset of the COVID-19 recession. But McConnell was roundly condemned in the press for using bankruptcy as a justification for not offering needed aid to states.[22] Other critics of state bankruptcy argued that states have lots of taxing authority and thus were not insolvent at the onset of the pandemic.[23] Still others argue that a state bankruptcy regime is just cover for a conservative effort to gut public employee pensions.[24]

But Skeel's proposal had more to it than his critics understood. Critics equate bankruptcy with default. As Chapters 2, 3, and 4 of this book demonstrate, states do not need the formal mechanisms of bankruptcy in order to default. States defaulted in the 1840s, the 1870s, and 1930s without help from a bankruptcy law.

When states default, they are protected by sovereign immunity from suits. A state does not even need to be insolvent, or without any capacity to pay its bills, to default. It is a political choice, not one that requires absolute penury. As a result, Vincent Buccola has argued that states would not file for Chapter 9 even if they could do so.[25] Filing for bankruptcy would put a state within the power of a bankruptcy court, limiting its options, while simply defaulting would give it free reign to pay some creditors and not others. States can already do everything critics of state bankruptcy argue they should not be able to do and more.

Buccola's article is excellent and he is absolutely right to argue that the most important question about state bankruptcy is how it would interact with sovereign immunity. But he underrates the benefits a state bankruptcy option would provide to state governments. While sovereign immunity renders legal claims against the state generally not enforceable, bankruptcy extinguishes legal claims, removing any legal risk going forward, giving a state a clean slate. Bankruptcy would allow states to break contracts without falling afoul of the Contract Clause.

Further, state officials may see some value in giving up the ability to pay some equally situated creditors but not others. Abandoning that power would also reduce pressure from politically powerful creditors on state officials that they use it. If Congress created a state bankruptcy regime and a state filed under it, the state would still retain authority to devise its plan of adjustment, just as cities have under Chapter 9. But a bankruptcy court would provide them with some political cover while making the tough decisions about who and how much to pay. Further, filing for bankruptcy might keep the federal government from doing what it did in the Arkansas road debt crisis, using federal aid as a cudgel on behalf of creditors. Concerns from federal officials that the state is acting abusively may be soothed because of court oversight.

A state bankruptcy system would also help establish to the public and to creditors the seriousness of a state's fiscal crisis. A state does not have to be insolvent to default. But justifying a decision not to make payments to creditors can be difficult even if it is wise.

As we saw in the *Detroit* and *Stockton* cases, "insolvency" as defined by courts under Chapter 9, does not require a city to lack any capacity at all to raise money or make payments. Instead, under the doctrine of "service delivery insolvency," courts determine whether current residents have already suffered from too much from the declining quality of public services to ask them to shoulder the costs of paying back bondholders and pensioners in full.

A judicial determination of insolvency can create space for politicians to make cuts or tax increases that they could not otherwise justify. The court, not the politicians, would be responsible for judging whether cuts had been sufficient. And bankruptcy might provide a signal to Congress that aid is needed. As we saw in the Detroit and New York City cases, after creditors take some losses, a higher level of government can provide aid in ways less likely to create moral hazard.

There would be a constitutional challenge to any state bankruptcy law. But because states would have to opt into a bankruptcy regime, the same logic the *Detroit* court used to dismiss a constitutional challenge to Chapter 9 should apply to state bankruptcy. A state bankruptcy regime would *increase* the power of a state government, giving it an option it did not previously have.

Chapter 9 allows for balanced solutions in the trilemma when cities are insolvent. Creating a similar option for states would be healthy. Congress should extend Chapter 9 to state governments.

9.3. Appendix to Chapter 9: The Constitutional Status of "Big MAC"s

The "Big MAC" bond structure has become more popular over the years, moving from New York to Puerto Rico to Illinois. But there remains an open question about its constitutionality.

As discussed in Chapter 3, the Supreme Court once decided that an effort by the state of Alabama to help the city of Mobile escape its debt was legally infirm.[26] When the city of Mobile couldn't pay its debts, Alabama created a new governmental entity, the Port of Mobile, and gave that entity most of the taxing authority that the city once had.[27] Mobile's bondholders were left with claims against an entity with no way to raise money. The Court—not relying clearly on any specific legal authority but possibly referring to the Contract Clause—held in *Port of Mobile v. Watson* that Port of Mobile was the successor to and responsible for the City of Mobile's debts.[28] The fact that there was a new legal entity did not mean the people of Mobile could escape their promises.

In theory, the *Watson* decision could be extended to nullify "Big MAC" style bonds. A court could hold that a state's decision to take taxes that once supported GO bonds and give them to new bondholders is an unconstitutional impairment of the contract between the GO bondholders and the city. *Watson* was not clear about what law it relied on, but other decisions from that period suggest the relevance of the Contract Clause. In *Wolff v. New Orleans*, the Court noted that state legislatures generally controlled the powers of municipalities, but that they could not use that power to impair municipal contracts "directly."[29] A state law removing local taxing authority leading to a local default violates the contract clause if the state law "directly . . . operate[s]" upon local ability to pay its debt, rather than the default being an "indirect[] . . . consequence of legitimate measures taken."

This suggests that state law changes to a municipality's taxing authority would violate the Contract Clause if they worsen the position of GO bondholders in an intentional and direct manner. Thus, as Clayton Gillette argues, there is a reasonable argument that Big MAC–style bonds violate the Constitution.[30]

However, there are good reasons to think that the Supreme Court would and should reject this argument. To start, in stark contrast with the decisions of the earlier railroad bond era, the Court has been clear for nearly 100 years that the Contract Clause imposes a pretty limited set of restrictions on state power.[31] In the 1930s, the Court issued important decisions that reduced the limitations the Contract Clause put on state regulation, moving away from prior doctrine. It is thus not obvious that cases like *Watson* and *Wolff* should be understood to have survived this revolution, at least not in a strong form.[32] The case law from that earlier period is far from consistent, anyway, and since then the Court has blessed state interventions reduced the value of local governmental municipal bonds.[33] The most notable of these was *Faitoute Iron & Steel v. City of Asbury Park*, discussed in Chapter 4 of this book, in which the Court rejected a challenge to what amounted to a state municipal bankruptcy law.[34]

The Court has imposed a higher standard under the Contract Clause when a state attempts to change the terms of contracts it signed itself.[35] But a challenge to "Big MAC"–style bonds would not implicate this higher standard. Before the New York City fiscal crisis, New York City (not the state government) entered into contracts with the general-obligation bond holders that were potentially impaired by state legislation removing from the city certain taxing authority and assigning it to support the MAC bonds.[36] The legal test applied to state laws that potentially impair city contracts should be no different from the loose test the Court applies when states pass laws that effect contracts between private parties.

Most importantly, there is a clear conflict between state sovereignty over municipalities and a reading of cases like *Watson* or *Wolff* to imperil "Big MAC" style bonds. The Court has consistently held that states are generally within their rights to reassign authority and power among local jurisdictions as they see fit.[37] This power is not without limit. Changes to jurisdictional lines can violate independent clauses of the Constitution, for instance if they are drawn intentionally to exclude African Americans, or to establish religious control of a municipality.[38] But outside of that, states can create, empower, disempower, shrink, or abolish local governments.[39]

The Court in *Wolff* argued that removing the city's taxing power violated an independent part of the Constitution. Specifically, the Court argued the legislature violated the Contract Clause because it "directly" interfered with a municipal contract by removing local taxing authority after having implicitly promised the city and its creditors that it would not do so.[40] "The control of the legislature over the power of taxation . . . is restrained to cases where such control does not impair the obligation of contracts made upon a pledge, expressly or impliedly given, that the power should be exercised for their fulfillment."[41]

But applying *Wolff* to limit state policies that reallocate taxing authority would be a very severe limitation on the right of states to control their municipalities. Even more problematically, it would allow municipalities to use their own bond contracts to attempt to freeze in place their powers. Simply by issuing a bond, a city would effectively be trapping the state government into assigning it the same or greater taxing authority for the life of that bond.

Unless *Wolff* and *Watson* are read *very* aggressively, courts should not find that "Big MAC"–style bonds violate the Constitution. "Big MAC"-style bonds do not "directly" interfere with contract rights at all, but rather, reallocate the power to tax among municipal entities in order to improve the quality of services available for local residents. Such bonds do not remove local governments' ability to pay back their general obligation bonds entirely, the way Alabama did to Mobile prior to the *Watson* decision. Nor do they even operate on the most traditional forms of local taxing authority (the "Big MAC" bonds did not reallocate property tax revenue, for instance).

Instead, Big MAC–style bonds just reallocate a specific source of revenue—most often sales taxes, but also other types of revenue—to a new government to support new bondholders.[42] Finding that this kind of structure violates the Contract Clause implies that a decision by a city to issue bonds can block the state from taking away its current powers to tax simply by issuing debt. That argument just can't be right or be made consistent with the long line of decisions allowing states to organize and reorganize their municipalities as they see fit.

Given the strength of the Court's commitment to allowing states to determine the powers of their own local governments without federal interference, and the weakness of Contract Clause restrictions in situations other than those in which a state binds itself, a court probably would not invalidate "Big MAC"-style bonds.[43]

Even so, it is fair to say that the Court's Contract Clause jurisprudence on this score is not perfectly clear!

Building Better Forms of State and Local Austerity

The one universal feature of all state and local budget crises is that there is at least some austerity. Unless they have saved enough beforehand, state and local governments facing balanced-budget requirements, debt limits, and political and market-driven limitations on borrowing will make spending cuts and/or increase taxes during recessions. At some point in a true crisis, these cuts may be relieved by federal aid or by making creditors take haircuts. However, the first, and in most cases the only, response will be spending cuts and tax increases.

The harms of spending cuts and tax increases will be determined in part by what gets cut. Clearly, a general discussion like this one cannot say too much about what should be cut from any particular state or city budget. However, there are two types of general reforms that can make austerity less painful.

First, the federal government can help make state taxation more efficient. Second, states can make legal changes that would allow them to address their pension funding problems in recessions.

10.1. Separating State and Local Tax Bases

In the 19th century, federal and state and local tax systems were often quite distinct: they taxed different things. However, over the course of the 20th century, federal and state tax bases began to resemble each other to a greater degree. Particularly in the last number of years, many states have become more reliant on progressive income and/or capital gains taxes, just like the federal government.[1]

The move toward relying on income and capital gains taxes has made state taxes more progressive, but it also has had two big effects on state tax systems during crises. First, state revenue has become more cyclical. Income taxes and capital gains taxes usually swing more during the business cycle than property or sales taxes, thereby providing more revenue in good times but less in bad times. In theory, states can save across the business cycle, but they have trouble doing so politically.[2] As a result, recessions create greater problems than ever for state budgets.

Second, the fact that federal and state taxes cover the same base makes them both less efficient. Basic tax economics shows that taxes become increasingly inefficient as rates go up.[3] An increase of a tax from 5% to 6% will create more economic harm than an increase from 2% to 3% because the increase from 5% to 6% will deter more valuable activity. Because both states and the federal government tax incomes, combined income tax rates get substantially higher and the tax becomes more inefficient. States have incentives to push tax rates past the (combined) efficient point, because the state does not really care that its taxes have the effect of decreasing federal tax revenue. States generally piggyback on federal tax base-definition rules for corporate and personal income taxes (although there was some breakdown of this following the 2017 federal tax changes), making this problem worse.[4]

This means that state income and capital gains tax increases have the effect of making federal taxes less efficient (and vice versa). These "vertical tax externalities" have gotten substantially worse over time.[5] For some taxes, the combined federal/state tax levels may even exceed the revenue-maximizing level, even if one were to put aside the economic harms associated with such high levels of taxation.[6]

Ideally, states and the federal government would tax different things, reducing vertical tax externalities. But creating and operating a new tax on a different base would be quite difficult for state and local governments as an operational matter.

David Gamage and Darien Shanske have a clever proposal for how the federal government can encourage states to tax something different from what the federal government taxes.[7] The federal government could do the work of creating a Value Added Tax (VAT) system—the type of comprehensive consumption tax seen in most European tax systems—but not actually collect taxes (or collect them and give the revenue to the states). This would leave states free to set whatever rates they wanted on consumption without taxing the same base as the federal government.

VATs are famously unpopular. Economist and former Treasury secretary Larry Summers once noted, "Liberals think it's regressive and conservatives think it's a money machine." He then quipped that a VAT would only pass if the parties switched their respective opinions.[8] It is hard to imagine Congress passing such a momentous tax change, let alone giving all of the revenue to state governments. Only in a context where the other choices are as bad as the other legs of the trilemma—federal bailouts or state defaults—is it even possible to imagine this type of political change.

Even so, this type of reform could help avoid some of the downsides of austerity.

10.2. Pension Reform

Underfunded pensions have become the major source of debt for our most indebted states and cities.[9] This has led many commentators to discuss the problems of state and local debt as if they were primarily about pensions and to think that the solutions are to be found in pension reform.[10] Municipal finance expert James Spiotto, for instance, argued that Congress should authorize a new bankruptcy system that applied only to public employee pensions.[11]

However, this argument misunderstands the nature of the problem of underfunded pensions. Underfunded pensions and Other Post-Employment Benefits (OPEB) liabilities are a product of a refusal to save money, not necessarily of excessive spending on employees or pensions. There may be excessive spending on benefits in some cases, but expensive pensions are not a necessary condition for having underfunded pensions.

Underfunded pension systems are caused by a broader failure of a state political system, a refusal to pay for services when they are received. Taxpayers get services today and pay the workers who provide those services with both salaries and a promise to pay pensions tomorrow. But states with underfunded pensions are not saving money today to make payments tomorrow. Underfunded pensions are also a legal problem, as constitutional debt limitations and balanced budget rules do not count pension underfunding as debt, even though an underfunded pension system, just like a bond, creates unavoidable future obligation. There is no reason to think that it is somehow less important to pay obligations to pensioners than it is to pay other creditors.

Instead, if a default is necessary, it would be wiser to make pensioners and bondholders share in losses, contrary to Spiotto's argument. Bankrupt cities have often gone the other way, making pensioners take smaller haircuts than bondholders. Whether or not this is a good idea, proposals to punish pensioners alone do not accord with the preferences of jurisdictions or the real nature of pension underfunding. Debt is debt, and if a government is discharging its debts, it should make all creditors bear some of the cost.

Further, underfunded pensions have the same or stronger legal status as debt in most states.[12] Courts have approved state bankruptcy authorizations that likely will lead to pension reductions because bankruptcies by their very nature mean reducing debt, and there is no reason to treat pension debt differently from bonded debt.[13] But state authorization for a pension-specific bankruptcy filing very well might not pass state constitutional muster.

However, that the most aggressive ideas about cutting pensions are unwise does not mean that nothing should be done. States should reform their constitutional debt limitations to include pension underfunding, which would be consistent with the suggestions in Chapter 8 about accrual accounting. They should probably not create statutory liens for general obligation bondholders of the type discussed in Chapters 5 and 9. But they should also repeal the most aggressive constitutional protections for pensions.

The case for debt limit reform is straightforward enough. There is extensive debate about whether debt limits make any sense at all, as they limit the ability of governments to borrow and make investments. But if there are going to be debt limits (or balanced budget rules), there is no reason to exclude from those limits all obligations governments undertake and cannot easily ignore. As long as pensions are protected by state constitutions, underfunding pensions should be understood as debt.

Statutory liens for general obligation bondholders in theory put them in the front of the line in the case of a bankruptcy. Statutory liens turn bondholder claims to tax revenue into secured claim, with a property interest in the revenue stream. Jurisdictions do this to make creditors more likely to lend. But doing so puts them at risk of not being able to adequately protect pensions, which will negatively impact their ability to hire, as the *Detroit* plan of adjustment decision argued. And as we saw in *Central Falls*, they require an extreme solution, bondholders to get paid in full (or close) before pensions get paid at all. As a result, they hold up the ability of jurisdictions to design balanced solutions to their fiscal problems during bankruptcies.

State constitutional pension reform can also help. How pension obligations are protected by state constitutions varies by states. Under the "California Rule," the terms of public employee pensions are protected from revision on the day an employee's career begins, even for pensions they have not yet earned.[14] The California Rule, which applies in a number of states, limits the ability of a government to balance the costs of a fiscal crisis across multiple stakeholders by making it impossible for a jurisdiction to reduce not-yet-earned pensions for current workers, even as part of a broader package of reforms in which many interests see losses. Other states have less dramatic protections that only protect the parts of pensions that workers have already earned. These rules protect the interests of workers while allowing states flexibility to make all interested parties in the state take losses when times are tough. It would be wise to move away from the California Rule and toward state constitutional protections for pensions that lock in gains workers have already earned, but allow for future-oriented pension changes for current workers.

State constitutional changes—by amendment or by judicial interpretation—would make reform easier. There are real questions, though, whether state constitutional changes would help in a crisis, given the interaction between state law and the federal constitution. Most states consider pensions to be contracts with public workers. As such, the federal Contract Clause protects pensions.[15] If the state repeals its state constitutional pension clause and then seeks to reduce pensions, public workers can argue that the state has repealed of the terms of a public contract, violating the federal Contract Clause. Exactly how a court would decide such a case is uncertain.

However, the exact same logic presents an argument in favor of repeal in advance of a crisis. Not having to deal with strong-form California Rule protections would give a state or city with much more flexibility in how it responds to a debt crisis.

Strong state constitutional pension protections limit the ability of state governments to balance among competing demands along the trilemma. If a state is able to slightly impair pensioners on a going-forward basis during a crisis, reducing cost of living adjustments, say, or increasing the retirement age, it may be able to avoid a true crisis, and it may be able to avoid layoffs, salary reductions, or other types of cuts that create very substantial harms.

Resilience, or Building a Better Federal System

The United States is a big country, and there are always some places that are doing well economically and others that are doing poorly. Indeed, it would be a disaster if this wasn't true. Just as we would think of a country that had the same 500 firms in its "Fortune 500" for 50 years as a sclerotic disaster, economic growth and technological change create advantages for some places over others, leading to localized booms and busts.

Further, despite claims made during the "Great Moderation," the 21st century has already seen huge macroeconomic swings, both periods of growth and several massive declines.[1] Assuming that we will continue to see localized economic shocks and semiregular dips in the business cycle (or worse), there will be economic declines in particular regions. When there are, we can expect to see fiscal crises as well. Unless they have an unusual amount of foresight, jurisdictions facing economic decline and population outflows always face substantial fiscal pressure, as they frequently have fixed costs (bonds, pensions, collective bargaining agreements) and physical plants (housing stock, infrastructure) that were designed for different levels of population and wealth.

As a result, the problems of regionalized state and local fiscal crises are likely going to be with us for as long as we have fiscally independent states and cities. The prior three chapters asked how to design federal policy responses to state and local fiscal crises. But another question to ask is how to make the country more resilient against the economic shocks that lead to such fiscal crises. Relatedly, we can ask how to make the financial system, particularly the municipal bond market, able to cope with the inevitability of fiscal pressure on state and local governments.

In this section, I will offer four policy ideas to make the country's economy and state financing system more resilient against regional shocks.

11.1. Encouraging Inter-Regional Mobility

One of the largest changes in the national economy over the last 50 or so years has been the decline of regional mobility. People move between states less often than they used to, and are less likely to leave regions suffering from economic shocks.[2] As I have argued elsewhere, this has all sorts of bad effects on the economy. It reduces the ability of people to combine in ways that fit contemporary economic conditions.[3] Further, as migration decreases, monetary policy becomes more difficult, as the Federal Reserve is setting interest rates for labor markets that are quite different from one another. It is unclear what the effects of increases in working-from-home following the COVID-19 recession will be on this. But the trend is long-standing.

The causes of declining mobility are much debated.[4] But it is clear that federal, state, and local laws make inter-regional migration harder.

Most notably, zoning regulations and other land use policies increase the cost of housing in hot job markets by making it difficult to build new houses. Limits on building new housing ensure that economic booms do not create boomtowns, with people from all over moving in to take advantage of new opportunities. Silicon Valley's population has increased only slightly since the mid-1990s, while previous local economic booms, like Chicago at the turn of the last century, saw millions of people moving in to seek opportunity. The reason: there just aren't enough houses and apartments in Silicon Valley because local laws bar developers from building densely enough to meet the demand. Only people with high salaries can afford to move in, limiting who gets to experience the growing and intellectually rich region.

The effects of regional limits on entry on the economy are enormous. Workers cannot move to the best job opportunities, depressing national wages and output. Chang-Tai Hsieh and Enrico Moretti; Kyle Herkenhoff, Lee Ohanian, and Edward Prescott; and David Albouy and Gabriel Ehrlich each have estimated the economic effects of reducing excessively restrictive zoning rules using different empirical methods and assumptions.[5] Their estimates range from around 2% of GDP (which is huge) to 36% of GDP (an almost impossibly large amount).

But land use is not the only limitation on mobility. Occupational licensing rules—requirements that workers receive a certificate of some sort before practicing a trade—now govern around 25% of the labor market. Such rules are almost always state-based.[6] Being a licensed cosmetologist in one state does not necessarily give one a right to practice cosmetology in another.

Social benefits are rarely transferable either.[7] This is true even when they are formally transferable. For instance, federal housing vouchers are legally transferable across states. But in practice, the difficulty of transferring housing vouchers is so great that most analysts understand them to be, as a practical reality, limited to one housing market.

The combined effect of these regulations is that they make moving harder. In particular, they make localized economic shocks much worse for the poor than the rich. High-income workers can flee such shocks, and typically can afford housing in whatever market they choose. But lower income workers are increasingly stuck and left behind. Doctors can move from Detroit to San Francisco, from San Juan to New York City, but it is harder for janitors to do the same.

The inability of poor workers to move to opportunity also makes the fiscal crises that follow localized economic shocks worse. Fiscal shocks and debt crises often follow economic shocks. When a big industry moves out of town, cities are left with too much debt and a public sector that is outsized relative to a region's current economic capacity. Debt cannot simply be ignored, but it is also hard to reduce the size of the local public sector, as a local economic shock creates greater need for services.

If regulations limit the ability of people to move, declining places will still lose their richest and highest tax-paying residents during economic downturns. But land use and other regulations in rich regions make the less well-off residents of poorer areas less likely to move. As a result, they trap more people in places with declining economies and now-underfunded public services.

A national economy that was more flexible, particularly for those without high incomes, would thus be better for reducing the costs of localized economic shocks. And it would reduce the costs of fiscal shocks as well.

The federal government can play some role in encouraging states and cities to reduce barriers to entry. It can tie transportation spending or federal housing support to reducing land use barriers. The Biden administration announced plans to challenge some state occupational licensing rules. And it can reform the way it provides benefits to make them more portable across places.

Doing so would allow residents of places suffering from economic shock to move to opportunity more easily, reducing the cost born by jurisdictions facing shocks.

11.2. The Tentative Case for Keeping the Municipal Bond Interest Tax Exemption

As discussed in Chapters 1 and 4, the federal government supports the ability of state and local governments to borrow in a number of ways. The biggest and most prominent is the exemption from federal income taxes for interest on municipal debt. This subsidy, which allows subnational governments to borrow at lower rates, costs the federal government around $31B a year.[8]

That the federal government supports state and local debt is strong evidence that moral hazard and Keynesian theories of state fiscal crises miss something important. State and local debt is clearly bad under both of these theories, because high debt loads make bailouts *and* pro-cyclical layoffs during recessions more likely.

The reason the federal government supports municipal debt is that it wants to encourage states and cities to invest. Because of the political difficulties the federal government faces in directly building infrastructure, state and local investment is necessary, and so the federal government subsidizes it.

But it is not obvious that the tax exemption, rather than direct cash support for state and local borrowing, is the best way to achieve this end. The federal government could provide cash subsidies to states for issuing debt as it did in the Build America Bonds program.[9]

The best justification for using the tax exemption to subsidize state and local borrowing is that it is a way to reduce the "contagion" effects of defaults. That is, while the efficiency of tax exemption is debatable, the exemption also serves an important insurance function, protecting states and cities against wild swings in their ability to borrow when there is a default in one jurisdiction or another.

As long as there has been a tax exemption, there have been critics of it. When the exemption was first created, there was a common belief that it was constitutionally mandated. However, the Supreme Court has now clearly held that the federal government can tax interest on municipal bonds if it chooses to.[10] Since the creation of the exemption, presidents—perhaps most notably President Franklin Delano Roosevelt—have tried to get Congress to repeal it.[11] In the debates over tax reform in in 1986, Congress and President Ronald Reagan again considered repeal, but ultimately chose only to reduce tax incentives for banks to buy municipal bonds and to restrict the ability of states and cities to borrow on behalf of private actors, creating a state-specific cap on the number of "private activity bonds" that could be issued.[12] Then, in 2017, Congress once again considered repealing the exemption, but decided against it, choosing instead only to limit "advance refundings," or the ability of cities to use tax-exempt debt to pay back already-issued debt when interest rates fall.[13]

The central case against the exemption is based on basic ideas about tax fairness.[14] Like all tax exemptions, the municipal bond interest exemption violates the principle of horizontal equality. Exemptions mean that some income is taxed, while other income is not. Further, the interest exemption is highly regressive.[15] The benefits it provides to investors accrue mostly to the rich. Individuals in the highest tax bracket benefit more from tax-exempt income than others, and thus buy more municipal bonds. To the extent that non-top-bracket taxpayers are the marginal purchasers of municipal bonds, the benefit to the rich is even larger.[16] If tax-exempt bonds are sold with high-enough interest rates to be attractive to individuals who are not receiving income exempt from taxes at the highest bracket, individuals who buy them and do pay the top rate will get a windfall. In that instance, the exemption also becomes a less-than-efficient way to subsidize state and local investment and the federal government is effectively providing a tax windfall for wealthy bond buyers.

So why keep the exemption? To understand the case for the exemption, it is important to understand how it changes who buys municipal bonds. Particularly when combined with states that make interest on their own bonds exempt from state taxes and thus "double tax exempt,"[17] the tax exemption strongly encourages individual Americans and particularly in-state residents to buy municipal bonds.[18]

The development of state-specific pools of money has the effect of allowing smaller governments to borrow without having to convince global investors of their credit-worthiness.[19] This can remove the power banks have over those governments (as these governments likely would not be able to borrow from capital markets without there being pools of state-specific money out there). Researchers have found that this effect—displacing banks as funders of small local governments—reduces borrowing costs by substantially more than it costs the federal government.[20]

The exemption also crucially changes the effect state and local fiscal crises have on broader municipal investment. A classic concern in debt markets is "contagion," or the effect a default in one place will have on borrowing in another. In international sovereign debt markets, investors sometimes react to a financial crisis in one country by pulling money from others, retreating to safe assets like US Treasury bonds. This harms countries that had nothing to do with the initial default.

Linkages between jurisdictions can create contagion. Their economies might rise and fall together due to trade, meaning that one's default causes economic problems for the other. Or jurisdictions might have common investors, meaning that a default in one can lead investors to pull money from others to make up for losses.[21] Alternatively, contagion can be caused by informational problems. A default in one country may cause investors to update their beliefs about the likelihood of default for a whole class of investment.[22] Countries that did not default can be punished because investors can't tell the difference between good and bad credit risks.

As a class of bondholder, we can expect in-state individual holders and state-specific investment funds to be less likely to be subject to contagion than other types of investors.[23] In-state investors are likely better informed about local economies and fiscal affairs than distant foreigners. It stands to reason that a

Massachusetts investor is less likely than a German one to see risk to Boston's bonds because Detroit filed for bankruptcy. Also, having different municipal bond purchasers in different states reduces contagion through effects on investors' balance sheets.

None of this means that contagion in municipal bonds is impossible or never occurs.[24] Even investors well-placed to avoid panics will not always do so. And some contagion is rational. For instance, a Detroit default should cause Lansing bond purchasers to believe that the Michigan state legislature is in no mood to provide bailouts.

But even though subsidizing investment in infrastructure through a tax emption on state and local bonds' interest is somewhat inefficient and reduces the progressivity of the tax system, it also likely reduces the risk of contagion. There is some evidence that municipal bonds as they exist now do not feature contagion risk, but an almost opposite phenomenon, a "flight to quality."[25] A default in one place increases demand for other municipal bonds, as investors, still seeking tax-free income, shift their investments rather than exiting the broader market.

This is a major benefit, as it makes possible policies that force creditors to take deeper haircuts in crises. If there are real concerns that investment in the United States as a whole or municipal bonds as a class would dry up if defaults were permitted in small Iowa towns, policies like the Supreme Court's aggressive pro-bondholder decisions in the 1870s become more necessary.[26] But if the harms of defaults can be localized, then the need to intervene on behalf of bondholders falls. That is, while the exemption supports the municipal bond market in "peace time" it makes choosing the leg of the trilemma that involves harms to bondholders (relatively) more attractive during crises.

However, there is a case against the exemption that also turns on its effect on the investor profile for bonds and its relationship to fiscal crises.[27] By its very nature, the exemption reduces liquidity in the municipal bond market by ensuring that foreigners and tax-exempt entities have few reasons to buy municipal bonds. A reduced pool of investors means higher prices in all periods and it also exacerbates breakdowns in the market due to investor-side problems. In 2008 and 2020, flows out of mutual funds and breakdowns in auction-rate security markets led to crashes in the broader market; the limited number of buyers were forced to sell and there were not outside sources of demand.[28]

That is, while the exemption makes the municipal bond market more resilient in the face of one type of risk—contagion risk following a default—it makes it more subject to other types of risk in choppy financial markets. The exemption is probably worth keeping, although it may necessitate actions like those undertaken by the Federal Reserve in 2020 to calm municipal bond markets.

11.3. The Efficiency of Infrastructure Spending

It is important to remember *why* we care whether the municipal bond market is healthy. The bond market makes investment by states and cities possible, particularly in areas where the legal and political structure of the federal government makes investment unlikely. That is, the municipal bond market exists in large part to support infrastructure investment.

But how much infrastructure we get is not only a product of state capacity to borrow and spend. It is also a product of how efficiently we spend the money we have. Recent research has shown that in a number of areas, we are getting less infrastructure per dollar than we used to, and that we get far less per dollar than other countries get.

Economists Leah Brooks and Zach Liscow show that the real cost of building a mile of interstate highway has increased substantially since the 1960s. This is not a product of building more complicated highways or increased costs for labor or materials.[29] There is, however, some evidence that these costs are associated with "citizen voice." Litigation and political pressure from highly interested groups forces highways to be built along "squigglier" (i.e., less straight) routes and with greater protections for nearby property owners, increasing costs.

Transit expert Alon Levy and number of others, including economist Tracy Gordon and me, have shown that the cost of building underground subways in the United States is way, way higher than it is in other countries.[30] Subways built in New York are more than 8 times more expensive per kilometer than projects in Tokyo, and 36 times more expensive than projects in Madrid. Projects in the rest of the United States are cheaper than those in New York, but there is still a huge cost premium associated with a project being built in the United States.

The exact reasons why this is true are less than perfectly clear. Brooks and Liscow's theory—that it is related to litigation threats and the political influence of interest groups and homeowners—is powerful. But there are other stories one could tell. Levy points to a refusal among Americans to adopt international best practices, and to a lack of trained civil servants to supervise projects. One could focus on how the unelected boards in charge of many transportation projects are not politically accountable and thus waste money. Another possibility is that partial federal financing increases costs, as federal officials get credit for pork spending but are not held accountable for results.

We do not really know why infrastructure costs are high and rising. While there are reasons why the federal government is not able to be the major builder of infrastructure, there is no reason it cannot act as a resource for states and cities. The federal government should invest a good amount of money in studying best practices for bringing down infrastructure costs.

11.4. Nationalizing Parts of the Welfare State

Scholars have long critiqued our regular use of "cooperative federalism" programs for essential parts of the welfare state. Having states play an important role in funding, say, Medicaid leads to a great deal of horizontal inequity—poor people in Alabama get different levels of healthcare than poor people in California. And it leads to more federal money going to rich states than poor ones.[31] Although Medicaid matches the money spent by poorer states at a higher rate, the fact that richer states spend much more money means that the federal government provides more aid in absolute terms to rich states.

While the arguments around whether Medicaid and other cooperative federalism programs should be nationalized are well rehearsed, focusing on state and local budget crises adds to the case for nationalization.

Nationalizing cooperative federalism programs would make the country more resilient against state and local fiscal crises. As discussed in Chapter 1, in economic downturns, demand for social welfare programs goes up, but state tax revenue goes down. States cannot run deficits the way the federal government can. Declining revenue needs to be offset by tax increases or spending cuts. As a result, states are forced to either forgo matching funds or to make huge cuts in other areas—education, transportation, and so on—worsening recessions and public services more generally.

Further, state-specific versions of social welfare programs reduce labor mobility for people dependent on social services. Recipients of social welfare spending often cannot transfer benefits across state lines and sometimes get a worse deal in growing economies. The effect is to trap less well-off people in declining places. This is bad for them, clearly, but it is also bad for the jurisdictions they don't leave, as declining jurisdictions end up having to continue paying for the cost of supporting public services targeted at them.

When considering the cases for and against nationalizing social welfare programs, from housing to healthcare, the problems of state and local budgets should add to the case for nationalization.

PART IV

THE CONCLUSION, OR WHY STATES ARE OFTEN BAD

Why States Are Often Bad

This book has shown how federal government officials have addressed acute state and local fiscal crises in the past. And it has laid out arguments for how they should think about such crises in the future. Hopefully, for citizens and observers focused on national-level political figures (and for those national-level political figures themselves!), the analysis and recommendations are important and useful.

But the primary responsibility for addressing state and local fiscal problems lies with state and local governments themselves. While state and local governments are not to blame for things like the global financial crisis of 2008 or the COVID-19 pandemic and the resulting recession in 2020–21, many of them did not save enough during periods of relative prosperity before these crises. Savings would have given state and local governments the kind of cushion that would make riding out a crisis less painful. Instead, many of them came into these crises with lots of debt, often in the form of underfunded pension and other post-employment benefit liabilities.

Prudent budgeting requires political legitimacy. Whether it is done by raising taxes or cutting popular spending programs, fiscal restraint involves tough choices. State and local officials need to have a strong base of popular support to be able to forego benefits today for gains tomorrow, to avoid providing the sugar high of tax cuts now in order to properly fund pension funds or to spend money on unglamorous, future-oriented projects like infrastructure maintenance.

But today, state governments and many local governments are in an acute *political* crisis that makes them less able to cope with acute fiscal stress. The rickety nature of state finances in many places is downstream from their broken politics.

What do I mean when I say a political crisis? The central problem of state and local politics is that they lack functional popular politics. Most voters know little and care less about state politics, with state elections outside of gubernatorial races largely serving as referenda on the president of the United States.[1] The lack of broad public engagement with state politics leaves state and local politicians in hock to the narrow set of voters and lobbying groups who dominate low-information elections like legislative primaries or off-cycle local elections.[2]

These groups—whether they are powerful donors, ideological groups, firms seeking subsidies, homeowner groups, or public employee unions—want specific things from government. They are not doing anything wrong by asking government for things. Indeed such groups exist and are influential at all levels of government.

But state and local officials lack the ability to marshal mass support, as the voting public does not know who they are or what they are doing. As a result, they do not have the ability to push back the demands of narrow groups. The fact that state politicians are unknown to most of the public gives them little capacity to resist group pressure or ask the public to sacrifice for the greater good.

To unpack this a bit, political scientists and legal scholars, like Dan Hopkins, Steve Rogers, Chris Elmendorf, and I have shown that state and partisan local elections increasingly turn on voters' impressions of national politics.[3] Voters who like President Joe Biden or former House Speaker Nancy Pelosi vote for Democrats for state assembly and county commission; those who like former President Donald Trump or Senate Minority Leader Mitch McConnell vote for Republicans in these races. The correlation between national partisanship and state legislative voting is extremely strong. In the lingo of political scientists, these elections are "second-order," turning on events that happen entirely outside the purview of the officials running in them.[4]

The best explanation for why this is true is voter ignorance of state politics. More exactly, second-order state elections are a result of the way voter ignorance of state politics interacts with the media and the political party system.

Voters often know little about individual politicians at any level of government. But as local newspapers have closed and shrunk in recent years, this is even more dramatically true about state and local officials. As Hopkins shows in his brilliant book, *The Increasingly United States*, when local newspapers shut down, it has a causal effect on local voting—places where papers have closed have more straight-ticket partisan voting.[5]

Further, at the federal level, the cost of low-levels of political knowledge is limited. It doesn't matter much if a voter does not know much about his Congresswoman as long as she knows what party she's in. Knowing the political party affiliation of a candidate for Congress gives voters lots of useful information. Because the parties are increasingly polarized, learning that a candidate is a Republican or Democrat will tell you her position on almost every issue.[6] And because the parties have been relatively ideologically consistent over time, many voters are able to develop "running tallies" in their minds about which one they like better.[7]

As a result, voters can use party as a "heuristic," or short-cut, when voting in federal elections. Doing so allows voters to behave pretty rationally, punishing performances and policies they don't like and rewarding ones they do.

This doesn't work perfectly, as voters often put their "team" or party affiliation first and policies and outcomes second.[8] Or voters are myopic, only looking at factors like the unemployment rate right before the election, rather than the long-run performance of officials. But at the very least, the policies national-level parties propose and actual outcomes of those policies have some effect on federal elections. Because what party-allied public officials actually do—the laws they pass, the votes they take—can have some effect on voter beliefs, such officials have some incentives to make their parties popular, or at least popular enough, with the general public.

In state elections, voters also use national-party membership as a heuristic, but it has a very different effect. In state and partisan local elections, most of us have little else to go on other than party labels and our impressions of national party officials.[9] We don't know who state legislators or county commissioners are or what they do. So we just vote in state and local elections based on what national party candidates represent, which at least provides some information about what they will do.

But, because political party membership is defined at the national level, party heuristics are less informative in state elections.[10] While learning what party someone is in at the state level does contains some information about what they will do, the issue space of state and local politics is different from national politics. States have no control over questions of war and peace or foreign policy, no control over monetary policy (and hence little control over unemployment), and no real power over retirement policy. If part of the reason you are a Democrat or Republican is the way officials acted around the War in Iraq, the parties' responses to the 2008 financial crisis, Social Security, the Supreme Court, or Donald Trump's immigration stances, it is not obviously correct to apply your national party preference in state and local elections, where those issue areas are not on the table.

Also, party membership often does not tell us about the real divisions in a state. Almost everyone in the Massachusetts state legislature is a Democrat, so anything most Democrats agree on is already likely to be the law. Seeing that a candidate is Democrat won't tell a voter much about where she stands on an issue that is actually in dispute in state politics.

Although party membership is a weaker heuristic in state politics, almost all of us still rely on it, because it is better than nothing. In the absence of other information, national party endorsements remain powerful, even if they are an awkward fit with issues confronting states.

The feedback loop party voting creates for state officials is weaker as well. Party preference is almost entirely a result of national-level politics, whether one likes President Biden or former President Trump. It's not clear that what the state legislature actually does has any substantial effect on elections for state legislature in most years. So the need for state politicians to do things that appeal to a majority of voters is lower. And state officials can be less worried that the bad effects of policies they choose will have any effect on their re-election chances.

Races for governor and mayor sometimes stand outside this dynamic a bit, as executive officials can become famous enough for voters to be able to individually assess them. Because of this, you sometimes see "out party" governors, Republicans in Massachusetts or Maryland, Democrats in Montana or Kentucky. But most state and local elections are second-order.

Where general elections are determined by factors outside of the control of candidates, political competition is pushed into lower-visibility, low-turnout electoral contests. The key elections in New York City or Wyoming are party primaries, rather than general elections. But turnout in primaries is very low, and the ballot does not contain relevant information like which party faction a candidate is associated with. Nonpartisan local election ballots similarly give voters few cues about the beliefs of candidates.

Because participation and information is so low, these elections are dominated by highly motivated and highly informed groups of voters, like homeowner groups, and interest groups who can get voters to the polls. Politicians also compete for support from groups that will help them advance to higher office, such as cross-state issue advocacy groups like the American Legislative Exchange Council, or prized endorsements from national officials unlikely to care much about local policy.

That is, state and local politicians do not seek, and do not receive, a public mandate from ordinary voters. They are instead responsive to narrow and unrepresentative groups of voters and interests.[11] This directly affects the politics of state and local budgeting. Where elections are low-turnout and low-information, interest groups become more powerful. For instance, school districts that hold elections "off-cycle" (at times other than November of an even-numbered year) have lower turnout. As Sarah Anzia shows, these jursidctions pay their teachers more, as teachers unions, who can get voters to the polls, are more influential.[12] When local newspapers close, local governmental borrowing costs go up, as there is less monitoring and more power for intense policy demanders.[13]

In theory, politicians could resist these groups by appealing to broader citizen interest in economic growth and high-quality services. But if voters do not know who state-level politicians are, and do not credit them with success, those politicians have no ability to resist the narrower-demands of groups wanting something from government today.

That's the political crisis of states and cities. State democracy just does not work very well, given the media and political party system we have today.

As this book details, it is hard for the federal government to respond well to state-level fiscal crises. The federal government faces a "trilemma," and is unable to entirely avoid all three of the problems of moral hazard, pro-cyclical spending cuts that worsen recessions, and defaults that harm future state investment.

There are steps the federal government can take to make state fiscal crises less painful, as Chapters 8–11 discuss. But it would better still if there were fewer state fiscal crises. To avoid future crises, however, we would need to fix state and local politics.

There are lots of ideas out there about how to improve state politics, too many to review. Almost all of them, though, start with voters paying more attention to state and local politics. While institutions like newspapers and political parties do not provide adequate tools for most people to monitor state and local governments, citizens can overcome this, both by paying more attention themselves and demanding more focus from the media on what is going on in state capitols and city halls around the country. More and better state democracy would help state and local fiscal policy, and is something we can insist on.

Ultimately, that is the best way out of a bad state.

NOTES

Introduction

1. Ella Koze, "How the Economy Is Actually Doing, in 9 Charts," *New York Times*, Dec. 17, 2020; Nelson D. Schwartz, "Coronavirus Recession Looms, Its Course 'Unrecognizable,'" *New York Times*, Mar. 21, 2020.

2. Emily Badger and Quoctrung Bui, "The Recession Is About to Slam Cities. Not Just the Blue-State Ones," *New York Times*, Aug. 17, 2020; Heather Gillers and Gunjan Banjeree, "U.S. States Face Biggest Cash Crisis since the Great Depression," *Wall Street Journal*, Oct. 28, 2020; Elizabeth McNichol, "States Expect More Damaging Cuts without More Federal Aid," Center for Budget and Policy Priorities, Sept. 9, 2020, https://www.cbpp.org/blog/states-expect-more-damaging-cuts-without-more-federal-aid.

3. Tracy Gordon, "State and Local Budgets and the Great Recession," Brookings Institution, Dec. 31, 2012, https://www.brookings.edu/articles/state-and-local-budgets-and-the-great-recession/; Robert A. Moffitt, "The Great Recession and the Social Safety Net," *Annals of the American Academic of Politics and Social Science* 650 (2013): 143; The White House, "The Effect of State Fiscal Relief," n.d., last accessed September 24, 2021, https://obamawhitehouse.archives.gov/administration/eop/cea/EffectsofStatefiscalrelief/.

4. Gordon, "State and Local Budgets and the Great Recession"; Sara Hinkley, "Public Sector Impacts of the Great Recession and COVID-19," U.C. Berkeley Labor Center, June 2020, 4, https://laborcenter.berkeley.edu/wp-content/uploads/2020/06/Public-Sector-Impacts-of-the-Great-Recession-and-COVID-19.pdf.

5. Barb Rosewicz, Justin Theal, and Joe Fleming, "States' Financial Reserves Hit Record Highs," Pew Trust, Mar. 18, 2020, https://www.pewtrusts.org/en/research-and-analysis/articles/2020/03/18/states-financial-reserves-hit-record-highs; Brian Tumulty, "State Rainy Day Funds Reach Record High," *Bond Buyer*, Dec. 17, 2019.

6. Alicia H. Munnell and Jean-Pierre Aubry, "An Overview of the Pension/OPEB Landscape," Center for Retirement Research, Working Paper 2016-11 (2016), 8–11, https://papers.ssrn.com/sol3/papers.cfm?abstract_id=2847725; Michael Katz, "State Pensions Entered Pandemic in Worse Position Than in 2008," *Chief Investment Officer Magazine*, Aug. 20, 2020.

7. Gillers and Banjeree, "U.S. States Face Biggest Cash Crisis since the Great Depression."

8. Munnell and Aubry, "An Overview."

9. Justin Baer, "The Day Coronavirus Nearly Broke the Financial Markets," *Wall Street Journal*, May 20, 2020.

10. Michael Leachman, "States, Localities Need Federal Aid to Restore Jobs, Avoid More Layoffs," Center for Budget and Policy Priorities, Oct. 8, 2020 (more than a million layoffs or furloughs, more than after 2008); Barb Rosewicz and Mike Maciag, "How COVID-19 Is Driving Big Job Losses in State and Local Government," Pew Trust, June 16, 2020, https://

www.pewtrusts.org/en/research-and-analysis/articles/2020/06/16/how-covid-19-is-driv
ing-big-job-losses-in-state-and-local-government (1.5M layoffs and furloughs).

11. Jeff Chapman, "State and Local Governments Relied on Debt for Budgetary Help in 2020,"
    Pew Trust, Jan. 28, 2021, https://www.pewtrusts.org/en/research-and-analysis/articles/
    2021/01/28/state-and-local-governments-relied-on-debt-for-budgetary-help-in-2020
    (governments relied heavily on debts); Louise Sheiner, *Why Is State and Local Employment
    Falling Faster Than Revenues?*, Brookings Institution, Feb. 16, 2021 ("States that depend
    heavily on tourism or oil revenue have been hit much harder, transit agencies have seen their
    revenues collapse"), https://www.brookings.edu/blog/up-front/2020/12/23/why-is-state-
    and-local-employment-falling-faster-than-revenues/.

12. Greg Minis and Ben Henken, "New York Transit Authority Taps into Federal Reserve
    Borrowing Program," Pew Trust, Oct. 9, 2020, https://www.pewtrusts.org/ru/research-and-
    analysis/articles/2020/10/09/new-york-transit-authority-taps-into-federal-reserve-borrow
    ing-program; Alexandra Scaggs, "The MTA Could Be the Last to Tap the Fed's Muni Facility.
    Wall Street Watchers Fret Its End," *Barrons*, Nov. 24, 2020.

13. Rick Pearson, "Illinois Senate President Don Harmon Asks Feds for $41 Billion Coronavirus
    Bailout," *Chicago Tribune*, Apr. 18, 2020.

14. Alan Auerbach, Bill Gale, Byron Lutz, and Louise Sheiner, "Fiscal Effects of COVID-19,"
    Brookings Papers on Economic Activities Conference Drafts, Sept. 2020, https://www.
    brookings.edu/wp-content/uploads/2020/09/Auerbach-et-al-conference-draft.pdf) ("We
    estimate far smaller income tax losses than would have been expected on the basis of histor-
    ical experience, which we attribute to the fact that employment losses have been unusually
    concentrated on low-wage workers. . . ").

15. Ben Casselman, "How the U.S. Got It (Mostly) Right in the Economy's Rescue," *New York
    Times*, Mar. 21, 2021.

16. "Federal Reserve Takes Additional Actions to Provide up to $2.3 Trillion in Loans to Support
    the Economy," Board of Governors of the Federal Reserve, Apr. 9, 2020, https://www.fed
    eralreserve.gov/newsevents/pressreleases/monetary20200409a.htm#:~:text=The%20Treas
    ury%20will%20provide%20%2435,appropriated%20by%20the%20CARES%20Act.

17. Andrew Prokop, "The Debate Over State and Local Aid in Biden's Stimulus Bill, Explained
    Could Some of That $350 Billion Be Better Spent Elsewhere?," *Vox*, March 1, 2021; "State
    and Local Governments Do Not Need Half a Trillion in COVID Relief," Committee for a
    Responsible Federal Budget, Feb. 17, 2021, https://www.crfb.org/blogs/state-and-local-
    governments-do-not-need-half-trillion-covid-relief.

18. Samar Khurshid, "After Overstating Budget Deficits, Cuomo and De Blasio Get Big Federal
    Bailout," *Gotham Gazette*, Mar. 9, 2021 (discussing New York State's structural budget weak-
    ness that experts think will resurface after aid wears off).

19. Sabri Ben-Achour, "Aid for State, Local Governments a Sticking Point in Federal COVID-
    19 Relief," *Marketplace*, Oct. 6, 2020; Emily Cochrane and Nicholas Fandos, "McConnell
    Moves to Head Off Stimulus Deal as Pelosi Reports Progress," *New York Times*, Oct. 20,
    2020; Carl Hulse, "McConnell Says States Should Consider Bankruptcy, Rebuffing Calls for
    Aid," *New York Times*, Apr. 22, 2020; John Wagner, "McConnell Takes Flak after Suggesting
    Bankruptcy for States Rather Than Bailouts," *Washington Post*, Apr. 23, 2020.

20. Alexandra Hutzler, "Mitch McConnell Wants to Stop Blue State Bailouts, But Red States
    Need Help Too," *Newsweek*, May 4, 2020; Mary Williams Walsh, "Virus Did Not Bring
    Financial Rout That Many States Feared," *New York Times*, Mar. 1, 2021.

21. Emily Cochrane, "G.O.P. Split over State Aid That Could Mostly Go to Democratic
    Strongholds," *New York Times*, May 11, 2020; Jordan Weissman, "Republicans Are Absolutely
    Deluded if They Think Only Blue States Need a Bailout," *Slate*, Apr. 29, 2020.

22. Jordan Weissman, "Biden Wants to Give States $350 Billion. Do They Still Need It?," *Slate*,
    Feb. 12, 2021.

23. David Schleicher, "Reasonable Conditions for State and Local Aid," Niskanen Center, May
    11, 2020, https://www.niskanencenter.org/reasonable-conditions-for-state-and-local-aid/.

24. This event is discussed in Chapter 3.

25. Seymour P. Lachman and Robert Polner, *The Man Who Saved New York: Hugh Carey and the
    Great Fiscal Crisis of 1975* (Albany: SUNY Press, 2010).

26. The idea of a policy trilemma is taken from the famous Mundell-Fleming "impossibility trinity" that countries cannot have all three of a fixed foreign exchange rate, free capital movement, and an independent monetary policy, but instead have to pick two of these three ends. "Two Out of Three Ain't Bad," *Economist*, Aug. 27, 2016 (quoting economist Michael Stein as saying "Governments face the policy trilemma; the rest is commentary"); Marcus J. Fleming, "Domestic Financial Policies under Fixed and Floating Exchange Rates," *IMF Staff Papers* 9, no. 3 (Nov. 1962): 369; Robert Mundell, "Capital Mobility and Stabilization Policy under Fixed and Flexible Exchange Rates," *Canadian Journal of Economics and Political Science* 29, no. 4 (Nov. 1963): 475, https://doi.org/10.2307/139336.

27. Jonathan A. Rodden, *Hamilton's Paradox: The Promise and Peril of Fiscal Federalism* (Cambridge: Cambridge University Press, 2005).

28. Defaults still do substantial short-term economic harm, as pensioners and creditors lose money, but the macroeconomic harm is less than what we see from state austerity, as discussed in Chapter 1.

29. Li Zhou, "States Have the Power to Make or Break the Infrastructure Law," *Vox*, Nov. 15, 2021; "Infrastructure Investment and Jobs Act: Summary of Key Programs and Provisions," Akin, Gump, Strauss, Hauer, and Feld LLP, 2021 ("many grant programs have a nonfederal match requirement"), https://www.akingump.com/a/web/nufGmVifPeR8e58xtrpZDC/38cxSY/infrastructure-investment-and-jobs-act-summary-of-key-programs-and-provisions2.pdf.

30. For instance, if federal actors are confident the Federal Reserve will do a good job of macroeconomic stabilization, the case for bailouts falls. Similarly, if there is a glut of investable capital in national and global markets, policymakers may be less concerned about harms to municipal bond market.

31. That is not to say the book will ignore politics. Far from it. Each branch of the trilemma is based on assumptions about politics that are more and less true in different periods. Moral hazard is in part a prediction about how one set of politicians (state and local officials) will respond to decisions made by another set of politicians (federal officials). State and local austerity will only worsen recessions if Congress and the Federal Reserve are politically unable to spend enough in other ways to respond to recessions immediately. And the inability of the federal government to build infrastructure or make investments is not a fact of nature, but a downstream political implication of how Congress is structured. This book's policy analysis is built around theories of politics. Some of these factors change over time and the book will discuss how they have changed and why it matters.

But while it does not ignore politics, the history of state fiscal crises in Chapters 2 through 6 does not seek to uncover the political determinants of why particular federal officials did what they did, who they thought they were helping and hurting. And the policy advice provided in Chapters 7 through 11 does not take a strong view about how federal officials should weigh the downsides of different choices along the trilemma.

32. The fact that state and local fiscal crises are *crises* helps explains the scope of the trilemma. The federal government is involved in state and local affairs and finances in all sorts of ways. One could imagine policy responses to a crisis that involve radical shifts in those policies. The federal government in theory could respond to a fiscal crisis in Chicago with a huge shift of money away from rural areas and toward urban ones, say by shifting transportation spending formulas away from roads and toward mass transit. A response to a fiscal crisis in New York could be removing regulations on finance, which would help the city's economy and thus its budget. The effect of having a districted Congress on the capacity to provide infrastructure could be reduced by Congress allowing, and states adopting, statewide multimember congressional districting, so representatives no longer represent specific geographic parts of states.

But, in a crisis, there is little time to completely rejigger our institutional structure or change settled political determinations about the general flow of money or regulatory structures. Doing so takes a long political debate and complex negotiations, if it's even possible. A politician who responded to Illinois being on the edge of default by proposing to launch a national movement to change all of Congress to multimember congressional districts (or to abolish the US Senate) would rightfully be laughed out of the room for not responding to the problem before her.

33. *War Games*, directed by John Badham (1983; United Artists) ("A strange game. The only winning move is not to play").

Chapter 1

1. Marie-Laure Breuillé and Marianne Vigneaultb, "Overlapping Soft Budget Constraints," *Journal of Urban Economics* 67, no. 6 (2010): 269; Yingyi Qian and Gérard Roland, *Federalism and the Soft Budget Constraint, American Economic Review* 88, no. 5 (1998): 1144. This work draws on Janos Kornai's famous claims about how firms behave in socialist economies. Janos Kornai, "Resource-Constrained versus Demand-Constrained Systems," *Econometrica* 47, no. 4 (July 1979): 801; Janos Kornai, "The Soft Budget Constraint," *Kyklos* 39, no. 1 (Feb. 1986), 3.

2. Jonathan A. Rodden, *Hamilton's Paradox: The Promise and Peril of Fiscal Federalism* (New York: Cambridge University Press, 2005); Jonathan A. Rodden, "Soft Budget Constraints and German Federalism," in *Fiscal Decentralization and the Challenge of Hard Budget Constraints*, eds. Jonathan A. Rodden, Gunner S. Eskeland, and Jennie Litvack (Cambridge, MA: MIT Press), 161; Jonathan A. Rodden, "Federalism and Bailouts in Brazil," in *Fiscal Decentralization*, Rodden et al., eds., 213; Jonathan A. Rodden, "Market Discipline and U.S. Federalism," in *When States Go Broke: The Origins, Context, and Solutions for the American States in Fiscal Crisis*, eds. Peter Conti-Brown and David Skeel (New York: Cambridge University Press, 2012), 123.

3. Rodden, *Hamilton's Paradox*, 2–3.

4. Ibid., 1–8, 16–19, 270; Jonathan A. Rodden, "Reviving Leviathan: Fiscal Federalism and the Growth of Government," *International Organization* 77, no. 4 (Oct. 2003): 695 (arguing that decentralization only leads to smaller government if state and local governments are fiscally independent of central government).

5. Notably, I have argued elsewhere that there are other reasons to be skeptical of these claims. The benefits of density ("agglomeration economies") limit the extent to which people move to get preferred government services. David Schleicher, "The City as a Law and Economic Subject," *University of Illinois Law Review* 2010 (2010): 1507. Very rich people continue to live in New York City, and the reason is almost certainly not that they like the high tax rates or the city's failure to pick up garbage in the street. Further, there is a cost when people do move to get services, as our political system is effectively forcing people to move away from their preferred location and neighbors in order to get the package of services and taxes they want. Promoting state and local fiscal independence may promote matching of people with their preferred package of taxes and services, but does so at the cost of preserving a truly free internal market for location.

   Also, state and local elections are often not necessarily responsive to local opinion, as voters generally simply vote in these elections for the same political party as they prefer for President. The reason they do so is that most voters know almost nothing about state and local politics, and simply use the information they have about party affiliation to make voting decisions in state elections. As a result, there is little reason to believe that many state and local elections do much to hold politicians accountable (other than elections for big-city mayor or governor, where candidates are sometimes famous enough to have their own brands distinct from party brands). Declining local newspapers and the lack of parties defined around local issues makes local democracy much less effective. David Schleicher, "Federalism and State Democracy," *Texas Law Review* 95: 780, 790 (2017). Chapter 12 returns to these themes.

6. Rodden, *Hamilton's Paradox*, 6–8, 48–82.

7. Kornai, "Soft Budget," 3.

8. Rodden, *Hamilton's Paradox*, 272–73.

9. There is a clear correlation between the extent to which the national government does most of the taxing and state and local borrowing limits. Ibid. at 75–119. If a national government is providing most of the revenue, it usually will not allow the provinces to borrow too much.

10. Ibid., 272; Jonathan A. Rodden, "The Dilemma of Fiscal Federalism: Grants and Fiscal Performance around the World," *American Journal of Political Science* 46, no. 3 (July 2002): 670.

11. Rodden, *Hamilton's Paradox*, 272.

12. Ibid., 56–73; Rodden, *Market Discipline*, 139–41 (describing how credit default swaps for US states diverged after 2008, tracking their own budget performance and not pricing in a federal bailout, although pre-2008 the market had treated most states as having a similar very low likelihood of default).

13. Robert P. Inman, "Transfers and Bailouts: Institutions for Enforcing Local Fiscal Discipline with Lessons from U.S. Federalism," in *Fiscal Decentralization*, Rodden et al., eds., 58.

14. One part of Inman's analysis deserves a little more attention. He argues that it is important for the federal government to establish a strong bankruptcy regime that forces state and local governments to pay creditors as much as they can. But why? From the perspective of discouraging federal bailouts, this is a little confusing. If creditors take greater haircuts, there should be less pressure on the federal government to aid states. Instead, greater haircuts make the creditors who enabled state profligacy bear some of the costs.

    Inman argues that, absent a punishing bankruptcy regime, there will be a risk of "contagion," or defaults in one jurisdiction stopping lenders from offering loans to other jurisdictions. The threat of contagion creates pressure for the national government to bailout state governments. Perhaps. But this risk needs to be traded off against the fact that haircuts would reduce the need for bailouts in any given crisis situation. As I argue below, I think Inman is on to something very important here, but that it has more to do as encouraging the construction of infrastructure than limiting contagion, a concern addressed through tools like the municipal bond interest deduction, which I discuss in Chapter 11.

15. Inman, "Transfers and Bailouts," 70.

16. See Emily D. Johnson and Ernest A. Young, "The Constitutional Law of State Debt," *Duke Journal of Constitutional Law and Public Policy* 7, no. 1 (2012): 147 ("To be perfectly honest, we find all this continued confidence in the U.S. government's no-bailout guarantee a bit puzzling."); Michael S. Greve, "Our Federalism Is Not Europe's. It's Becoming Argentina's," *Duke Journal of Constitutional Law and Public Policy* 7, no. 1 (2012): 27–33, 37–40; Paul E. Peterson and Daniel Nadler, "Freedom to Fail: The Keystone of American Federalism," *University of Chicago Law Review* 79, no. 1 (2012): 253; Rodden, "Market Discipline," 141–43.

17. Anna Gelpern, "Bankruptcy, Backwards: The Problem of Quasi-Sovereign Debt," *Yale Law Journal* 121, no. 4 (2012): 888; Clayton P. Gillette, "What States Can Learn from Municipal Insolvency," in *When States Go Broke: The Origins, Context, and Solutions for the American States in Fiscal Crisis*, eds. Peter Conti-Brown and David Skeel (New York: Cambridge University Press, 2012).

18. Loans through the Federal Reserve's Municipal Liquidity Facility were clearly jurisdiction-specific, though.

19. Emily Maher, "State Uses of the CARES Act Coronavirus Relief Funds," *State Legislatures Magazine*, Aug. 5, 2020, https://www.ncsl.org/research/fiscal-policy/state-uses-of-the-cares-act-coronavirus-relief-funds-magazine2020.aspx.

20. Daniel Hemel, "Treasury's Noble Effort to Save the Net Tax Revenue Provision, Substance over Form," *Medium*, May 10, 2021, https://substanceoverform.substack.com/p/treasurys-noble-effort-to-save-the.

21. Cooper Howard, "Game Changer: How the American Rescue Plan Improved the Outlook for Munis," Charles Schwab, May 19, 2021, https://www.schwab.com/resource-center/insights/content/game-changer-how-american-rescue-plan-improved-outlook-munis ("Narrowing in on the different credit ratings within the muni market, we think lower-rated issuers are more attractive than higher-rated issuers. Spreads, which are the additional yield above a AAA-rated muni, have been declining for all credit ratings and are tight, as illustrated in the chart below.").

22. Amanda Vinicky, "Voters to Get Preelection Tax Relief," *WTTW*, Apr. 7, 2022, https://news.wttw.com/2022/04/07/voters-get-preelection-tax-relief (Republican legislative leader describing state budget as a "sugar high."); Bryan P. Sears, "Maryland Counties Cautioned about 'Sugar High' of Federal Virus Aid," *Daily Record*, Aug. 19, 2021; E. J. McMahon, "Andrew Cuomo's Crisis May Open the Door to State Fiscal Madness," *N.Y. Post*, Mar. 8, 2021 (quoting Governor Andrew Cuomo calling federal aid a "sugar high");

23. For instance, in fall of 2020, investing in bonds of the fiscally troubled Metropolitan Transit Authority became popular. The *New York Times* summarized the strategy: "You can make a

lot of money betting on government bailouts." Matt Phillips, "New York Subway's Pain Could Bring Riches for Bond Investors," *New York Times*, Oct. 30, 2020.

24. Robert S. Chirinko, Ryan Chiu, and Shaina Henderson, "What Went Wrong? The Puerto Rican Debt Crisis, the Treasury Put, and the Failure of Market Discipline," Cesifo Working Paper No. 7558 (2019), https://papers.ssrn.com/sol3/papers.cfm?abstract_id=3357135.

25. Richard Briffault, "Disfavored Constitution: State Fiscal Limits and State Constitutional Law," *Rutgers Law Journal* 34, no. 4 (2002–2003): 907.

26. State taxing capacity is more limited for a variety of reasons. Most notably, states and cities have to worry that people and businesses will leave the jurisdiction if taxes get too high.

27. Gary Burtless, "Private Sector Payrolls Finally Top Pre-Recession Peak," Brookings Institution, Apr. 4, 2014, https://www.brookings.edu/blog/jobs/2014/04/04/private-sec tor-payrolls-finally-top-pre-recession-peak/; Edwin Pome and Nicholas Saxon, "Private Industry Hit Harder but Bounced Back Faster," United States Census Bureau, Oct. 17, 2019, https://www.census.gov/library/stories/2019/10/effects-of-economic-downturn-private-and-public-employment.html.

28. David A. Super, "Rethinking Fiscal Federalism," *Harvard Law Review* 118, no. 8 (2005): 2544–52, 2586–93.

29. Damon Silvers, "Obligations without the Power to Fund Them," in *When States Go Broke*, Conti-Brown and Skeel, eds., 48–51; Super, "Rethinking Fiscal Federalism," 2586–98.

30. Silvers, "Obligations without the Power to Fund Them," 50–54.

31. Ibid., 55–57; Super, "Rethinking Fiscal Federalism," 2649–51.

32. Moral hazard and Keynesian state aid theorists often have very different accounts of *why* states and cities get into fiscal trouble. Moral hazard theorists put the blame on federal aid and the profligacy of state and local officials, while Keynesian types tend to focus on stories about economic shifts and the broad effect of recessions. In most cases, both are right to some degree. Take Detroit. Its political leaders spent money in many questionable ways (think of the infamous "People Mover," which economist Edward Glaeser has called "perhaps the most absurd public transit project in the country."). Edward Glaeser, *Triumph of the City: How Our Greatest Invention Makes Us Richer, Smarter, Greener, Healthier, and Happier* (New York: Penguin Publishing, 2012), 62. But it is also the case that the rise of automobile construction in Japan, Europe, and the south of the United States, and the general increase in suburbanization, led Detroit to lose firm and people, leaving the city with too big a footprint and debt and pension costs generated by a much bigger city. Further, stories that focus on political failures and stories that focus on exogenous forces are not entirely distinct. As exogenous shocks to the economy get worse, local politicians face greater pressure to take risks and/or to provide resources to now-declining areas or interest groups.

33. Yair Listokin, *Law and Macroeconomics: Legal Remedies to Recessions* (Cambridge, MA: Harvard University Press, 2019).

34. Inman discusses the history of pro-creditor policies quite brilliantly, but focuses mostly on their potential effect on bailouts. Inman, "Transfers and Bailouts," 60.

35. Department of Treasury, "Tax Expenditures," Budget of the United States Government, Fiscal Year 2022, 161, June 3, 2021, https://home.treasury.gov/system/files/131/Tax-Expenditu res-FY2022.pdf; "What Are Municipal Bonds and How Are They Used?," Tax Policy Center Briefing Book, 2019, https://www.taxpolicycenter.org/briefing-book/what-are-munici pal-bonds-and-how-are-they-used.

36. "Federal Support for Financing State and Local Transportation and Water Infrastructure," Congressional Budget Office, Oct. 2018, 4, 11–13, https://www.cbo.gov/system/files/2018-10/54549-InfrastructureFinancing.pdf (describing the range of direct federal credit programs for infrastructure, and noting they total less than 1/10 the size of investment 2007 to 2017, through the municipal bond interest income tax exemption).

37. Charles D. Jacobson and Joel A. Tarr, "Ownership and Financing of Infrastructure: Historical Perspectives," World Bank Working Paper 1466, https://elibrary.worldbank.org/doi/abs/ 10.1596/1813-9450-1466 ("Although the size and relative importance of the federal government has greatly increased since the 1930s, a large proportion of policymaking concerning infrastructures continues to take place at local and state levels."); "Public Spending on Transportation and Water Infrastructure, 1956 to 2017," Congressional Budget Office, Oct.

2018, 5, 8 https://www.cbo.gov/system/files/2018-10/54539-Infrastructure.pdf (today, states provide 59% of capital spending and 90% of operation and maintenance spending for transportation and water infrastructure, and states have outspent federal government by a substantial amount every year since 1957).

38. Li Zhou, "States Have the Power to Make or Break the Infrastructure Law," *Vox*, Nov. 15, 2021; "Infrastructure Investment and Jobs Act: Summary of Key Programs and Provisions."

39. Determining exactly what can be described as "infrastructure" became a heavily debated topic in 2021, as a result of a debate over whether things like childcare should be included in President Biden's American Jobs Plan. Bryce Covert, "The Debate over What 'Infrastructure' Is Is Ridiculous," *New York Times*, Apr. 26, 2021; William Saletan, "Americans Are Fine with a Broad Definition of 'Infrastructure,'" *Slate*, May 26, 2021. For the purposes of this book, infrastructure can be understood as investments in the future that ought to be debt-financed to spread the costs across the universe of users over time. Investments in human capital—like schools—are on the edge of this definition, as they are investments in the future but for which there is little need to spread the costs out by financing them with debt, because there are new costs each and every year. But state and local governments provide most financing for schools as well. From the perspective of Congress, schools and universities are also more like the post offices or lighthouses that are regularly supported by federal spending than like other types of infrastructure, in that they are needed in most jurisdictions, making concerns about the inefficiency of log-rolling less important.

40. John Ferejohn, Morris Fiorina, and Richard D. McKelvey, "Sophisticated Voting and Agenda Independence in the Distributive Politics Setting," *American Journal of Political Science* 31 (1987): 169; Barry R. Weingast, "Reflections on Distributive Politics and Universalism," *Political Research Quarterly* (June 1994): 319. John Ferejohn, *Pork Barrel Politics: Rivers and Harbors Legislation 1947–68* (Stanford, CA: Stanford University Press, 1974).

41. John J. Wallis and Barry Weingast, "Dysfunctional or Optimal Institutions? State Debt Limitations, the Structure of State and Local Governments, and the Finance of American Infrastructure," in *Fiscal Challenges: An Interdisciplinary Approach to Budget Policy*, eds. Elizabeth Garrett, Elizabeth A. Graddy, and Howell E. Jackson (Cambridge: Cambridge University Press, 2008) (noting that federal spending is usually either determined by formula so that every state gets some or doled out into tiny projects into lots of legislative districts); John J. Wallis and Barry Weingast, "Equilibrium Impotence: Why the States and Not the American National Government Financed Economic Development in the Antebellum Era," *Journal of Public Finance and Public Choice* 33 (2018): 19.

42. Gary W. Cox and Mathew D. McCubbins, *Legislative Leviathan: Party Government in the House*, 2d ed. (New York: Cambridge University Press, 2007); Gary W. Cox and Mathew D. McCubbins, *Setting the Agenda: Responsible Party Government in the U.S. House of Representatives* (2005); D. Roderick Kiewiet and Mathew D. McCubbins, *The Logic of Delegation: Congressional Parties and the Appropriations Process* (1991).

43. David Harrison, "Infrastructure Bill Gives Biden Administration Greater Say over Projects," *Wall Street Journal*, Nov. 7, 2021.

44. Also, the interstate highway system is spread out around the country!

45. Larry Summers, "From Bridges to Education: Best Bets for Public Investment," Brookings Institution, Jan. 2017, https://www.brookings.edu/wp-content/uploads/2017/01/200170109_public_investment_transcript.pdf (describing the economic case for more federal spending on infrastructure "overwhelming"). Notably, federal government subsidies for infrastructure also help overcome state parochialism or short-sightedness. Infrastructure can create cross-jurisdictional and temporal spillovers. Roads, bridges, and ports facilitate trade and travel between states. Further, states and cities may not consider the benefits for future residents, as future migrants are not voters in those states and cities today.

46. Super, "Rethinking Fiscal Federalism" (discussing advantages of federal over state and local taxes).

47. See Lynn Baker, Clayton Gillette, and David Schleicher, *Local Government Law: Cases and Materials*, 5th ed. (New York: Foundation Press, 2015), 620–21.

48. For a discussion of credit limitations on local governments and how the municipal bond interest tax exemption helps them overcome them, see Daniel Garrett, Andrey Ordin, James

W. Roberts, and Juan Carlos Suárez Serrato, "Tax Advantages and Imperfect Competition in Auctions for Municipal Bonds," National Bureau of Economic Research Working Paper No. 23473 (2017), https://www.nber.org/papers/w23473.

49. Other federal policies also seek to reduce contagion. As I will argue in Chapter 11, the most important is the income tax exemption for interest income on municipal debt (and state equivalents).

50. In theory, it is less than *perfectly* clear that protecting creditors will lead to more debt being issued in the future. States and cities may be more willing to borrow if they know that in the future they will be able to default. But this effect is likely dominated by the effect on lenders. A default is a loss for the lender himself. Politicians who make spending and borrowing decisions do not fully internalize the effect of long-in-the-future defaults. It is not their money, after all. Also, politicians' time horizons are likely shorter than investors. An investor who buys a 30-year bond will still hold the bond 10 years from now (or will have sold it, with the price reflecting the buyer's predictions about the future). In contrast, in 20 years, most politicians will be out of office. Where state or local government bonds are voted on by the public, in a referendum, the case gets a bit closer, as property owners provide both most of the electorate and most of the tax base (and local debt may get capitalized into their property values as future taxes.). But overall, defaults are very likely to reduce future lending and thus borrowing, both by the jurisdiction that is forced to default and by other jurisdictions.

51. Thanks to Zach Liscow for recommending including this table.

52. Creditor losses also reduce economic activity during a recession. But the macroeconomic effect of lost money for creditors is outweighed by gains for the government from not having to make cuts. Governments spend what they have, particularly in recessions, directly employing people and increasing output. Creditors—whether they are bondholders or pensioners—save some of the money, meaning that the "multiplier" of money paid to them, rather than kept by the government, is lower. Further, one major class of state and local debt, municipal bonds, is mostly in the hands of richer people who have a higher propensity to save. As a result, it makes sense to think of defaults as sparing short-term macroeconomic harm.

53. There is a countervailing force that is worth considering. Cities and states plan for a level of population growth, but are sometimes wrong about it. The absence of a way to default on debt may lead to them being too conservative about population projections, and thus being interested in building too little infrastructure. Having a mechanism for defaulting on debt may lead to more investment, or at least more desire to invest, on the part of local and state governments. It is certainly the case that bankruptcy provides real benefits to places that have seen big population declines and are left with public debt (and infrastructure) fit for a bigger city. David Schleicher, "Stuck! The Law and Economics of Residential Stagnation," *Yale Law Journal* 126, no. 1 (2017): 127, 145–49. The effect this has on willingness to borrow—and whether it simply balances against the optimism of politicians—is a bit speculative, however. In contrast, the increased borrowing costs created by defaults (or even the sheer lack of willingness of markets to lend) has a direct effect on borrowing.

54. Hunter v. City of Pittsburgh, 207 U.S. 161, 179 (1907); Nikolas Bowie, "The Constitutional Right to Self-Government," *Yale Law Journal* 130, no. 7 (2021).

55. For a discussion of sovereign immunity, see Chapter 4.

56. Amy B. Monohan, "When a Promise Is Not a Promise: Chicago-Style Pensions," *University of California Los Angeles Law Review* 65 (2017): 356, 392–98 (discussing challenges facing creditors in recovering against municipalities); Fred Smith, "Local Sovereign Immunity," *Columbia Law Review* 116 (2016): 409 (discussing legal rules that make it hard to recover against local governments).

57. Compare "A Recovery for All of Us: Fiscal Year 2022," New York City Mayor's Office of Management and Budget (proposing a $98.6B budget), Apr. 26, 2021, with Gray Rohrer, "DeSantis Signs $101 Billion Budget Laden with Federal COVID-19 Money," *Orlando Sentinel*, Jun. 2, 2021 (Florida budget for 21–22 is $101.5B).

58. "Los Angeles County Population vs. State Populations," *L.A. Almanac*, n.d., last visited Sept. 24, 2021 http://www.laalmanac.com/population/po04a.php.

59. The important policymaking role played by federal courts in fiscal federalism is not only a blind spot in the literature on fiscal federalism; it is a blind spot in studies of federal courts.

Legal scholar Alison LaCroix argues that one of the central innovations of American federalism was the decision to leave a great deal of the line-drawing over the powers of the federal and state governments to federal courts, making the jurisdiction of the courts a crucial battleground in determining how federalism operates. Alison C. LaCroix, *The Ideological Origins of American Federalism* (Cambridge, MA: Harvard University Press, 2010). So too with fiscal federalism. A law school course in Federal Courts could be taught partially as a course in how the Supreme Court resolved fights over fiscal federalism, with important doctrines like Article III limits on federal question jurisdiction, the extent of federal court common-law power in diversity cases before the Supreme Court abandoned it, and sovereign immunity coming out of fights over state fiscal policy. Osborn v. Bank of the United States, 22 U.S. (9 Wheat.) 738, 824 (1824) (establishing the "original ingredient" test for Article III federal question jurisdiction in the context of allowing the Bank of the United States to challenge an effort by a state to tax the bank); Gelpcke v. Dubuque, 67 U.S. 599, 603 (1862) (applying the court's federal common-law powers in an unusually aggressive way to force an Iowa city to make payments on municipal bonds issued to support a railroad); Hans v. Louisiana, 134 U.S. 1 (1890) (establishing that sovereign immunity protected states from suits in federal court by citizens of their own state in the context of Louisiana's post-Reconstruction repudiation of its debts).

Chapter 2

1. The focus fiscal federalism scholars put on the Johnson Report can be a little funny. The leading scholar in the field, Jonathan Rodden, wrote, "However, in a pivotal moment in the history of U.S. federalism, the bailout proposal failed in the legislature." Jonathan A. Rodden, "Market Discipline," in *When States Go Broke: Origins, Context, and Solutions for the American States in Fiscal Crisis*, eds. Peter Conti-Brown and David Skeel (New York: Cambridge University Press, 2012), 123. Most people would say that events like the beginning and end of the Civil War, the end of Reconstruction, and the passage of the Civil Rights and Voting Rights Acts were pivotal moments in the history of American federalism. But for those deep in the fiscal federalism literature, the rejection of the Johnson Report is on a par with those other events.
2. Ron Chernow, *Alexander Hamilton* (New York: Penguin, 2004), 297 (discussing the situation leading to Hamilton publishing the Report on Public Credit).
3. David Currie, "The Constitution in Congress: Substantive Issues in the First Congress, 1789–1791," *University of Chicago Law Review* 61, no. 3 (1994): 775 (discussing Hamilton's proposal); Max M. Edling, "So Immense a Power in the Affairs of War: Alexander Hamilton and the Restoration of Public Credit," *William & Mary Quarterly* 64, no. 2 (Apr. 2007): 287.
4. Alexander Hamilton, "Report Relative to a Provision for the Support of Public Credit," Department of Treasury, 1790, https://founders.archives.gov/documents/Hamilton/01-06-02-0076-0002-0001.
5. Hamilton, "Report Relative to a Provision for the Support of Public Credit" ("But there is a consequence of this, less obvious, though not less true, in which every other citizen is interested. It is a well-known fact, that in countries in which the national debt is properly funded, and an object of established confidence, it answers most of the purposes of money. Transfers of stock or public debt are there equivalent to payments in specie; or in other words, stock, in the principal transactions of business, passes current as specie. The same thing would, in all probability happen here, under the like circumstances."); Edling, "So Immense a Power in the Affairs of War," 294; Chernow, *Alexander Hamilton*, 270–77.
6. Robert P. Inman, "Transfers and Bailouts: Institutions for Enforcing Local Fiscal Discipline with Lessons from U.S. Federalism," in *Fiscal Decentralization and the Challenge of Hard Budget Constraints*, eds. Jonathan Rodden, Gunnar Eskelund, and Jennie Litvack (Cambridge, MA: MIT Press 2003), 58, 64 (quoting Hamilton).
7. Lin-Manuel Miranda, "Cabinet Battle # 1," *Hamilton*, Atlantic Records, 2015.
8. Chernow, *Alexander Hamilton*, at 270–77. This issue emerges in many fiscal crises, with governments skeptical of the value of paying off "vulture funds."

9. Currie, "The Constitution in Congress: Substantive Issues in the First Congress, 1789–1791," 808 (discussing the deal); Lin-Manuel Miranda, "The Room Where It Happens," *Hamilton*, Atlantic Records, 2015 (turning the deal into an amazing song).

10. Inman, "Transfers and Bailouts,"

11. Theodore Sky, *The National Road and the Difficult Path to Sustainable National Investment* (Wilmington: University of Delaware, 2011); Carter Goodrich, *Government Promotion of American Canals and Railroads 1800–1890* (New York: Columbia University Press, 1960); Charles Heckman, "Establishing the Basis for Local Financing of American Railroad Construction in the Nineteenth Century: From *City of Bridgeport v. The Housatonic Railroad Company* to *Gelpcke v. City of Dubuque*," *American Journal of Legislative History* 32, no. 3 (July 1988): 263, 264; John Joseph Wallis and Barry R. Weingast, "Equilibrium Impotence: Why the States and Not the American National Government Financed Economic Development in the Antebellum Era," *Journal of Public Finance and Public Choice* 33 (2005): 28.

12. Wallis and Weingast, "Equilibrium Independence," 20.

13. Roderick D. Hills Jr., *The Gentry, the Saints, and the Federal Republic: The Rise and Fall of Constitutional Decentralization in America*" (on draft with author: 2021); Lee W. Formwalt, "Benjamin Henry Latrobe and the Revival of the Gallatin Plan of 1808," *Pennsylvania History: A Journal of Mid-Atlantic Studies* 48, no. 2 (Apr. 1981): 99, 120; Carter Goodrich, *Government Promotion of American Canals and Railroads 1800–1890*, 43–48.

14. David P. Currie, *The Constitution in Congress: The Jeffersonians, 1801–1829* (Chicago: University of Chicago Press, 2001), 265; Ronald E. Shaw, *Canals for a Nation: The Canal Era in the United States, 1790–1860* (2014), 26.

15. Hills, *The Gentry, the Saints*; Brian Balough, *A Government Out of Sight: The Mystery of National Authority in Nineteenth-Century America* (New York: Cambridge University Press, 2009), 138; John Larson, *Internal Improvement: National Public Works and the Promise of Popular Government in the Early United States, 1783–1863* (Chapel Hill: University of North Carolina Press, 2001), 141–50.

16. Hills, *The Gentry, the Saints*.

17. Pamela L. Baker, "The Washington National Road Bill and the Struggle to Adopt a Federal System of Internal Improvement," *Journal of the Early Republic* 22, no. 3 (Autumn, 2002): 437, 456–60; Hills, *The Gentry, the Saints*.

18. Currie, "The Constitution in Congress: Substantive Issues," 15–30; Hills, *The Gentry, the Saints*.

19. Alberta M. Sbragia, *Debt Wish: Entrepreneurial Cities, U.S. Federalism and Economic Development* (Pittsburgh: University of Pittsburgh Press, 1996), 23–24 ("the federal role in assisting transportation was a subordinate one. . . . State and local governments became, by default, the major public financial actors in the field of public investment").

20. Ibid., 28–29 (noting the enormous economic success of the Erie Canal at transforming the economy of the Midwest, upstate New York, and New York City).

21. Ibid., 33; Nathan Miller, *The Enterprise of a Free People: Aspects of Economic Development in New York State during the Canal Period, 1792–1838* (Ithaca, NY: Cornell University Press, 1962), 68–73 (describing the taxes that were devoted to support bonds issued to build the canal). New York State had previously floated "public and transferable stock" in 1815 with "limited success" but mostly relied on bank loans. Ibid. 79–81.

22. Ibid., 85–111.

23. Ibid., 115.

24. Harry N. Scheiber, "State Law and 'Industrial Policy' in American Development, 1790–1987," *California Law Review* 75, no. 1 (Jan. 1987): 415, 422 (discussing uses of Canal Fund money); Miller, *The Enterprise of a Free People*, 138–44, 172–93.

25. Sbragia, *Debt Wish*, 29 (discussing galvanizing effect of Erie Canal on other states).

26. John J. Wallis, "Constitutions, Corporations, and Corruption: American States and Constitutional Change, 1842 to 1852," *Journal of Economic History* 65, no. 1 (Mar. 2005): 211, 222–24, 228–30. Notably, these projects were not like modern user-fee-supported projects in that the bonds were not funded with "revenue bonds." This meant that if the user fees were insufficient, the state was on the hook. For a discussion of revenue bonds, see Chapter 3.

27. Rodden, *Hamilton's Paradox*, 58 (discussing popularity of state infrastructure investments with British and Dutch investors); Sbragia, *Debt Wish*, 34 (same).

28. Sbragia, *Debt Wish*, 29–30; Wallis and Weingast, *"Equilibrium Impotence,"* 25–26; John Joseph Wallis, Richard Sylla, and Arthur Grinath III, "Sovereign Debt and Repudiation: The Emerging-Market Debt Crisis in the U.S. States, 1839–1843," NBER Working Paper 10753 (2004), 7, 11 (noting the difference between the original Erie Canal and Ohio bonds, backed by taxes as well as tolls, and investments in other states, including the later New York and Ohio investments, which were not).

29. Ibid., 5–8.

30. Sbragia, *Debt Wish*, 33–34; Isabel Rodriguez-Tejedo and John Joseph Wallis, "Fiscal Institutions and Fiscal Crises," in *When States Go Broke*, eds. Peter Conti-Brown and David Skeel (New York: Cambridge University Press, 2012), 14–15. By comparison, federal debt was only 0.3% of GDP.

31. Wallis, Sylla, and Grinath, "Sovereign Debt and Repudiation," 5–8.

32. Ibid.

33. Rodden, *Hamilton's Paradox*, at 58; Sbragia, *Debt Wish*, 35 (noting that Biddle's efforts seemed like a federal government endorsement to many foreign investors because the U.S. Bank of Pennsylvania was the successor to the Second Bank of the United States.) More than half of outstanding state debt in 1841 had been borrowed after 1837. Wallis, Sylla, and Grinnath, "Sovereign Debt and Repudiation," 6.

34. Namsuk Kim and John Joseph Wallis, "The Market for American State Government Bonds in Britain and the United States, 1830 to 1843," *Economic History Review* 58, no. 4 (Nov. 2005): 736, 760.

35. Wallis, Sylla, and Grinnath, "Sovereign Debt and Repudiation," 15–25.

36. Ibid; Sbragia, *Debt Wish*, 36–39.

37. Wallis, Sylla, and Grinnath, "Sovereign Debt and Repudiation," 22–25. Much of the difference between Pennsylvania, which defaulted, and New York, which did not, came down to Pennsylvania's initial refusal to raise taxes. Ibid., 23. But once it did, it could make its payments.

38. Ibid., 17–25; Sbragia, *Debt Wish*, 36.

39. Wallis, Sylla, and Grinnath, "Sovereign Debt and Repudiation,"17–25; Christopher Shortell, *Rights, Remedies, and the Impact of State Sovereign Immunity* (Albany: SUNY Press, 2008), 58–67 (describing partial repudiations in Arkansas, Louisiana, Michigan, and full repudiations in Florida and Mississippi).

40. Rodden, *Hamilton's Paradox*, 68.

41. Ibid., 59–60.

42. Ibid., 61–62.

43. Congress's decision not to bail out the states was surely aided in that, by 1843, when it finally voted on the Johnson Report, it had become clear that big states like Maryland and Pennsylvania at least were going to be able to resume payments after passing new taxes. Ibid., 67.

44. For example, consider Rodden, "Market Discipline," 123.

45. Rodriguez-Tejado and Wallis, "Fiscal Institutions and Fiscal Crises," 24–35; John A. Dove, "Credible Commitments and Constitutional Constraints: State Debt Repudiation and Default in Nineteenth Century America," *Constitutional Political Economy* 23, no. 1 (2012): 66.

46. Dove, "Credible Commitments" (detailing the range of state constitutional changes); John Joseph Wallis, "Constitutions, Corporations and Corruption," *Journal of Economic History* 65 no. 1 (2005): 230–33 (same).

47. Richard Briffault, "The Disfavored Constitution: State Fiscal Limits and State Constitutional Law," *Rutgers Law Journal* 34 (Summer 2003): 907, 911–14. Notably, courts have repeatedly weakened public purpose requirements over time, rendering them "largely rhetorical." Ibid., at 914.

48. Wallis, "Constitutions, Corporations and Corruption," 230–33 (discussing state constitutional changes, including Indiana's absolute ban on debt).

49. Exactly what work debt limits do is a subject of a long debate. Richard Briffault argues, as most legal scholars do, that debt limits and balanced budget rules can easily be circumvented

by state officials (using tools ranging from the creation of special authorities to lease-and-buy-back arrangements). Briffault, "The Disfavored Constitution," 915–17. Economists have generally found that state fiscal constitutions affect state budget practice in aggregate, with stricter rules leading to more prudent budgeting. James Poterba, "Budget Institutions and Fiscal Policy in the U.S. States," *American Economic Review* 86, no. 2 (May 1996): 395; Tracy Gordon, "State and Local Fiscal Institutions in Recession and Recovery," in *Oxford Handbook on State and Local Government Finance*, eds. Robert Ebel and John Petersen (Oxford: Oxford University Press, 2012). These claims can be harmonized if debt limits matter—either by creating real limits or by raising the political costs of excessive borrowing—until a state faces real problems, in which case they do not, as officials can come up with avoidance strategies.

50. Shortell, *Rights, Remedies, and the Impact of State Sovereign Immunity*, 78–80.
51. State governments did not grow relative to GDP, and state debts declined over the rest of the 19th century. Rodriguez-Tejado and Wallis, *Fiscal Institutions and Fiscal Crises*, 13.
52. States were not *entirely* out of the infrastructure improvements game, but they were not involved the way they were before the 1840s. Carter Goodrich, "The Revulsion against Internal Improvements," *Journal of Economic History* 10, no. 2 (1950): 145, 149–55 (discussing state financing of internal improvements after the 1840s and then the return to funding improvements by some states later).
53. There is another view of this change. John Wallis and Barry Weingast argue that moving infrastructure investment from states to cities was a positive adaptation. John Joseph Wallis and Barry Weingast, "Dysfunctional or Optimal Institutions? State Debt Limitations, the Structure of State and Local Governments, and the Finance of American Infrastructure," in *Fiscal Challenges: An Interdisciplinary Approach to Budget Policy*, Garrett, Graddy, and Jackson, eds. (Cambridge: Cambridge University Press, 2008). They argue that local governments, and later special purpose local governments, are better suited to invest in infrastructure as they can make the main beneficiaries of these projects pay for them. This is a very powerful argument. Often, making local governments pay for infrastructure does mean that the ultimate beneficiaries end up paying for them, creating incentives for efficient building. I will return to this question in Chapter 3.

   However, their argument is much harder to justify for the period after the Civil War. During this period, the biggest investments were in railroads, which by their nature are not local. Further, because of agglomeration economies, railroad subsidies had large effects beyond local governments where they encouraged firms to concentrate in a few hubs. The intense competition between cities to be hubs—and the overinvestment that ensued—was surely economically wasteful in ways that state governmental direction might have avoided. David Schleicher, "The City as a Law and Economic Subject," *University of Illinois Law Review* 2010 (2010): 1507, 1554. Similarly, when states came back into the picture as funders of infrastructure, it was to build intercity roads, another type of infrastructure for which local governments and special districts were largely inappropriate. Jon C. Teaford, *The Rise of the States: Evolution of American State Government* (Baltimore: Johns Hopkins University Press, 2002), 96–97, 100.

Chapter 3

1. Avis Thomas-Lester, "Forgotten in the Classroom: The Reconstruction Era," *Washington Post*, Jan. 14, 2018.
2. William Novak argues that beliefs that the United States has historically been a "weak state" are too focused on the admitted historically limited capacity of the federal government to govern behavior, on its weak potential "despotic power." William Novak, "The Myth of the 'Weak' American State," *American History Review* 113 (2008): 752, 763. In contrast, Novak argues the United States has always had a very substantial "infrastructural power," although this power to build civic infrastructure has been disguised due to its distribution among a huge number of state and local entities. Ibid., 763–67. This book argues that the need to distribute "infrastructural power" does more than make it hard for historians to see, but also creates a set of tradeoffs between maintaining that infrastructural power, macroeconomic stability, and the capacity of federal officials to make states internalize their own costs.

3. A. M. Hillhouse, *Municipal Bonds: A Century of Experience* (New York: Prentice-Hall, 1936), 34 ("With state aid for internal improvements checked, municipal aid filled the gap."); Alberta M. Sbragia, *Debt Wish: Entrepreneurial Cities, U.S. Federalism, and Economic Development* (Pittsburgh: University of Pittsburgh Press, 1996), 56. In 1873, the value of bonds issued by local governments equaled the total amount of bonds issued by both the states and the federal government combined. Charles Fairman, *The Oliver Wendell Holmes Devise History of the Supreme Court of the United States*, eds. Paul A. Freund and Stanley N. Katz, vol. 6 (New York: Macmillan, 1971), 926.

4. Hillhouse, *Municipal Bonds*, 40–44, 195 ("railroad aid bond defaults . . . have furnished nearly half of all bonds held void" from 1835–1930); James E. Spiotto, "The Myth and Reality of State and Local Governments Debt Financing in the U.S.A. in Times of Financial Emergency," Presentation to the SEC (July 25, 2011), https://www.sec.gov/spotlight/municipalsecurit ies/statements072911/spiotto-slides1.pdf.

5. Hillhouse, *Municipal Bonds* 44, 195; Sbragia, *Debt Wish*, 56–60.

6. Paul Stephen Dempsey, "Transportation: A Legal History," *Transportation Law Journal* 30, no. 2–3: 235, 249–51 (discussing subsidies for intercontinental rail); Lloyd J. Mercer, "Taxpayers or Investors: Who Paid for the Land-Grant Railroads?," *Business History Review* 46 (1972): 279 (discussing historical debate over what percentage of funding for intercontinentals came from government subsidies and finding that subsidies were "very substantial."); Sbragia, *Debt Wish*, 53.

7. Brian Balough, *A Government Out of Sight: The Mystery of National Authority in Nineteenth-Century America* (Cambridge: Cambridge University Press, 2009), 286–89.

8. The size of the land grants was enormous, equal to just less than 7% of the continental land mass of the United States. Lloyd J. Mercer, *Railroads and Land Grant Policy: A Study in Government Intervention* (New York: Academic Press, 1982); Douglas W. Allen, "Establishing Economic Property Rights by Giving Away an Empire," *Journal of Law and Economics* 62 (2019): 251.

9. As Alison LaCroix shows, the use of land grants was designed to overcome the legal position of opponents of internal improvements. The federal government funded railroad construction by transferring federally owned land to state governments, conditioned on its use to support the building of railroads. Alison L. LaCroix, "The Interbellum Constitution, Federalism in the Long Founding Moment," *Stanford Law Review* 67, no. 2 (2015): 397, 432–39. The land was generally granted in a "checkerboard" fashion, with the federal government holding on to every other chunk of land, so that it would see financial upsides, tempering claims that it was providing aid to particular areas rather than seeking to provide general benefits.

10. The total amount actually transferred by the federal government was less than the size of Texas, but when state governmental transfers are included, the actual amount transferred is more than the total size of Texas. David Maldwyn Ellis, "Railroad Land Grant Rates, 1850–1945," *Journal of Land and Public Utility Economics* 21, no. 3 (1945): 207, 208–09.

11. It is no accident that almost all major American cities were built around ports or railroad hubs, a result of high shipping costs and the agglomeration gains to be made from being a transportation hub. Firms wanted to locate near transportation hubs to reduce shipping costs, and producers of input goods wanted to locate near those firms to reduce their shipping costs. Edward L. Glaeser and Janet E. Kohlhase, "Cities, Regions and the Decline of Transport Costs," *Papers in Regional Science* 83 (2004): 197–99;

12. David Schleicher, "The City as a Law and Economic Subject," *University of Illinois Law Review* 2010, no. 5 (2010): 1555.

13. It is genuinely hard to describe how fast Chicago grew in such a short amount of time, going from just over 30,000 people to over 2 million over the course of just 60 years. Chicago's growth was also driven by the development of its port, which allowed shipping connections between the east cost and the Mississippi River. Emily Badger, "What Happened to the American Boomtown?," *New York Times*, Dec. 6, 2017 (quoting me saying, "You see these numbers, and they just look fake").

14. "Cities had visions of metropolitan greatness, and they indulged in numerous ill-considered enterprises. They competed with each other for railroad transportation and subscribed freely for railroad stocks." E. Blythe Stason, "State Administrative Supervision of Municipal Indebtedness," *Michigan Law Review* 30 (1932): 833, 837. The exact amounts are hard to

calculate, but local governments seem to have contributed about $125M in the antebellum period to rail improvements and around $175M between 1860 and 1890. Sbragia, *Debt Wish*, 51. Railroad promoters took advantage of this competition between cities, getting them to bid against one another. Hillhouse, *Municipal Bonds*, 149.

15. Stanley L. Engerman, "Some Economic Issues Relating to Railroad Subsidies and the Evaluation of Land Grants," *Journal of Economic History* 30 (1972): 443, 451 ("capital market conditions were crucial in determining the extent of the government role."); Hillhouse, *Municipal Bonds*, 150 (describing private money raised by railroad promoters among local residents). Because the projects were speculative and the towns supporting them small, interest rates were high and often the bonds sold for below par. Ibid.,150. Shady railroad promoters would sell shares to local residents, selling them on a rich potential future. Ibid., 148–51.

16. Hillhouse, *Municipal Bonds*, 151–52. Railroad salesmen traveled across the west convincing towns and counties to buy shares with promises of glory. The stories of cities during this period are much like the famous episode of *The Simpsons* in which a canny salesman woos local voters to build a new train with the song: "Monorail, Monorail, Monorail." Sean Cole, "Marge and the Monorail," *Vice*, Nov. 5, 2020, https://www.vice.com/en/article/akdzx5/an-oral-history-of-marge-vs-the-monorail-the-simpsons.

17. See Schleicher, "The City," 1549–55.

18. Herbert Hovenkamp, "Regulatory Conflict in the Gilded Age: Federalism and the Railroad Problem," *Yale Law Journal* 97, no. 6 (1988): 1017, 1035.

19. Ibid.,1038 n. 101; Senate Report. No. 46, 49th Cong., 1st Sess. 48–51 (1886).

20. John A. Dove, "Financial Markets, Fiscal Constraints, and Municipal Debt: Lessons and Evidence from the Panic of 1873," *Journal of Institutional Economics* 10 (2014): 71, 75 (spike in municipal defaults after Panic of 1873).

21. Ibid. (estimating that nearly 20% of all municipal debt was in default); Hillhouse, *supra* note 3, at 39 (same).

22. Charles Warren, *The Supreme Court in United States History*, vol. 2 (1932), 532 (more than 200 Supreme Court cases on municipal bonds during this period, more than on any other subject).

23. As a point of contrast, a recent paper disputes the conventional wisdom that investors were wildly successful in the municipal bond Supreme Court cases of the era. It argues instead the municipal bond cases had a reasonable, formalistic logic, resulting in issuers winning more often than is commonly understood. Allison Buccola and Vincent J. Buccola, "The Municipal Bond Cases Revisited," *American Bankruptcy Law Journal* 94 (2020): 591. Even by the terms of this argument, however, the Court's approach to these was not required by existing legal materials and was broadly pro-bondholder, if not as aggressively lawless in their favor as the conventional wisdom suggests.

24. The first important state case to rule on the issue was Goddin v. Crump, 35 Va. 120 (1837) (finding that Richmond could invest in railroad stock). But as Charles Heckman notes, the factual nature of the local investment in railroads at issue in *Goddin* was different from the cases that followed, as the State of Virginia was the principal owner of the railroad. Charles Heckman, "Establishing the Basis for Local Financing of American Railroad Construction in the Nineteenth Century: From *City of Bridgeport v. The Housatonic Railroad Company* to *Gelpcke v. City of Dubuque*," *American Journal of Legislative History* 32, no. 3 (July 1988): 241. Thus *Sharpless*, not *Goldin*, become the leading case.

25. 21 Pa. 147 (Penn. 1853) ("If all municipal subscriptions are void, railroads, which are necessary to give the state those advantages to which everything else entitles her, must stand unfinished for years to come, and large sums, already expended on them, must be lost.")

26. Ibid.

27. Hillhouse, *Municipal Bonds*, 145–47; Fairman, *Oliver Wendell Holmes Device*, 927–31; Sbragia, *Debt Wish*, at 94–95.

28. Sbragia, *Debt Wish*, 94 (discussing state court opinions).

29. Hillhouse, *Municipal Bonds*, 161–64 (describing conflict between elected state court judges and appointed federal judges with lifetime tenure).

30. The parties in these cases often relied on the character of bondholders—the nationality, ethnicity, and investment-timing—in their arguments. In the arguments in *Gelpcke v. Dubuque*, the city's attorney noted that Gelpcke, a New York banker, represented Jewish bond holders from Germany: "Then, the question is . . . whether . . . people upon the 'Rhine'—the respectable citizens of the Juden-Gasse of Frankfurt-am-Maine—[who] have brought these bonds at large discounts, on account of those doubts of their legality which everywhere have attended the issue of them, shall have them enforced in the face of constitutions and solemn decisions of the State courts, simply because they have bought and yet hold them." Heckman, "Establishing the Basis," 255. The reference to a Jewish neighborhood in Munich was surely not lost anyone.

31. 4 Greene 1 (1853); Michael A. Ross, *Justice of Shattered Dreams: Samuel Freeman Miller and the Supreme Court* (Baton Rouge: Louisiana State University Press, 2003), 34–35 ("In 1853, the Iowa Supreme Court, in a brief but sweeping opinion, did its best to squelch any concerns about the legality of municipal railroad bonds.")

32. Ross, *Shattered Dreams*, 35 ("The court's decision [in *Dubuque County*] opened the floodgates for the river of Iowa bonds that followed.")

33. Hillhouse, *Municipal Bonds*, 153.

34. Ross, *Shattered Dreams*, 88–93.

35. State ex rel. Burlington & M. R. R. Co. v. County of Wapello, 13 Iowa 388, 400–03 (1862).

36. Ibid., 423.

37. Ibid. This is best read as snidely pouring salt into the bondholders' wounds rather than as a real suggestion. See Heckman, "Establishing the Basis," 254 (describing the passage as a "piece of hypocrisy.")

38. Joan C. Williams, "The Constitutional Vulnerability of American Local Government: The Politics of City Status in American Law," *Wisconsin Law Review* 83 (1986): 94.

39. Ross, *Shattered Dreams*, at 22–24, 256.

40. Keokuk was in the 1850s a fast-growing town with delusions of grandeur, a belief that it might not only emerge as a piece of the St. Louis economic region but was, according to locals, an "infant Hercules" that would "eclipse both Chicago and St. Louis." Ibid., at 22, 22–24.

41. Miller's involvement in fighting railroad bridges is a fascinating story. In the 1850s, a railroad bridge crossed the Mississippi River in Davenport, Iowa, and then ran to Chicago. The cities along the River realized this would be a major blow, as their dreams of urban growth were premised on a belief that they would the terminus of a railroad, with cargo being ferried across the Mississippi through their ports or shipped down the River. If railroads could simply cross the Mississippi River, there would not be much need for River port towns.

Following the crash of a steamship called the *Effie Afton*, lawsuits were filed in Illinois and Iowa, claiming that the bridge was a hazard to shipping down the Mississippi. (When he was US secretary of war, later president of the Confederacy, Jefferson Davis had previously tried to block the same bridge, hoping that a railroad bridge across the Mississippi would be built further south first to encourage settlement of western territories by southerners.) St. Louis merchants supported the lawsuit, seeking to keep commerce flowing down the Mississippi rather than going by rail to Chicago. The trial was a major regional news story, helping build the reputation for a trial lawyer for the railroad in the Illinois suit: Abraham Lincoln.

The Illinois case ended in a hung jury. In the Iowa suit, the plaintiffs were represented by none other than Samuel Freeman Miller. Miller not only wanted to preserve shipping on the Mississippi and the role for river towns generally; he also wanted to give Keokuk time to catch up with Davenport. Miller won the case at trial, in front of a judge from Keokuk who, before going on the bench, had ties to Miller's law firm. The Iowa suit eventually made it up to the Supreme Court in 1862, after the President Lincoln appointed Miller to the Supreme Court. With Miller forced to abstain, the Court ruled in favor of the railroad.

Interestingly, Lincoln had not met Miller before appointing him, and there is no evidence he knew about Miller's role in railroad litigation. (For much of the time leading up to the nomination, Lincoln did not even realize the Miller he was considering was Samuel Miller, confusing him with another Republican Party lawyer named Miller from Iowa.) It seems somewhat unlikely that Lincoln would have appointed Miller had he known that he held a diametrically opposing position on one of the central issues of Lincoln's legal career. Ross,

Shattered Dreams, 40; Brian McGinty, *Lincoln's Greatest Case: The River, the Bridge, and the Making of America*, 35–36, 64–69, 75–107, 166–67 (2015); Larry A. Riney, *Hell Gate of the Mississippi: The Effie Afton Trial and Abraham Lincoln's Role in It* (New York: Talesman Press, 2006); David A. Pfeiffer, "Bridging the Mississippi: The Railroads and Steamboats Clash at the Rock Island Bridge," *Prologue Magazine* 36 (2004).

42. Ross, *Shattered Dreams*, 41–44.

43. Ibid., 53. Keokuk tried over the years to renegotiate or repudiate its debts to no avail. Ibid., 177. Miller was heavily involved in one of these efforts as a sitting Supreme Court justice, even as he was regularly deciding cases involving municipal bonds.

44. Ibid., 236–37.

45. In *Chisholm v. Georgia*, the absence of sovereign immunity for municipalities was the basis for Chief Justice John Jay's critique of the doctrine of sovereign immunity for states. 2 U.S. 419, 472 (1793) ("Will it be said, that the fifty odd thousand citizens in Delaware stand in a rank so superior to the forty odd thousand of Philadelphia?") The Court has also long interpreted the Eleventh Amendment not to provide sovereign immunity for local governments. Fred Smith, "Local Sovereign Immunity," *Columbia Law Review* 116 (2016): 412–13 (reviewing the case law, but arguing that although municipalities lack sovereign immunity, they have been granted many other forms of immunity from claims that amount to a very substantial amount of protection from suits).

46. 67 U.S. 599, 603 (1862). As Allison and Vincent Buccola note, *Leffingwell* was not completely settled precedent. Allison Buccola and Vincent Buccola, "The Municipal Bond Cases Revisited." In *East Oakland Township v. Skinner*, the Court states: "If the Supreme Court of a State gives construction to the language of a statute, and there have been no conflicting decisions, this court, as a general rule, follows the construction thus given." 94 U.S. 255, 257 (1873). Were this the Court's approach at the time, Buccola and Buccola argue, it would make sense of cases like *Gelpcke*, which one could understand as simply reversing the state court on the meaning of state law, an exception to the "general rule," to be sure, but not a replacement of state law with federal law. But *Leffingwell* was decided only one year before *Gelpcke*, suggesting that its stronger statement about the dominance of state courts over state law should have governed. As a result, *Gelpcke* is probably best understood as it traditionally is, an aggressive application of the Court's common-law powers in a diversity case. Either way, the Court was doing something aggressive in *Gelpcke*, either using its common-law powers or its strangely acquired capacity to understand the content of Iowa law better than the Iowa Supreme Court.

47. 68 U.S. at 175.

48. U.S. Const. Art 1, Sec. 10 ("No State shall . . . pass any Bill of Attainder, ex post facto Law, or Law impairing the Obligation of Contracts.")

49. Commercial Bank v. Buckingham's Executors, 5 How. 317, 343 (U.S. 1847) ("The power delegated to us is for the restraint of unconstitutional legislation by the States, and not for the correction of alleged errors committed by their judiciary.")

50. 68 U.S. at 206. The Court does not actually mention the Contract Clause in *Gelpcke*, but does quote an earlier decision made on Contract Clause grounds for the proposition: "The sound and true rule is, that if the contract, when made, was valid by the laws of the State as then expounded by all departments of the government, and administered in its courts of justice, its validity and obligation cannot be impaired by any subsequent action of legislation, or decision of its courts altering the construction of the law." Gelpcke, 68 U.S. at 206 (quoting The Ohio Life & Trust Co. v. Debolt, 16 Howard, 432 (1854) (decided on contract clause grounds).

As David Curie notes, because the language of the Contract Clause only refers to "Law[s]" that impair contract obligations, if the Court "did mean to hold that the Constitution forbade judicial impairment of contract, [it] had some explaining to do." David Curie, "The Constitution in the Supreme Court: Contracts and Commerce, 1836–1864," *Duke Law Journal* (1983): 493–95 (1983). In Tidal Oil Co. v. Flanagan, 263 U.S. 444, 451–52 (1923), the Court explicitly foreswore the importance of the Contract Clause to *Gelpcke*, making clear that, at least from the perspective of the 1920s, the *Gelpcke* Court was relying exclusively on its power to make rules of decision in diversity cases.

51. Gelpcke, 68 U.S. at 206–207. Later cases took the *Gelpcke* decision and overturned state court decisions holding that bonds were unenforceable even when there had been no earlier decision approving of them. The most dramatic of these was probably *Pine Grove v. Talcott*, in which the Court rejected the Michigan Supreme Court's decision to hold railroad bonds unenforceable—not because the Michigan Supreme Court had reversed a prior decision, but merely because the Court found that the state court's decision "not satisfactory to our minds." Ouch! *Pine Grove v. Talcott*, 86 U.S. 666, 677–78 (1874); *Olcott v. The Supervisors*, 83 U.S. 678, 689 (1872) (finding enforceable bonds used to fund a donation to a railroad despite a state court decision that did not explicitly reverse any prior decision that such bonds were illegally issued). For a nice discussion of these cases, consider L. A. Powe Jr. "Rehearsal for Substantive Due Process: The Municipal Bond Cases," *University of Texas Law Review* 53 (1975): 744 ("The Court's opinions . . . pretended to follow *Gelpke*, but in fact they significantly expanded that decision."); Fairman, *The Oliver Wendell Holmes Device*, 1021–22 (discussing *Pine Grove*).

52. "[W]e are to have two courts . . . sitting within the same jurisdiction, deciding upon the same rights, arising out of the same statute, yet always arriving at opposite results." *Gelpcke*, 68 U.S. at 208–09 (J. Miller, dissenting). Miller also claimed that Iowa law pre-*Wapello* had not been clear because there had been dissenting opinions, ibid., 207, a point on which Heckman rightfully describes the opinion as "poor." Heckman, "Establishing the Basis," 257.

53. *Gelpcke* has been much criticized over the years, most famously by Justice Holmes. *Muhlker v. New York & H. R. Co.*, 197 U.S. 544, 573 (Holmes, J. dissenting) ("we are asked to extend to the present case the principle of *Gelpcke v. Dubuque* . . . . That seems to me a great, unwarranted and undesirable extension of a doctrine which it took this court a good while to explain."); *Kuhn v. Fairmont Coal Co.*, 215 U.S. 349, 372 (J. Holmes dissenting) ("I know of no authority in this court to say that in general state decisions shall make law only for the future. Judicial decisions have had retrospective operation for near a thousand years. There were enough difficulties in the way, even in cases like *Gelpcke v. Dubuque*."). For more skepticism about the reasoning in *Gelpcke*, see Fairman, *Oliver Wendell Holmes Device*, 937 ("For years afterward the Justices were at a loss to find any adequate justification [for *Gelpcke*]—and so too were the commentators."); Jan Deutch, "Property, The Individual, and Governmental Power: The Meaning of *Gelpcke v. Dubuque*," *Journal for Corporate Law* 4 (1979): 357. *Gelpcke* does have its supporters, most notably James Bradley Thayer, "The Case of Gelpcke v. Dubuque," *Harvard Law Review* 4 (1891): 311, 319; Heckman, "Establishing the Basis," 255–60.

54. Fairman, *Oliver Wendell Holmes Device*, 945–47 (describing numerous unsuccessful lawsuits brought in a federal court by municipalities seeking to evade bonds on the basis of fraud or illegality).

55. 24 How. 376 (1861); *Marcy v. Township of Oswego*, 92 U.S. 637 (1876); *Humboldt Township v. Long*, 92 U.S. 642 (1876); Fairman, *Oliver Wendell Holmes Device*, 931–33 (discussing these opinions). Robert Amdusrky, Clayton Gillette, and Allen Bass argue compellingly that these cases encourage efficient risk allocation—the city is reasonably allocated the risk because it is in the best position to monitor compliance with procedural compliance. Robert S. Amdursky, Clayton P. Gillette, and Allen Bass, *Municipal Debt Finance Law: Theory and Practice*, 2nd ed. (Wolters Kluwer Law and Business, 2020) at section 5.12.

56. 68 U.S. 83, 95 (1863).

57. Ibid., 96.

58. *Coloma v. Eaves*, 92 U.S. 484, 487–88 (1876) (holding that bonds issued without a required vote among residents were nonetheless enforceable).

59. Ibid., 489.

60. *Venice v. Murdock*, 92 U.S. 494, 497 (1876). There were a few cases that went the other way. *The Mayor v. Ray*, 86 U.S. 468 (1873) (where a government has no legal right to borrow money even innocent secondary market purchasers cannot recover); *Williams v. Louisiana*, 103 U.S. 637 (1880) (same).

61. 71 U.S. 535 (1867). See also *Benbow v. Iowa City*, 7 Wall 313 (1869).

62. 75 U.S. (8 Wall.) 575, 582 (1869); Fairman, *Oliver Wendell Holmes Device*, 1000 ("The tax limit was brushed aside as applicable only to 'the ordinary course of . . . municipal action.'"); *City of Galena v. Amy*, 72 U.S. 705 (1867); *Meyer v. Muscatine*, 68 U.S. 384 (1864).

63. Butz v. City of Muscatine, 75 U.S. (8 Wall.) 575, 582 (1869).

64. Hillhouse, *Municipal Bonds*, 169–70. Compare Supervisor v. Rogers, 74 U.S. 175 (1869) (Iowa state law allowed for appointment of a marshal to levy taxes, and therefore federal court could make this happen) with Rees v. Watertown, 86 U.S. 107 (1873) (Wisconsin law does not allow for appointment of marshals, so creditor has to wait until new city officials are elected upon whom the federal court can order to raise taxes through an *mandamus* order). The Court described this period dramatically in Faitoute Iron & Steel Co. v. City of Asbury Park, 316 U.S. 502, 513 (1942) ("we have had the spectacle of taxing officials resigning from office in order to frustrate tax levies through mandamus, and officials running on a platform of willingness to go to jail, rather than to enforce a tax levy . . . and evasion of service by tax collectors, thus making impotent a court's mandate") (citations and quotation marks omitted).

65. Hillhouse, *Municipal Bonds*, 169.

66. Fairman, *Oliver Wendell Holmes Device*, 968.

67. Ibid., 962–89 (describing Iowa's state courts and local government officials resisting orders from the federal judiciary). Iowa was not the only state in which such a rebellion took place. Missouri in the late 1870s threw up a huge number of barriers to the enforcement of railroad bonds ordered by the Supreme Court, including passing laws specifically barring cities from passing new taxes without an order by a Missouri state court (effectively barring federal mandamus actions). Eventually, though, Missouri too backed down. Ibid., 1100–11. See also Hillhouse, *Municipal Bonds*, 65–67 (describing organized political response to federal court orders, including state Democratic conventions in Arkansas and Missouri calling for legislation barring federal courts from making mandamus orders to local governments to raise taxes).

68. Riggs v. Johnson County, 73 U.S. 166, 195 (1868) ("State courts are exempt from all interference by the Federal tribunals, but they are destitute of all power to restrain either the process or proceedings in the national courts.");Weber v. Lee County, 73 U.S. 210 (1868) (same).

69. Fairman, *Oliver Wendell Holmes Device*, 966–67.

70. Ibid., 985.

71. For instance, cities and states started taxing interest on bonds, effectively reducing debt burdens. The Court struck these down as violations of the Contract Clause. Murray v. Charleston, 96 U.S. 432 (1877); Hartman v. Greenhow, 102 U.S. 672 (1881).

72. Hillhouse, *Municipal Bonds*, 327–28 (describing corporate suicides).

73. 116 U.S. at 304 ("The laws which establish local municipal corporations cannot be altered or repealed so as to invade the constitutional rights of creditors.").

74. The decisions in this area were hardly uniform. In Meriwether v. Garrett, 102 U.S. 472, 504 (1880), the court let a corporate suicide serve as a defense against bondholders on the grounds that there were no longer city officers who could be subject to a *mandamus* order. On the other hand, in Wolff v. New Orleans, 103 U.S. 358, 365 (1880), the Court held that a state law violated the Contract Clause because it removed taxing authority from a city after that city had defaulted. The harm to creditors was "not indirectly as a consequence of legitimate measures taken, as will sometimes happen, but directly by operating upon" the ability of a city to pay its debts.

75. Shapleigh v. San Angelo, 167 U.S. 646 (1887) ("The State's plenary power over its municipal corporations to change their organization . . . or to abolish them altogether, is not restricted by contracts entered into by the municipality with its creditors. . . . An absolute repeal of a municipal charter is therefore effectual so far as it abolishes the old corporate organization; but when the same or substantially the same inhabitants are erected into a new corporation . . . such new corporation is treated as in law the successor of the old one, entitled to its property rights, and subject to its liabilities.")

76. Miller was more than willing to use the Court's *Swift*-based common-law powers aggressively when he saw fit. See Loan Ass'n v. Topeka, 87 U.S. 655 (1876) (Miller opinion finding that municipal bonds issued to aid an iron works were illegally issued and were thus unenforceable despite a state court decision approving them); Yates v. Milwaukee, 77 U.S. 497, 506 (1870) (Miller opinion applying general common law over state court rule, noting "[t]he law which governs the case is the common law, on which this court has never acknowledged the right of

the State courts to control our decisions."); Tony Freyer, *Harmony and Dissonance: The Swift and Erie Cases in American Federalism*, vol. 4 (New York: New York University Press, 1981), 61 ("Miller . . . consistently dissented in the bond cases. These dissents, however, seem not to have represented a rejection of the fundamental nature of general law, as much as an unwillingness to sanction its application in particular instances.").

77. Charles Fairman, *Mr. Justice Miller and the Supreme Court 1862–1890* (Cambridge, MA: Harvard University Press, 1939), 231 (1939) (quoting letter from Miller to William Ballinger).

78. Gelpcke, 68 U.S. at 214 (Miller, J. dissenting).

79. Ross, *Shattered Dreams*, 175 (quoting Miller letter to William Ballinger).

80. Randall Bridwell and Ralph U. Whitten, *The Constitution and the Common Law: The Decline of the Doctrines of Separation of Powers and Federalism* (Lexington: Lexington Free Press, 1977), 115 ("The characteristic of the common law that [prior to the 1860s] prevented violations of federalism and separation of powers restrictions by the federal courts in diversity cases was its private or customary character."); Freyer, *Harmony and Dissonance*, 4 ("But if neither federalism nor national commerce were the central questions in Swift, what was the main issue . . . . Throughout the antebellum period, federal courts were conceived of as alternate forums to the tribunals of states . . . [so] nonresidents might have the means to avoid the uncertainties and sporadic prejudices of local law.").

81. Bridwell and Whitten, *The Constitution and the Common Law*, 116 ("[T[he federal courts . . . began to depart . . . in important ways which violated both restrictions of federalism and separation of powers. . . . The cases in which these deviations occurred involved municipal bond and tort disputes."); Freyer, *Harmony and Dissonance*, 56–58 ("From 1860 on, judges . . . displayed a willingness to apply the 'general law' in a growing number of cases. . . . The Supreme Court also continued to enlarge the 'general law' despite state court decisions and statutes to the contrary. The two main categories of cases in which this enlargement took place involved tort liability in accidents and recovery on municipal bonds.")

82. Powe, "Rehearsal," 755.

83. Ibid.

84. Munn v. Illinois, 94 U.S. 113 (1876). Further, Miller's opposition to big business interests did not stop him from writing the majority opinion in Wabash, St. L. & Pac. Ry. v. Illinois, 118 U.S. 557 (1886), which sharply limited state authority to regulate inter-state railway shipping. For an excellent discussion of the underlying economics of the *Granger* cases and the wisdom of Miller's opinion in *Wabash Railway*, see Hovenkamp, "Regulatory Conflict," 1062–76. The politics of federal railroad rate regulation, both in the courts and in Congress, did not feature the same ideological coherence and came a bit later, as the dominant Republican coalition frayed. As Stephen Skowronek argues, the politics of railroad rate regulation was quite pluralistic, with a variety of different groups and interests playing important roles. Stephen Skowronek, *Building a New American State: The Expansion of National Administrative Capacities, 1877–1920* (1982); 123–62.

85. Loan Association, 87 U.S. at 655.

86. Powe, "Rehearsal," 746.

87. Interestingly, despite the pro-creditor position taken by the Supreme Court, most of the debt was eventually renegotiated on decently favorable terms for the debtors. Hillhouse, *Municipal Bonds*, 173–75 (describing results of compromises with bondholders). Randall Picker and Michael McConnell credit this to the extremity of mandamus as a remedy, as efforts to raise taxes on local governments without strong economies would not produce much revenue, leaving the creditors with outstanding claims for long periods of time. See Michael W. McConnell and Randal C. Picker, "When Cities Go Broke: A Conceptual Introduction to Municipal Bankruptcy," *University of Chicago Law Review* 60 (1996): 450.

88. Dove, "Financial Markets," 77–80 (discussing types of municipal debt limits, procedural requirements governing debt issuance, and tax caps).

89. Ibid., 78. These restrictions became less strict over time, allowing much more aid to private activity than was originally allowed. Richard Briffault, "The Disfavored Constitution: State Fiscal Limits and State Constitutional Law," *Rutgers Law Journal* 34 (Summer 2003): 915–18.

90. Ibid., 79; Sbragia, *Debt Wish*, 83.

91. Dove, "Financial Markets," 80.
92. See Fairman, *Mr. Justice Miller and the Supreme Court,* 243 (describing Miller and Dillon's relationship).
93. John F. Dillon, *Treatise on the Law of Municipal Corporations* (Chicago: J. Cockcraft 1872), 20–25; Gerald E. Frug, "The City as a Legal Concept," *Harvard Law Review* 93 (1980): 1109 (describing Dillon's Rule). Dillon also issued a well-known opinion in 1868, affirming the decision in *Wapello* that found that the use of municipal debt to support railroads was unconstitutional under the Iowa Constitution. Hanson v. Vernon, 27 Iowa 28 (1868). The Iowa Supreme Court later reversed Dillon's decision in Hanson. Stewart v. Board of Supervisors, 30 Iowa 9 (1870).
94. Dillon, *Treatise,* 101–102.
95. Frug, "The City as a Legal Concept," 1108–1120.
96. The winner-take-most nature of agglomeration economies of the time, caused by the high cost of shipping and the attendant need to co-locate industry and input suppliers, meant that states had good reason to worry that aid to industry would have a beggar-thy-neighbor effect, attempting to lure growth in one direction at the expense of others. Schleicher, "The City," 1549–55.
97. Dillon, *Treatise,* 556.
98. "[W]here the purpose for which the tax was to be issued could no longer be justly claimed to have [a] public character, . . . but was purely in aid of private or personal objects, the law authorizing it was beyond the legislative power, and was an unauthorized invasion of private right." Loan Association, 87 U.S. at 662 (citing Dillon, *Treatise,* 556). This decision overruled lower court opinions and rejected state legislation to the contrary, showing that Miller's opposition to *Gelpcke* was ideological, rather than jurisprudential in nature.
99. Dove, *Financial Markets,* 92.
100. Isabel Rodriguez-Tejedo and John Joseph Wallis, "Fiscal Institutions and Fiscal Crises," in *When States Go Broke,* eds. Peter Conti-Brown and David Skeel (New York: Cambridge University Press, 2012), 13. Local revenues as a share of GDP fell slightly between 1870 and 1880, from 2.6% to 2.2%, but rose thereafter, increasing to 2.8% in 1890 and 4.0% in 1902 (compared with around 7% today). Id.
101. Sbragia, *Debt Wish,* 104.
102. This is not meant to be a full list. For instance, both states and cities rely on leases and long-term contracts to avoid debt limits. Briffault, "The Disfavored Constitution," 919–20. And states regularly use subject-to-appropriation or "moral obligation" debt, bonds that are backed solely by the legislature's willingness to spend money and not by the state's full faith and credit. Ibid., 922–24. These are not subject to debt limits either.
103. There's nothing that stops governments from using other revenues to pay back revenue bonds, and often there is substantial pressure for them to do so, as defaulting can lead to worries about the jurisdiction's other debts.
104. Special assessments are charges levied on property owners near infrastructure (or other) improvements that are benefited by those improvements. Because debt issued to fund projects backed by assessments did not count toward debt limits, localities and states moved more projects into assessments and out of general taxes. Sbragia, *Debt Wish,* 114. Revenue bonds are, very generally, bonds backed by funds generated by the specific project built with the revenues from the bond. Courts determined that revenue bonds were not backed by the full faith and credit of local governments and thus were not subject to debt limits. Ibid., 118–22. Traditionally, the "special fund" doctrine meant that only those bonds solely backed by the revenues from the funded project itself were exempt from debt limits. But a broader version of the "special fund" doctrine, allowing other revenues to back such bonds, was adopted by courts, increasing what revenue bonds may be used for. By 1930, many states allowed jurisdictions to use revenue bonds, creating another way for governments to borrow outside of their debt limits. Briffault, "The Disfavored Constitution"; Benjamin Ulysses Ratchford, *American State Debts* (Durham, NC: Duke University Press, 1941), 446.
105. Briffault, "The Disfavored Constitution," 147–62. Wallis and Weingast argue that the rise of special authorities, like the transition from state borrowing pre-1840 to local borrowing afterward, was an evolution that better matched the beneficiaries of infrastructure with those

paying for it. John Joseph Wallis and Barry Weingast, "Dysfunctional or Optimal Institutions? State Debt Limitations, the Structure of State and Local Governments, and the Finance of American Infrastructure," in *Fiscal Challenges: An Interdisciplinary Approach to Budget Policy*, eds. Elizabeth Garrett, Elizabeth A. Graddy, and Howell E. Jackson (Cambridge: Cambridge University Press, 2008), 47–50. Notably, they argue that state constitutional guarantees that such authorities issue debt themselves, often backed by fees like tolls, made users of infrastructure pay for it. This, they argue, led to a more efficient provision of infrastructure.

There are situations where there is power to this argument, but there is also much left out. First, the fact that legally states and cities are not on the hook for the debt of authorities formally does not mean that they are not on the hook for it in practice. If creditors blame states for defaults from associated entities, then there is little difference between special authority debt and state debt. On top of this, while funding infrastructure with user fees or by taxes on the most effected residents works for some types of infrastructure, it does not work well for others. For instance, subways or light rail are unlikely to be built efficiently through user fees or even specific local taxes. The benefits of such projects are not fully captured by users (rail reduces traffic on roads and reduces pollution). Having special authorities fund infrastructure also often means that one type of fee (say tolls on roads and bridges) often cannot cross-subsidize other types (like rail). Wallis and Weingast also ignore the afterlife of the special purpose local governments, implicitly assuming institutional forms evolve effortlessly over time. In practice many special purpose governments live on well after their justification for existing, creating all sorts of problems through complicating government and encouraging excessive spending. They can also have a distortionary effect on the bond market. Aurelia Chaudhury, Adam J. Levitin, and David Schleicher, "Junk Cities: Resolving Insolvency Crises in Overlapping Local Governments," *California Law Review* 107, no. 2 (2019): 459 (discussing problem of overlapping local governments).

106. Sbragia, *Debt Wish*, 109.
107. Jon Teaford, *The Unheralded Triumph: City Government in America*, 1870–1900 (Baltimore: Johns Hopkins University Press, 1984),1–5 (describing widespread belief in inefficiency and corruption of city governments of the late 1800s.)
108. Ibid., 217–82.
109. Notably, many services—particularly policing and aid to the poor—lagged substantially behind European counterparts. Ibid., 268–78. The efficiency of municipal debt markets did not help cities provide services that are not and should not be debt financed. And, as Teaford notes, political machines were deeply involved in these areas, while they largely left city treasurers and chief engineers alone. Ibid., 7.
110. Ibid., 280–81; Sbragia, *Debt Wish*, 62–80 (discussing superiority of American urban civic infrastructure at the turn of the century).
111. Teaford, *The Unheralded Triumph*, 219–26.
112. Ibid., 227–32. The same is true for parks, where American cities exceeded British and German ones in square footage (with the exception of London), and public libraries, where all big American cities outdid all German ones in number of books, and generally exceeded British ones as well. Ibid., 252–58.
113. Ibid., 234–38. To be fair, Glasgow, by far the leader in the United Kingdom and Germany, had marginally fewer rides per capita than the biggest American cities except for New York, Chicago, Philadelphia, and Boston. Ibid.
114. Sbragia, *Debt Wish*, 20, 62–79.
115. Amend. XIV, § 4 ("But neither the United States nor any state shall assume or pay any debt or obligation incurred in aid of insurrection or rebellion against the United States, or any claim for the loss or emancipation of any slave; but all such debts, obligations and claims shall be held illegal and void."); Sarah Ludington, Mitu Gulati, and Alfred L. Brophy, "Applied Legal History: Demystifying the Doctrine of Odious Debts," *Theoretical Inquiries in Law* 11 (2010): 247, 272–74 (discussing fate of Confederate debt after passage of Fourteenth Amendment).
116. Ratchford, *American State Debts*, 163 (former confederate states owed $112M in pre–Confederate War debts and interest payments in 1865).

117. John J. Gibbons, "The Eleventh Amendment and State Sovereign Immunity: A Reinterpretation," *Columbia Law Review* 83 (1983): 1976–77 (describing debt issuance and spending during Reconstruction); Ratchford, *American State Debts*, 164–84 (describing debt issuance of the period through an extremely pro-Redeemer lens).

118. John V. Orth, *The Judicial Power of the United States: The Eleventh Amendment in American History* (New York: Oxford University Press, 1987), 94–96.

119. Ludington et al., "Applied Legal History," 276.

120. V. Markham Lester, "The Effect of Southern State Bond Repudiation and British Debt Collection Efforts on Anglo-American Relations, 1840–1940," *Journal British Studies* 52, no. 2 (2013): 415.

121. Christopher Shortell, *Rights, Remedies, and the Impact of State Sovereign Immunity* (Albany: SUNY Press, 2008), 87–90. However, Virginia was less successful than other states in repudiating its debts. Virginia bonds had been written in a way that allowed them to be used to pay state taxes, a promise the Court held it could less easily revoke. See *McGahey v. Virginia*, 135 U.S. 662, 664–65 (1890); *In re Ayers*, 123 U.S. 443, 507–08 (1887); *Virginia Coupon Cases*, 114 U.S. 269, 269–70 (1885); *Antoni v. Greenhow*, 107 U.S. 769, 782 (1883); *Hartman v. Greenhow*, 102 U.S. 672, 685 (1881).

122. Luddington et al., "Applied Legal History," 277–78 ("Viewed through the lens of the times, the post-Reconstruction repudiations by Southern states were paradigmatic odious debt cases").

123. Ibid., 248.

124. That these arguments could be used by post-Reconstruction southern states highlights the central problem of the odious debt doctrine, that what appears to be odious to one group looks completely ordinary (or better) to another, and vice versa. The deep irony of the invocation of odious debt arguments by post-Reconstruction southern states is that these White-dominated, segregationist successor regimes were far more unrepresentative and oppressive than the mixed-race Reconstruction era governments that issued the debt. Ibid., 278 ("This further illustrates the difficulty in making moral judgments about the despotic nature of a prior government. Such judgments are all too fluid; what may appear to be a legitimate government to one set of voters and judges can soon be seen as despotic.").

125. Ibid., 277. Histories of the period accepted Southern odious debt arguments in, well, odious terms. For example, Ratchford argued that because "negroes and carpetbaggers predominated" in state legislatures, "the most ignorant, corrupt and venal lawmakers ever to hold office in this country" and that corruption, the lack of benefit for residents, and the huge size of the debts made repudiation acceptable. Ratchford, *American State Debts*, 169, 192–94.

126. Orth, *The Judicial Power*, 1–9; Gibbons, "The Eleventh Amendment," 1989–91.

127. U.S. Const. amend. XI.

128. Osborn, 22 U.S. at 824; Orth, *The Judicial Power*, 58–61 (describing the holding in *Osborn*). But see *Governor of Georgia v. Madrazo*, 26 U.S. (1 Pet.) 110 (1828) (suggesting exceptions to the rule in *Osborn*); Michael G. Collins, "The Conspiracy Theory of the Eleventh Amendment," *Columbia Law Review* 88, no. 1 (1988): 212 (reviewing Orth's book and arguing that he overstates the extent of the change in the doctrine announced in *Louisiana v. Jumel*, although agreeing that "precedent hardly foreordained the result").

129. Board of Liquidation v. McComb, 92 U.S. 531 (1875).

130. Orth, *The Judicial Power*, 60–70; Gibbons, "The Eleventh Amendment," 1992 ("Chief Justice Waite's majority opinion in *Jumel* is no more than a pathetic effort to distinguish [the Court's long-standing precedent].")

131. See Gibbons, "The Eleventh Amendment," 1980–2002 (summarizing the sovereign immunity cases of the period); *Louisiana v. Jumel*, 107 U.S. 711, 721 (1883) (describing Louisiana's repudiation law).

132. The Court argued that the central distinction between *McComb*, the 1775 case allowing a *mandamus* remedy, and *Jumel* was that in the prior case the money was held in trust for the creditors. *Jumel*, 107 U.S. at 727. Orth calls this distinction "specious." Orth, *The Judicial Power*, 66–68.

133. 107 U.S at 726 (distinguishing McComb); 107 U.S. at 728, 733 (Field, J. dissenting) (Louisiana's repudiation is "a direct violation of the inhibition of the Federal Constitution against the impairment of the obligation of contracts. Is this inhibition against the repudiation by the State of her engagements of any efficacy? The majority of the court answer No.'"); 107 U.S. at 746, 748–9 (Harlan, J. dissenting) ("Here are contract rights which, but for the nullifying provisions in the new Constitution of Louisiana, the courts ... unquestionably protect by the process of injunction, and also, if need be, by mandamus .... Now ... the judicial arm of the nation is hopelessly paralyzed in the presence of an ordinance, destructive of those rights, and passed in admitted violation of the Constitution of the United States.")
134. 108 U.S. 76 (1883).
135. 134 U.S. 1 (1890).
136. Orth, *The Judicial Power*, 1–10; Gibbons, "The Eleventh Amendment," 1976–2002.
137. Notably, near the same time, Minnesota also repudiated its debts, but after a state court held that the repudiation violated the Contract Clause, the state reversed itself and paid off the debt. Ratchford, *American State Debts*, 230–32.
138. Shortell, *Rights, Remedies*, 110.
139. Lester, "The Effect of Southern State Bond Repudiation," 427–28. British lenders attempted to make the federal government accept repudiated Southern bonds to offset British World War I debts to no avail. Ibid., 429–33.
140. See Richard Franklin Bensel, *The Political Economy of American Industrialization, 1877–1900* (New York: Cambridge University Press, 2000).
141. Jeremy Atack, Robert A. Margo, and Paul Rhode, "Industrialization and Urbanization in Nineteenth Century America," NBER Working Paper 28597 (2021), https://www.nber.org/papers/w28597.

Chapter 4

1. US Department of the Treasury, "Tax Expenditures," Nov. 11, 2015, https://www.treasury.gov/resource-center/tax-policy/Documents/Tax-Expenditures-FY2017.pdf. I will discuss the exemption at length in Chapter 11.
2. See Isabel Rodriguez-Tejedo and John Joseph Wallis, "Fiscal Institutions and Fiscal Crises," in *When States Go Broke*, eds. Peter Conti-Brown and David Skeel (New York: Cambridge University Press, 2012), 13–15 . It went up to 27.9% of GDP in 1932, but this huge spike was in large part due to declining GDP in the Great Depression. Ibid. Even so, local capital expenditures doubled between 1920 and 1930. Robert P. Inman, "Transfers and Bailouts: Institutions for Enforcing Local Fiscal Discipline with Lessons from U.S. Federalism," in *Fiscal Decentralization and the Challenge of Hard Budget Constraints*, eds. Jonathan Rodden, Gunnar Eskelund, and Jennie Litvack (Cambridge, MA: MIT Press, 2003), 58.
3. Rodriguez-Tejedo and Wallis, "Fiscal Institutions and Fiscal Crises," 13–15.
4. Jon C. Teaford, *The Rise of the States: Evolution of American State Government* (Baltimore: Johns Hopkins University Press, 2002), 96–97, 100.
5. Inman, "Transfers and Bailouts," 58–59; Omer Kimhi, "Chapter 9 of the Bankruptcy Code: A Solution in Search of a Problem," *Yale Journal on Regulation* 27, no. 2 (2010): 351, 361–62.
6. Inman, "Transfers and Bailouts," at 58.
7. Ibid., 59.
8. A. M. Hillhouse, *Municipal Bonds: A Century of Experience* (New York: Prentice-Hall, 1936), 9.
9. John Joseph Wallace and Wallace E. Oates, "The Impact of the New Deal on American Federalism," in *The Defining Moment: The Great Depression and the American Economy in the Twentieth Century*, eds. Michael D. Bordo, Claudia Goldin, and Eugene N. White (Chicago: University of Chicago Press, 1998); James T. Patterson, "The New Deal and the States," *American Historical Review* 73, no. 1 (Oct. 1979): 70; John Joseph Wallis, "The Birth of the Old Federalism: Financing the New Deal, 1932–1940," *Journal of Economic History* 44, no. 1 (Mar. 1984): 139. Also, due to patterns of federal aid distribution, there was also a change in the relative power of state and local governments, with state governments growing very substantially over this period. See Karen M. Tani, *States of Dependency: Welfare, Rights, and American Governance, 1935–1972* (New York: Cambridge University Press, 2016)

(discussing how federal role in welfare spending increased power of state officials relative to local officials); Ronald Snell, "State Finance in the Great Depression," *National Conference of State Legislatures*, Mar. 5, 2009, https://www.ncsl.org/research/fiscal-policy/state-finance-in-the-great-depression.aspx (describing increasing role of states and federal government and declining relative role of local governments after the Great Depression).

10. After the New Deal, most federal money continued to be provided through specific programs aimed at specific policy ends, rather than broad grants of cash to states. In the 1970s, the federal government briefly adopted "general revenue sharing," a program under which the federal government gave states and localities money with only the loosest of conditions. General revenue sharing was short-lived, though, eliminated in the 1980s under President Ronald Reagan. Rena I. Steinzor, "Unfunded Environmental Mandates and the 'New (New) Federalism': Devolution, Revolution, or Reform?," *Minnesota Law Review* 81, no. 97 (1996) (describing demise of general revenue sharing); Robert P. Hey, "A Federal Era Ends," *Christian Science Monitor*, Oct. 6, 1986; James K. Galbraith, Michael Lind, and Martin J. Luby, "The Case for Revenue Sharing: Fiscal Equalization and the COVID-19 Recession," Texas LBJ School, Dec. 8, 2020, https://lbj.utexas.edu/resiliency-toolkit/revenue-sharing.

11. Eric Weiner, "What Happens When City Hall Goes Bankrupt?," *National Public Radio*, Feb. 28, 2008.

12. Kimhi, "Chapter 9 of the Bankruptcy Code," 362.

13. Ibid., 364.

14. Faitoute Iron & Steel Co. v. City of Asbury Park, 316 U.S. 502, 514–15 (1942).

15. Alan Schwartz, "A Normative Theory of Business Bankruptcy," *Virginia Law Review* 91, no. 5 (2005) (arguing that reducing the cost of capital should be the only goal of bankruptcy law). This is not to minimize the enormous conceptual differences between municipal and corporate bankruptcy, a subject which I will return to in Chapter 5. Adam J. Levitin, "Bankrupt Politics and the Politics of Bankruptcy," *Cornell Law Review* 97 (2012)(discussing differences between municipal and corporate bankruptcy).

16. Michael W. McConnell and Randal C. Picker, "When Cities Go Broke: A Conceptual Introduction to Municipal Bankruptcy," *University of Chicago Law Review* 60 (1996): 450–54; Kimhi, "Chapter 9 of the Bankruptcy Code," 365.

17. 298 U.S. 513 (1936).

18. Ibid., 531 ("[States or their political subdivisions] are no longer free to manage their own affairs; the will of Congress prevails over them: although inhibited, the right to tax might be less sinister.")

19. See Kimhi, "Chapter 9 of the Bankruptcy Code," 366.

20. 304 U.S. 27, 52–53 (1938) ("The statute is carefully drawn so as not to impinge upon the sovereignty of the State").

21. Ibid., 54.

22. See Juliet M. Moringiello, "Goals and Governance in Municipal Bankruptcy," *Washington & Lee Law Review* 71, no. 1 (2016): 403 (arguing that Chapter 9 was designed to facilitate state oversight of municipalities, allowing them to overcome holdout problems in limited circumstances as part of a broader state response to local fiscal problems).

23. John Patrick Hunt, "Taxes and Ability to Pay in Municipal Bankruptcy," *Washington Law Review* 515 (2016): 531–39 (reviewing legislative history).

24. O. Emre Ergungor, "Sovereign Default in the US," Federal Reserve Cleveland Working Paper 16–09, Mar. 2016, https://www.clevelandfed.org/newsroom-and-events/publications/working-papers/2016-working-papers/wp-1609-sovereign-default-in-the-us.aspx; Benjamin Ulysses Ratchford, *American State Debts* (Durham, NC: Duke University Press, 1941), 383.

25. Ergungor, "Sovereign Default," 3.

26. Ibid.; Ratchford, *American State Debts*, 386.

27. Ergungor, "Sovereign Default," 4.

28. Lee Reaves, "Highway Bond Refunding in Arkansas," *Arkansas History Quarterly* 2 (1943): 316, 318.

29. Ratchford, *American State Debts*, 386.

30. Robert Slavin, "Arkansas' 1930s Default Foreshadowed Puerto Rico," *Bond Buyer*, Nov. 2, 2015.

31. Ergungor, "Sovereign Default," 4.

32. Ibid.

33. Ibid., at 6. Ratchford, *American State Debts*, 395; Reaves, "Highway Bond Refunding," 319–20.

34. Ratchford, *American State Debts*, 395; Ergungor, "Sovereign Default," 6.

35. Ratchford, *American State Debts*, 397–98.

36. Ergungor, "Sovereign Default," 7.

37. See Chapter 3(b).

38. Hubbell v. Leonard, 6 F. Supp. 145, 151 (E.D. Ark. 1934) (creating injunction against state treasurer from allocating tax money to purposes other than paying debts). This decision was legally dubious, given that the Treasurer was representing the state, which had sovereign immunity. Anna Gelpern, "Bankruptcy, Backwards: The Problem of Quasi-Sovereign Debt," *Yale Law Journal* 121, no. 4 (2012): 898 n.29 (describing *Hubbell* as an "outlier"); Clayton P. Gillette, "What States Can Learn from Municipal Insolvency," in *When States Go Broke*, eds. Peter Conti-Brown and David A. Skeel Jr. (Cambridge: Cambridge University Press, 2012), 112, 112 n. 56 (arguing that *Hubbell* was wrongly decided). Amazingly, one of judges in the case was John Martineau, who had been governor when some of the bonds were issued. See Hubbell, 6 F. Supp. at 145; Robert Slavin, "How Arkansas Solved Its 1930s Debt Crisis," *Bond Buyer* (Nov. 3, 2015).

39. Ergungor, "Sovereign Default," 8.

40. Slavin, "How Arkansas Solved," 38.

41. Ergungor, "Sovereign Default," 10–11.

42. Ibid., 12. An initial refunding plan was rejected by voters.

43. Ibid., 12; Reaves, "Highway Bond Refunding," 326–28.

44. Rodriguez-Tejedo and Wallis, "Fiscal Institutions and Fiscal Crises," 13–15.

45. Colin H. McCubbins and Mat McCubbins, "Cheating on Their Taxes: When Are Tax Limitations Effective at Limiting State Taxes, Expenditures, and Budgets?," *Tax Law Review* 67 (2014): 507; Kirk J. Stark, "The Right to Vote on Taxes," *Northwestern University Law Review* 97, no. 1 (2001): 191.

46. Shayak Sarkar and Josh Rosenthal, "Exclusionary Taxation," *Harvard Civil Rights and Civil Liberties* 53 (2018): 619.

47. McCubbins and McCubbins, "Cheating on Their Taxes," 46.

48. Congressional Budget Office, "Public Spending on Transportation and Water Infrastructure, 1956 to 2017," Oct. 2018, https://www.cbo.gov/publication/54539.

49. There are other examples, Cleveland in the 1970s most notably, but I am going to focus on the centers of financial and political power. Emily D. Johnson and Ernest Young, "The Constitutional Law of State Debt," *Duke Journal of Constitutional Law and Public Policy* 117, no. 149 (2012) (discussing Cleveland default); Todd Swanstrom, *The Crisis of Growth Politics: Cleveland, Kucinich, and the Challenge of Urban Populism* (1985), 1–9.

50. There are other examples, Cleveland in the 1970s most notably, but I am going to focus on the centers of financial and political power. Emily D. Johnson and Ernest Young, "The Constitutional Law of State Debt," *Duke Journal of Constitutional Law and Public Policy* 117, no. 149 (2012) (discussing Cleveland default); Todd Swanstrom, *The Crisis of Growth Politics: Cleveland, Kucinich, and the Challenge of Urban Populism* (1985), 1–9.

51. ("There are four basic reasons for the condition of New York City's finances in 1975. They are: 1) changing population and economic characteristics; 2) national economic difficulties; 3) state and federal government action; 4) inaction and weaknesses in the political system itself.")

52. Ibid., 1121 ("The fact that the City performs so many functions is not only a matter of taste or choice. No other large city in this country has as many services assigned to it as the City of New York."); Omer Kimhi, "A Tale of Four Cities—Models of State Intervention in Distressed Localities Fiscal Affairs," *University of Cincinnati Law Review* 80 (2012): 881, 918 n.205 ("In 1975, New York's labor costs per capita were between two and five times bigger than those of most other major cities in the U.S.").

53. Shalala and Bellamy, "A State Saves a City," 1122.

54. Ibid., 1119–22.

55. Ibid., 1124–26.

56. Notably, when the City's budget started getting very tight, rather than giving aid, Governor Nelson Rockefeller backed increasing the city's ability to borrow short-term. Before the change, the city could only borrow short-term what it earned in revenues the year before. Rockefeller backed legislation to allow the city to borrow as much as it expected to receive in revenue that year, a number the city could stretch if it wanted to borrow. Richard Ravitch, *So Much to Do: A Full Life of Business, Politics, and Confronting Fiscal Crises* 81 (New York: Public Affairs, 2014).

57. Ibid., 45–53 (discussing UDC crisis).

58. Lizbeth Cohen, *Saving America's Cities: Ed Logue and the Struggle to Renew Urban America in the Suburban Age* (New York: Farrar Strous & Giroux, 2019) (discussing creation of UDC).

59. Ravitch, *So Much to Do*, 55–70.

60. Ibid., 75.

61. Ravitch, *So Much to Do*, 55–70; Shalala and Bellamy, "A State Saves a City," 1124.

62. Quirk v. Mun. Assistance Corp. for City of N.Y., 41 N.Y.2d 644 (1977) (describing how MAC bonds worked).

63. Seymour P. Lachman, and Robert Polner, *The Man Who Saved New York: Hugh Carey and the Great Fiscal Crisis of 1975* (Albany: SUNY Press Excelsior Editions, 2011), 114 (discussing relationship between MAC and PFA); Ravitch, *So Much To Do*, 55–70 (describing how MAC built on PFA approach).

64. Shalala and Bellamy, "A State Saves a City," 1128; Ravitch, *So Much to Do*, 90–93.

65. Clayton P. Gillette, "Dictatorships for Democracy: Takeovers of Financially Failed Cities," *Columbia Law Review* 114 (2014): 1373, 1462; Robert W. Bailey, *The Crisis Regime: The MAC, the EFCB, and the Impact of the New York City Financial Crisis* (Albany: SUNY Press, 1984), 23–46.

66. Gillette, "Dictatorships," 1394.

67. Flushing Nat'l Bank v. Mun. Assistance Corp. for City of N.Y., 40 N.Y.2d 731 (1976) (holding that the Moratorium Act unconstitutionally replaced Full Faith and Credit with moral debt). Notably, the Court of Appeals decided the case on state constitutional grounds, rendering Supreme Court review impossible, and gave the City and State a substantial amount of time to respond to the decision, an outcome that was not too unfavorable. Ibid., 741. Although the City lost the case, the Court of Appeals decision ensured that the Supreme Court would not issue an opinion that truly upset the recovery of the City's finances.

68. Scholars tell the same story. "The reluctance of the federal government to bail out local governments in distress continues to this day best symbolized by President Ford's response to New York City's request for federal assistance following its 1974–75 default." Inman, "Transfers and Bailouts," 59.

69. Frank Van Riper, "Ford to City: Drop Dead," *New York Daily News*, Oct. 30, 1975, A1; Clayton P. Gillette and David A. Skeel Jr., "Governance Reform and the Judicial Role in Municipal Bankruptcy," *Yale Law Journal* 125 (2016): 1150, 1237.

70. See Clayton P. Gillette, "Fiscal Federalism, Political Will, and Strategic Use of Municipal Bankruptcy," *University of Chicago Law Review* 79 (2012): 304 (reviewing literature showing that the problems New York City's fiscal crisis created for municipal bond market and for banks created political pressure on Ford to support aid); Ravitch, *So Much to Do*, 90 (discussing pressure put on Ford by European leaders).

71. Gillette and Skeel, "Governance Reform," 1181. New York City Seasonal Financing Act of 1975, 31 U.S.C.A. §§ 1501–10 (1976). The effect of Ford's speech being what was remembered surely had the effect of reducing moral hazard, despite the federal government actually providing aid. Were this intentional, it would have been a masterstroke, but I am not sure that it was.

72. Nor were they very harsh, to be fair. Gillette, "Fiscal Federalism," 307 (arguing that conditions in Seasonal Financing Act are less harsh than one generally sees in state aid).

73. Ibid., 304 ("The few recent instances of imminent default by major cities provide some additional evidence that centralized governments that intervene in the face of municipal fiscal distress are motivated largely by a perception of contagion risk.")

74. Ravitch, *So Much to Do*, 92–94.

75. Ibid.

76. For a full discussion of this issue, see the Appendix to Chapter 10.

77. Gillette and Skeel, "Governance Reform," 1180–83.

78. Kimhi, "Chapter 9 of the Bankruptcy Code," 359–61.

79. Inman, "Transfers and Bailouts," 70.

80. Another possibility, of course, is that some people worry too much about moral hazard.

81. See "Note, Democracy or Distrust? Restoring Home Rule for the District of Columbia in the Post-Control Board Era," *Harvard Law Review* 111 (1998): 2045, 2049 (describing the coming of home rule in 1973).

82. Alice Rivlin, "The Fiscal Problem of Being Washington D.C." in *Building the Best Capital City in the World,* DC Appleseed and Our Nation's Capital, 2008, 23–27, https://www.brookings.edu/wp-content/uploads/2016/07/table_of_contents.pdf. . Rivlin served as Chair of the DC Control Board from 1998–2000.

83. Carol O'Cleireacain, *The Orphaned Capital: Adopting the Right Revenues for the District of Columbia* (Washington, DC: Brookings Institution Press, 1997), 103–05.

84. Rivlin, "The Fiscal Problem," 26.

85. Jon Bouker, "The D.C. Revitalization Act: History, Provisions and Promises" in *Building the Best Capital City in the World* (describing fiscal imposition associated with home rule)

86. Ibid., 81.

87. Campbell Gibson and Kay Jung, "Historical Census Statistics on Population Totals by Race, 1790 to 1990, and by Hispanic Origin, 1970 to 1990, For Large Cities and Other Urban Places in the United States," U.S. Census Population Division Working Paper 76 (2005), https://www.census.gov/content/dam/Census/library/working-papers/2002/demo/POP-twps0 056.pdf (DC population fell from 756,510 in 1970 to 606,900 in 1990); Yesim Sayin Taylor, "Twenty Years after the Revitalization Act, the District of Columbia Is a Different City," D.C. Policy Center, Dec. 19, 2017, https://www.dcpolicycenter.org/publications/twenty-years-revitalization-act-district-columbia-different-city/ (DC lost 12% of its population between 1990 and 1997).

88. Metropolitan Police Department District of Columbia, "A Study of Homicides in the District of Columbia" (Oct. 2001): 2, https://mpdc.dc.gov/sites/default/files/dc/sites/mpdc/publ ication/attachments/homicidereport_0.pdf; Natalie Delgado, "Murders in D.C. Jumped 40 Percent in 2018," WAMU, Dec. 2018, https://wamu.org/story/18/12/28/murders-in-d-c-jumped-40-percent-in-2018/.

89. "Democracy or Distrust," 2051; Bouker, "The D.C. Revitalization Act," 82–84.

90. Bouker, "The D.C. Revitalization Act," 86–98.

91. Ibid., 87.

92. Taylor, "Twenty Years After."

93. Not to say the reforms will necessarily be good, or that the suspension of local democracy will lead to good outcomes. Gillette, "Dictatorships," 1414–16 (discussing the debate over and then laying out the case for emergency managers as a response to fiscal crises.)

94. Stephen Eide, "Connecticut's Broken Cities: Laying the Conditions for Growth in Poor Urban Communities," Manhattan Institute (Jan. 2017) https://media4.manhattan-instit ute.org/sites/default/files/Broken-Cities-FINAL-for-WEB.pdf (describing Hartford's fiscal challenges).

95. Amanda Albright, "Any Deeply Indebted City Might Want the Bailout Hartford Got," *Bloomberg,* March 28, 2018, https://www.bloomberg.com/news/articles/2018-03-28/any-deeply-indebted-city-might-want-the-bailout-hartford-got (describing aid to Hartford); Christopher Keating, "Gov. Malloy Defends Long-Term Hartford Bailout," *Harford Courant,* Apr. 13, 2018.

96. In Connecticut, the state government created something called the Municipal Assistance Review Board (MARB), which gave Hartford access to extra municipal assistance. See Municipal Accountability Review Board (MARB) Sections 349 to 376 of Public Act 17–2, June Special Session https://portal.ct.gov/-/media/OPM/Secretary/MARBsummary pdf.pdf?la=en; Paul Burton, "Connecticut Assumption of Hartford Debt Pays Immediate Dividend to City's Credit," *Bond Buyer,* Mar. 27, 2018. As Hartford is a "Tier III" city in that system, MARB reviews the city's budget. City of Hartford, "FY2019 Adopted Budget," 5, https://www.hartfordct.gov/files/assets/public/ombg/mgmt-budget-documents/new-fol

der/fy2019adoptedbudgetfinalrgb.pdf. Needless to say, these governance requirements are a far cry from the massive changes the federal government required in DC.

97. Eide, "Connecticut's Broken Cities" (describing fiscal problems in other Connecticut cities); Keith Phaneuf, "Gubernatorial Rivals Find Rare Common Ground on Municipal Bailouts," *CT. Mirror*, Oct. 8, 2018 (describing how both Democratic and Republican candidates for governor oppose bailouts for other Connecticut cities).

Chapter 5

1. They don't all go down by the same amounts. Income tax revenue is more procyclical than sale tax revenue, which itself is more procyclical than property tax revenue, as property values are steadier and not always reassessed frequently (and are assessed using prior sales, creating a backward-looking bias.) Jiri Jonas, "Great Recession and Fiscal Squeeze at U.S. Subnational Government Level," International Monetary Fund Working Paper 12/184 (2012).

2. Tracy Gordon, "State and Local Budgets and the Great Recession," Brookings Institution, Dec. 31, 2012, https://www.brookings.edu/articles/state-and-local-budgets-and-the-great-recession/.

3. Ibid. Notably, state tax increases were a small part of the broader effort to rebalance state budgets; states cut spending by far more. Ibid. ("Despite its severity, states relied less on revenue increases as a solution in the recent downturn."). Despite the collapse of the housing market being central to the economic crisis, local property tax revenue did not fall too far, because reassessments lag property value changes and because property tax rates increased substantially (meaning that property owners were having more taken out of their pockets despite an economic collapse). Byron F. Lutz, Raven Molloy, and Hui Shan, "The Housing Crisis and State and Local Government Tax Revenue: Five Channels," *Regional Science and Urban Economics* 41, no. 4 (2011): 306, 308–10.

4. Robert A. Moffitt, "The Great Recession and the Social Safety Net," *Annals of the American Academy of Political and Social Science* 650, no. 1 (2013): 143–66, https://doi.org/10.1177/0002716213499532.

5. The White House, "The Effect of State Fiscal Relief," n.d., https://obamawhitehouse.archives.gov/administration/eop/cea/EffectsofStatefiscalrelief/.

6. "Private Industry Hit Harder but Bounced Back Faster," Census Bureau (2019), https://www.census.gov/library/stories/2019/10/effects-of-economic-downturn-private-and-public-employment.html.

7. Gordon, "State and Local Budgets and the Great Recession."

8. Josh Bivens, "Why Is Recovery Taking So Long—and Who's to Blame?," Economic Policy Institute, 2016, https://files.epi.org/pdf/110211.pdf.

9. Patrice Hill, "Government Job Cuts Create a Historically Slow Recession Recovery," *Washington Times*, Sept.17, 2013 ("The biggest downsizing of state and local government in modern history has proved to be a . . . a primary reason the four-year-long recovery is more sluggish than other recoveries since World War II,").

10. California did come somewhat close, due to a budget impasse, and was forced at one point to issue what were, in effect, IOUs to pay its bills. Dan Whitcomb and Ciara Linnane, "California Set to Issue IOUs as Fiscal Crisis Weighs," *Reuters*, June 24, 2009.

11. American Recovery and Reinvestment Act of 2009 (Stimulus Bill), Pub. L. No. 111–5, 123 Stat. 115 (codified in scattered sections of 19, 26, 42, 47 U.S.C.); Kimberly Amadeo, "ARRA, Its Details, with Pros and Cons," *Balance*, Apr. 11, 2020, https://www.thebalance.com/arra-details-3306299.

12. Phil Oliff, John Shure, and Nicholas Johnson, "Federal Fiscal Relief Is Working as Intended," Center for Budget and Policy Priorities, June 29, 2009, https://www.cbpp.org/research/federal-fiscal-relief-is-working-as-intended; https://www.commonwealthfund.org/publications/newsletter-article/early-federal-action-health-policy-impact-states. The "match" is how much federal government money is given to a state per dollar that state spends on Medicaid, and varies by state based on wealth levels. "Federal Medical Assistance Percentage (FMAP) for Medicaid and Multiplier," Kaiser Family Foundation, n.d. https://www.kff.org/medicaid/state-indicator/federal-matching-rate-and-multiplier/?currentTimeframe=0&sortMo

del=%7B%22colId%22:%22Location%22,%22sort%22:%22asc%22%7D (listing different matching rates for states).

13. Oliff, Shure, and Johnson, "Federal Fiscal Relief Is Working as Intended."

14. Congressional Research Service, "Federal Grants to State and Local Governments: A Historical Perspective on Contemporary Issues," CRS Report no. R40638 (Washington, DC: Congressional Research Service, 2019), https://fas.org/sgp/crs/misc/R40638.pdf; Oliff, Shure, and Johnson, "Federal Fiscal Relief Is Working as Intended,"

15. Oliff, Shure, and Johnson, "Federal Fiscal Relief Is Working as Intended"; Robert P. Inman, "States in Fiscal Distress," National Bureau of Economic Research, Working Paper No. 16086 (2010) https://www.nber.org/papers/w16086.pdf.

16. "Viewing total ARRA funding as a single federal policy, it is best described as a three-year formula grant providing temporary fiscal relief from rising Medicaid costs and short-term fiscal stress with a few dollars for highway construction and a lot of lump-sum aid per capita in the guise of expanded and new program initiatives." Inman, "States in Fiscal Distress."

17. Gabriel Chodorow-Reich, Laura Feiveson, Zachary Liscow, and William Gui Woolston, "Does State Fiscal Relief during Recessions Increase Employment? Evidence from the American Recovery and Reinvestment Act," American Journal of Economic Policy 4, no. 3 (Aug. 2012): 118, 121.

18. Michael Grunwald, The New New Deal: The Hidden Story of Change in the Obama Era (New York: Simon & Schuster, 2013).

19. "Ten Years Later: How the Financial Crisis Reverberated into Municipal Bonds," Bond Buyer, Oct. 28, 2018.

20. "Timeline: Bond Insurers' Ratings," Reuters, Feb. 14, 2008.

21. Christine R. Martell and Robert S. Kravchuk, "The Liquidity Crisis: The 2007–2009 Market Impacts on Municipal Securities," Public Administration Review 72, no. 5 (Sept. 2012): 668, 669, 671.

22. Blaine G. Saito, "Building a Better America: Tax Expenditure Reform and the Case of State and Local Government Bonds and Build America Bonds," Georgetown Journal of Law and Public Policy 11, no. 2 (May 2013): 577, 599–602.

23. Internal Revenue Service, "Tax-Exempt Governmental Bonds" (2019), https://www.irs.gov/pub/irs-pdf/3p4079.pdf, 2.

24. SIFMA, "SIFMA Fact Sheet: About Build America Bonds," 1, https://www.sifma.org/wp-content/uploads/2018/01/Build-America-Bond-Factsheet-08-2009.pdf.

25. Ibid.

26. Treasury Department, "Build America Bonds Are Helping State and Local Governments Finance Infrastructure Projects and Create Jobs While Saving Taxpayers Billions," June 2010, https://www.treasury.gov/initiatives/recovery/Documents/Build%20America%20Bonds%20Fact%20Sheet,%2006-10-10.pdf; Andrew Ang, Vineer Bhansali, and Yuhang Xing, "Build America Bonds," 1–2, National Bureau of Economic Research Working Paper, 16008 (2010), https://www.nber.org/system/files/working_papers/w16008/w16008.pdf.

27. Ang et al, "Build America Bonds."

28. Dario Cestau, Richard C. Green, and Norman Schurhoff, "Tax-Subsidized Underpricing: The Market for Build America Bonds," Journal of Monetary Economics 60, no. 5 (July 2013): 593.

29. See Chapter 11 for a more extensive discussion.

30. Jordan Eizenga and Seth Hanlon, "Bring Back BABs: A Proposal to Strengthen the Municipal Bond Market with Build America Bonds," Center for American Progress, 5–6 (Apr. 2011), https://www.americanprogress.org/wp-content/uploads/issues/2011/04/pdf/build_america_bonds.pdf.

31. Robert Puents, Patrick Sabol, and Joseph Kane, "Revive Build America Bonds (BABs) to Support State and Local Investments," Brookings Institution, Aug. 2013, https://www.brookings.edu/wp-content/uploads/2016/06/Fed-Series-Babs-82813.pdf.

32. Ibid.

33. Ibid.

34. Brian Tumulty, "Revival of Build America Bonds Receives Bipartisan Support," Bond Buyer, May 18, 2021.

35. Barb Rosewicz and Daniel Newman, "Decade after Recession Began, Tax Revenue Higher in 34 States," Pew Research Center, May 2, 2018, https://www.pewtrusts.org/en/research-and-analysis/articles/2018/05/02/decade-after-recession-began-tax-revenue-higher-in-34-states (showing slow recovery of state tax revenue after recession).

36. Sara Hinkley, "Public Sector Impacts of the Great Recession and COVID-19," University of California Berkeley Labor Center 4 (2020), https://laborcenter.berkeley.edu/wp-content/uploads/2020/06/Public-Sector-Impacts-of-the-Great-Recession-and-COVID-19.pdf. Also, overall population and total output increased, meaning that state and local employment was still lower relative to a bigger, richer country.

37. State Budget Crisis Task Force, "Report of the State Budget Crisis Task Force: Final Report," Peter G. Peterson Foundation, Jan. 2014, https://www.volckeralliance.org/publications/report-state-budget-crisis-task-force, 10. They could have, of course, raised taxes more. But revenue increases were only a small part of state responses to the Great Recession.

38. Ibid. Medicaid spending increased by more than ordinary health care spending, in fact.

39. Heather Gillers, "The Long Bull Market Has Failed to Fix Public Pensions, "*Wall Street Journal*, Apr. 10, 2019, A1; Alicia H. Munnell, Jean-Pierre Aubry, and Caroline V. Crawford, "How Big a Burden Are State and Local OPEB Benefits," Center for Retirement Research, Mar. 2016, https://crr.bc.edu/wp-content/uploads/2016/03/slp_48.pdf.

40. Alicia H. Munnell and Jean-Pierre Aubry, "An Overview of the Pension/OPEB Landscape," Center for Retirement Research Working Paper 2016–11 (2016), https://papers.ssrn.com/sol3/papers.cfm?abstract_id=2847725, 8–11.

41. "State and Local Finance Initiative," Urban Institute (2011), https://www.urban.org/policy-centers/cross-center-initiatives/state-and-local-finance-initiative/projects/state-and-local-backgrounders/state-and-local-government-pensions.

42. Alicia H. Munnell, Jean-Pierre Aubry, Josh Hurwitz, and Laura Quinby, "Comparing Compensation: State-Local versus Private Sector Workers," Center for Retirement Research, Sept. 2011, http://crr.bc.edu/wp-content/uploads/2011/09/slp_20-508.pdf.

43. Jack M. Beerman, "The Public Pension Crisis," *Washington and Lee Law Review* 70, no. 1 (Winter 2013): 3, 7, 26–31.

44. Munnell and Aubry, "An Overview of the Pension/OPEB Landscape," 8–11.

45. Heaton v. Quinn (In re Pension Reform Litig.), 32 N.E.3d 1 (Ill. 2015); Beerman, "The Public Pension Crisis," at 3, 7, 26–31; Amy Monahan, "Statutes as Contracts? The 'California Rule' and Its Impact on Public Pension Reform," *Iowa Law Review* 97 (2012): 1029, 1032–1033.

46. Monahan, "Statutes as Contracts?"

47. Ibid.

48. Mary Williams Walsh, "Rhode Island Averts Pension Disaster without Raising Taxes," *New York Times*, Sept. 25, 2015.

49. Alameda City Deputy Sheriff's Association v. Alameda City Employees' Retirement Association, 9 Cal. 5th 1032 (2020) (changes to pension spiking rules are constitutional); Justus v. State, 2014 Co. 75, 336 P.3d 202 (2014) (changes to cost of living adjustments are constitutional).

50. In 2015, the Illinois Supreme Court found that a series of state pension reforms violated Illinois's strong California-Rule protections for pensions. Heaton, 32 N.E.3d at 3. In so doing, the court noted that when Illinois's constitution was passed, the authors of the pension clause openly considered and rejected a provision requiring the state to fund its pensions, arguing instead that legal protections for pensioners would force the state to save enough. Ibid., 12–14.

51. Beerman, "The Public Pension Crisis," 26–31.

52. Tom Sgouros, "The Case for New Pension Accounting Standards," National Conference Public Employee Retirement Systems (May 2019), https://www.ncpers.org/files/The%20Case%20for%20New%20Pension%20Accounting%20Standards_May%202019.pdf.

53. Jeffrey R. Brown and David W. Wilcox, "Discounting State and Local Pension Liabilities," *American Economic Review* 99, no. 2 (2009): 538–42.

54. "Pension Plan Valuation: Views on Using Multiple Measures to Offer a More Complete Financial Picture," Government Accountability Office, GAO-14–264 (2014), https://www.gao.gov/products/gao-14-264, 1.

55. The Government Accounting Standards Board (GASB) forced state and local governments to reduce the discount rate for the underfunded portion of their pensions in 2015 in a complex way (give or take, it applied a lower discount rate to the unfunded portion of their pensions, but not to the funded portion.) But GASB's rules only apply to states' backward-looking accounting statements, not to their budgeting decisions on a going-forward basis. Even so, the huge reduction in published "funded ratios" (or the amount of future benefits governments had saved for) that resulted from GASB's changes did encourage many governments to save more. Aleksandar Andonov, Rob Bauer, and Martijn Cremers, "Pension Fund Asset Allocation and Liability Discount Rates: Camouflage and Reckless Risk Taking by U.S. Public Plans?," *Review of Financial Studies* 30 (2017): 2555 (describing discount rates); Sheila Weinberg, "GASB 67 and GASB 68: What the New Accounting Standards Mean for Public Pension Reporting," Mercatus Center, June 15, 2017, https://www.mercatus.org/publicati ons/urban-economics/gasb-67-and-gasb-68-what-new-accounting-standards-mean-public-pension (explaining GASB rules); Divya Anantharaman and Elizabeth Chuk, "The Impact of Governmental Accounting Standards on Public-Sector Pension Funding," SSRN Working Paper (2019), https://papers.ssrn.com/sol3/papers.cfm?abstract_id=3438074 (showing GASB rules did effect funding decisions by governments).

56. Amy B. Monahan, "Inviolable—or Not: The Legal Status of Retiree Medical Benefits for State and Local Employees," Manhattan Institute, March 31, 2016, https://www.manhattan-instit ute.org/html/inviolable-or-not-legal-status-retiree-medical-benefits-state-and-local-employ ees-8698.html.

57. "Research Announcement: Moody's—US States' Pension Liabilities Fall in Fiscal 2018 amid Higher Investment Returns," Moody's Investors Service, 1 (Sept. 17, 2019), https:// m.moodys.com/research/Moodys-US-states-pension-liabilities-fall-in-fiscal-2018-amid— PBM_1195186.

58. Munnell and Aubry, "An Overview of the Pension/OPEB Landscape" (showing Illinois, New Jersey, Connecticut, Hawaii, and Kentucky as the most indebted states relative to revenue; and Chicago as the most-indebted city relative to revenue).

59. "Municipal Securities: Financing the Nation's Infrastructure" Municipal Securities Rulemaking Board, 2019, http://www.msrb.org/~~~/media/Files/Resources/MSRB-Inf rastructure-Primer.ashx.

60. Jenifer C. Merkel, "Financing Public Infrastructure: Generational Equity and Municipal Debt," Municipal Research and Service Center, Sept. 1, 2012, http://mrsc.org/Home/Stay-Informed/MRSC-Insight/September-2012/Financing-Public-Infrastructure-Generational-Equit.aspx.

61. In the case of teacher pensions, you could understand today's workforce's productivity to be the product of those past wages, as better teachers improve students' productivity and future happiness. But this is somewhat attenuated by the fact that schoolchildren can move out of a state (and certainly out of a school district). It is hard to understand the pensions owed to, say, police or sanitation workers as anything other than past consumption.

62. Jean-Pierre Aubry, Alicia H. Munnell, and Kevin Wandrei, "2020 Update: Market Decline Worsens the Outlook for Public Plans," Center for Retirement Research, May 2020.

63. Jamie Lenney, Byron Lutz, and Louise Sheiner, "The Sustainability of State and Local Government Pensions: A Public Finance Approach," Brookings Institution, 2–3 (July 14, 2019), https://www.brookings.edu/wp-content/uploads/2019/07/lenney_lutz_sheiner_ MFC_Final.pdf.

64. Ironically, they argue it is not the states with the most underfunded pensions that have the most to worry about, as many of these states have made changes in the pension saving policies that have at least stopped making the problem worse. They argue the biggest problems are in those states that did not reform their pension systems recently.

65. Robert M. Costrell and Josh McGee, "Sins of the Past, Present, and Future: Alternative Pension Funding Policies," Brookings Municipal Finance Conference (July 13–14, 2020), https://www.brookings.edu/wp-content/uploads/2020/07/Sins-of-the-Past-Present-and-Future_Costrell-and-McGee_July-10-2020.pdf.

66. "Tax-Exempt Bonds: A Description of State and Local Government Debt," Congressional Research Service, Feb. 15, 2018, https://crsreports.congress.gov/product/pdf/RL/RL30

638 ("Total debt issuances have slowly increased in the past few years, but have been relatively flat since 2008, . . . The lack of growth in debt outstanding in recent years could be explained by a hesitation to engage in new long-term capital projects given the budget challenges and economic uncertainties facing municipal governments.").

67. Elizabeth McNichol, "It's Time for States to Invest in Infrastructure," Center for Budget and Policy Priorities (Mar. 19, 2019), https://www.cbpp.org/research/state-budget-and-tax/its-time-for-states-to-invest-in-infrastructure (describing need for infrastructure investment); Alexis Madrigal, "The Toxic Bubble of Technical Debt Threatening America," *Atlantic*, Oct. 29, 2019 ("For decades, corporate executives, as well as city, county, state, and federal officials, not to mention voters, have decided against doing the routine maintenance and deeper upgrades to ensure that electrical systems, roads, bridges, dams, and other infrastructure can function properly under a range of conditions. . . . [I]t's really borrowing against the future, without putting that debt on the books.").

68. Jean-Pierre Aubry, Caroline V. Crawford, and Alicia H. Munnell, "How Have Municipal Bond Markets Reacted to Pension Reforms," Center for Retirement Research (2017), http://crr.bc.edu/wp-content/uploads/2017/10/slp_57.pdf; This interacts with aging of a population. Alexander W. Butler and Hanyi Yi, "Aging and Public Financing Costs: Evidence from U.S. Municipal Bond Markets," Draft Paper, Jan. 6, 2020, https://papers.ssrn.com/sol3/papers.cfm?abstract_id=3301648.

69. Juliet M. Moringiello, "Chapter 9 Plan Confirmation Standards and the Role of State Choices," *Campbell Law Review* 37, no. 1 (Symposium 2015).

70. Ibid. The most notable case after the Great Depression and before the Great Recession was probably Orange County, CA, which filed following the failure of a series of investments by its treasurer. County of Orange v. Merrill Lynch & Co., 191 B.R. 1005, 1019–20 (Bankr. C.D. Cal. 1996); Richard W. Trotter, "Running on Empty: Municipal Insolvency and Rejection of Collective Bargaining Agreements in Chapter 9 Bankruptcy," *Southern Illinois University Law Journal* 36, no. 1 (Fall 2011)(discussing Orange County case).

71. 11 U.S.C. § 109(c)(2); The specific authorization language was added to Chapter 9 following a case involving Bridgeport, CT. A court ruled that the state authorized Bridgeport to file by granting it general home rule powers (although it was later deemed ineligible for other reasons). *In re* City of Bridgeport, 128 B.R. 686, 691 (Bankr. D. Conn. 1991) (holding that Bridgeport's home rule authority allowed it to file); *In re* City of Bridgeport, 129 B.R. 332, 339 (Bankr. D. Conn. 1991) (finding that Bridgeport was not insolvent and thus not eligible to file for bankruptcy). Congress responded by passing the new language. Laura Napoli Coordes, "Restructuring Municipal Bankruptcy," *Utah Law Review* 2016, no. 2 (2016): 307, 314–15 (discussing passage of new language).

72. M. Heath Frost, "States as Chapter 9 Bankruptcy Gatekeepers: Federalism, Specific Authorization, and the Protection of Municipal Economic Health," *Mississippi Law Journal* 84 (2015): 817, 834–49 (2015) (surveying the different approaches states take to authorization).

73. "If debt is a promise, default is an acknowledgment that the country was lying, and the 'contagion effect' is the paranoia that there are more liars." Derek Thomson, "What Is the 'Contagion Effect,'" *The Atlantic*, May 18, 2010, https://www.theatlantic.com/business/archive/2010/05/what-is-the-contagion-effect/56858/.

74. For a summary, see Aurelia Chaudhury, Adam J. Levitin, and David Schleicher, "Junk Cities: Resolving Insolvency Crises in Overlapping Local Governments," *California Law Review* 107, no. 2 (Apr. 2019): 459, 483–84.

75. Adam J. Levitin, "Bankrupt Politics and the Politics of Bankruptcy," *Cornell Law Review* 97, no. 6 (Sept. 2012)(noting vast differences between municipal and corporate bankruptcy).

76. 11 U.S.C. § 903.

77. See 11 U.S.C. § 109(c) (2012); Laura Napoli Coordes, "Restructuring Municipal Bankruptcy," *Utah Law Review* 2016, no. 2 (2016): 307, 316–24 (discussing eligibility requirements).

78. Note 70.

79. 11 U.S.C. § 109(c).

80. 11 U.S.C. §§ 362, 901(a), 922 (2012).

81. There are some conditions on the ability to reject collective bargaining agreements. In re City of Vallejo, 403 B.R. 72, 74 (Bankr. E.D. Cal. 2009) (requiring rejections of CBAs to only

happen after reasonable efforts to resolve contract issues and a consideration of the hardships of the rejection on employees). Other bankruptcy courts have used state law governing emergency modifications of contracts as a baseline for this inquiry. See In re County of Orange, 179 B.R. 177, 179 (Bankr. C.D. Cal. 1995).

82. 11 U.S.C. § 903–904.

83. Michael W. McConnell and Randal C. Picker, "When Cities Go Broke: A Conceptual Introduction to Municipal Bankruptcy," *University of Chicago Law Review* 60 (1996): 450–54; Clayton P. Gillette and David A. Skeel Jr., "Governance Reform and the Judicial Role in Municipal Bankruptcy," *Yale Law Journal* 125 (2016): 1150, 1185.

84. 11 U.S.C. § 941.

85. 11 U.S.C. § 943(b)(7). In re Mount Carbon Metropolitan District, 242 B.R. 18, 32 (Bankr. D. Colo. 1999) (holding that, to be feasible, a plan must ensure that the "debtor can both pay pre-petition debt and provide future public services at the level necessary to its viability as a municipality" and must not be "visionary schemes which promise creditors more under a proposed plan than the debtor can possibly attain after confirmation") (citations and quotations omitted); Anderson M. Shackelford, "Is the § 943(b)(7) Feasibility Requirement Feasible? Why Congress Should Clarify Its Chapter 9 Bankruptcy Plan Requirements," *Campbell Law Review* 37, no. 1 (Symposium 2015)(discussing feasibility requirements).

86. 11 U.S.C. § 943(b)(7).

87. *In re* Mount Carbon, 242 B.R. at 34 (applying best interests test); *In re* Sanitary & Improvement District, # 7, 98 B.R. 970 at 975–76 (Bankr. D. Neb. 1989) (same); Moringiello, "Chapter 9 Plan," 79 (best interests tests only requires showing creditors would fare better under the plan than they would outside of bankruptcy").

88. 11 US.C. § 1126(c).

89. 11 U.S.C. § 1129(b) (incorporated into Chapter 9 by 11 U.S.C. § 943 and 11 U.S.C. § 901).

90. Ibid. Lorber v. Vista Irrigation Dist., 127 F.2d 628, 639 (9th Cir. 1942) (citations and quotation marks omitted) ("the test as to the fairness of the plan [is] whether or not the amount to be received by the bondholders is all that they can reasonably expect in the circumstances.")

91. For discussions of the case, see Robin R. Smith, "Southern Discomfort: An Examination of the Financial Crisis in Jefferson County, Alabama," *Houston Business and Tax Law Journal* 10, no. 3 (2010): 363; Mary Jane Richardson, "The Disguise of Municipal Bonds: How a Safe Bet in Investing Can Become an Unexpected Uncertainty during Municipal Bankruptcy," *Campbell Law Review* 37, no. 1 (2015): 187; "The State Role in Local Government Financial Distress," Pew Trust, Apr. 2016, https://www.pewtrusts.org/~/media/assets/2016/04/pew_state_role_in_local_government_financial_distress.pdf, 4, 10, 24–26.

92. Christine Sgarlata Chung, "Government Budgets as the Hunger Games: The Brutal Competition for State and Local Government Resources Given Municipal Securities Debt, Pension and OBEP Obligations, and Taxpayer Needs," *Review of Banking and Financial Law* 33, no. 2 (Mar. 2014): 663.

93. The story of these swaps, and the corruption surrounding them, is wild. Bond Girl, "The Incredible Story of the Jefferson County Bankruptcy—One of the Greatest Financial Rip-offs of All Time," *Business Insider*, Oct. 23, 2011, https://www.businessinsider.com/the-incredible-story-of-the-jefferson-county-bankruptcy-one-of-the-greatest-financial-ripoffs-of-all-time-2011-10.

94. Chung, "Government Budgets as the Hunger Games," 698.

95. Jefferson County v. Weissman, 69 So. 3d 827, 844–45 (Ala. 2011). As with most things about the Jefferson County bankruptcy, the saga of Jefferson County's taxing authority was extremely convoluted. Ibid. ("The case underlying this appeal continues [an] exquisitely complex sequence of legislative enactments and related litigation.") (internal citations and quotations omitted). State courts had invalidated a previous County occupational tax, causing the governor to call the legislature in to an emergency special session in 2009 to give the County the power to impose occupational taxes again. It did so, but the Alabama Supreme Court found that the legislature had not complied with a provision of the state constitution that required the posting of notice in the county for any "special or local law" that only applies to one or several local governments. As a result, the reimposed power to tax was unconstitutional.

96. Richardson, "The Disguise," 198–99. The central legal question in the case involved what the County could do with the revenues still coming in through the sewer system. As the bonds were secured by the revenue from the sewer system, bondholders were entitled to the revenue, but Chapter 9 allows debtors to withhold money for "necessary operating expenses." 11 U.S.C. § 928(b). But it was unclear whether "necessary operating expenses" included (1) capital expenses and depreciation on the sewer system; (2) legal costs associated with bankruptcy. Ibid. The bondholders won on the question of capital expenses and lost on the question of fees associated with the bankruptcy. Bank of N.Y. Mellon v. Jefferson County (In re Jefferson County), 482 B.R. 404, 430–34. After this, the County came forward with a plan of adjustment that included heavy sewer fee increases and substantial write-downs of debt.

97. "Jefferson County Bankruptcy: A Timeline from Beginning to End," AL, June 4, 2013, https://www.al.com/spotnews/2013/06/jefferson_county_bankruptcy_a.html (providing a timeline of the state legislature responses to Jefferson County's crisis).

98. Maria O'Brien Hylton, "Central Falls Retirees v. Bondholders: Assessing Fear of Contagion in Chapter 9 Proceedings," Wayne Law Review 59 (Fall 2013): 525, 526–36; Katherine Newby Kishfy, "Preserving Local Autonomy in the Face of Municipal Financial Crisis: Reconciling Rhode Island's Response to the Central Falls Financial Crisis with the State's Home Rule Tradition," Roger Williams University Law Review 16, no. 2 (Spring 2011): 348, 348–53; "The State Role in Local Government Financial Distress," Pew Trust, Apr. 2016, https://www.pewtrusts.org/~/media/assets/2016/04/pew_state_role_in_local_government_financial_distress.pdf.

99. Hylton, "Central Fall Retirees," 530.

100. Ibid., 526.

101. Central Falls asked a court to appoint its own receiver, but Rhode Island passed a new law to give the state the power to take over the city, which preempted the city's efforts. Moreau v. Flanders, 15 A.3d 565 (R.I. 2011) (ruling that the state receiver law was constitutional and preempted any effort by city to have the court appoint a receiver).

102. R.I. Gen. Laws § 45–12–1 (2013) ("The faith and credit, ad valorem taxes, and general fund revenues of each city, town and district shall be pledged for the payment of the principal of, premium and the interest on, all general obligation bonds and notes of the city or town whether or not the pledge is stated in the bonds or notes, or in the proceedings authorizing their issue and shall constitute a first lien on such ad valorem taxes and general fund revenues."); Hylton, supra note 109, at 526–27.

103. Richard M. Hynes and Steven D. Walt, "Pensions and Property Rights in Municipal Bankruptcy," Review of Banking and Financial Law 33 (2014): 609, 613.

104. Ibid.

105. Hylton, "Central Falls Retirees v. Bondholders," 526.

106. Ibid.

107. Ibid.

108. "The State Role in Local Government Financial Distress," Pew Trust, Apr. 2016, 4, 10, 36, https://www.pewtrusts.org/~/media/assets/2016/04/pew_state_role_in_local_government_financial_distress.pdf (quoting state revenue director Rosemary Booth Gallogly).

109. For discussions of these cases, see Alexandru V. Roman, "Financial Crisis Is a Political Crisis First: How Politics Trumps Sound Fiscal Management—A Case Study of the San Bernardino Bankruptcy," American Bankruptcy Law Journal 90, no. 4 (Dec. 2016): 677; "Modifying or Terminating Pension Plans through Chapter 9 Bankruptcies with a Focus on California," Fordham Urban Law Journal 40, no. 5 (Symposium Mar. 2016): 1975; Christopher J. Tyson, "Exploring the Boundaries of Municipal Bankruptcy," Willamette Law Review 50 (Summer 2014): 661; Laura Napoli Coordes, "Restructuring Municipal Bankruptcy," Utah Law Review 2016, no. 2 (2016): 307; Moringiello, "Goals and Governance in Municipal Bankruptcy," 403.

110. Coordes, "Restructuring Municipal Bankruptcy," 324–25 (discussing length of insolvency determinations).

111. 11 U.S.C. § 109(c)(3) (requiring insolvency); 11 U.S.C. § 101(32)(C) (defining insolvency).

112. In re City of Stockton, 493 B.R. 772, 778–81 (Bankr. E.D. Cal. 2013) (describing conditions in Stockton).

113. Ibid., 788.
114. Ibid., 790.
115. Ibid., 789–90.
116. Ibid.
117. *In re* City of Detroit, 504 B.R. 97, 169 (Bankr. E.D. Mich. 2013) (applying service-delivery insolvency).
118. The exception to this is education. State constitutions include clauses guaranteeing the right to a public education, and courts have interpreted those clauses to give residents the ability to sue to force the state to spend more and differently on public education.
119. Michelle Wilde Anderson, "The New Minimal Cities," *Yale Law Journal* 123, no. 5 (March 2014); 1118, 1195 (describing the lack of a baseline in constitutional law for service delivery insolvency).
120. For instance, in Detroit, the court noted that 40% of the city's 88,000 streetlights were not functioning and the police department's average response time was 58 minutes. In Re: City of Detroit, 504 B.R. at 120 (describing the wait time for ambulance services in Detroit). But how many streetlights are there in a rural area of the Upper Peninsula in Michigan? How long does it take for the police or an ambulance to respond to a call?
121. Anderson, "New Minimal Cities," 1196 (critiquing revenue hill model of service delivery insolvency).
122. Clayton P. Gillette, "How Cities Fail: Service Delivery Insolvency and Municipal Bankruptcy," *Michigan State Law Review*, 2019 (2019); 1238–48 (arguing that population declines among economically integrated actors who would otherwise benefit from agglomeration economies of the city is a good indicia of insolvency); Anderson, "New Minimal Cities," 1196–1200 (discussing possible minimum standards for municipal services).
123. *In re* City of Stockton, 493 B.R. at 790.
124. In addition to the plan of adjustment there was another major pension question in the case. Diane Lourdes Dick, "Bondholders vs Retirees in Municipal Bankruptcies: The Political Economy of Chapter 9," *American Bankruptcy Law Journal* 92, no. 1 (Winter 2018): 73 (discussing the issue). Stockton's pensions are managed by a state agency, CalPERS. The first question the court needed to resolve was whether CalPERS was a contractor or a creditor. The court held that CalPERS was only a creditor for fees, and that its servicing contract in theory could be rejected. Pensioners, and not the state agency, were the true largest creditors. *In re* City of Stockton, 526 B.R. 35, 59 (2015); However, this was not actually invoked, as pensions were not cut in the plan of adjustment. Dick, "Bondholders vs Retirees in Municipal Bankruptcies," 90.
125. Sam Katz and James McGovern (directors), *Gradually, then Suddenly: The Detroit Bankruptcy* (film) (History Making Productions, 2022); Nathan Bomey, *Detroit Resurrected: To Bankruptcy and Back* (New York: W.W. Norton & Company, Inc., 2017) (invoking *The Sun Also Rises*); Jodie Adams Kirshner and Michael Eric Dyson, *Broke: Hardship and Resilience in a City of Broken Promises* (New York: St. Martin's Press, 2019) Ernest Hemingway, *The Sun Also Rises* (New York: Scribner, 2016, originally published 1926), 109.
126. Nathan Bomey and John Gallagher, "How Detroit Went Broke: The Answers May Surprise You—And Blame Coleman Young," *Detroit Free Press*, Sept. 15, 2013 (explaining that city own-source revenue declined by 40% in real terms despite adding income tax, utility tax, and casino gambling tax).
127. Edward L. Glaeser, "Can Detroit Find the Road Forward," *New York Times Economix*, Feb. 22, 2011, https://economix.blogs.nytimes.com/2011/02/22/can-detroit-find-the-road-forward/ (discussing the People Mover); Bomey and Gallagher, "How Detroit Went Broke" (discussing fiscal cost of subsidies to General Motors).
128. Bomey and Gallagher, "How Detroit Went Broke," 2–3.
129. Brian Merchant, "The Ultimate Detroit Ruin Porn," *Vice*, Dec. 10, 2013, https://www.vice.com/en/article/xyw8g7/the-ultimate-detroit-ruin-porn-skiing-through-the-apocalypse.
130. Bomey and Gallagher, "How Detroit Went Broke"
131. "Detroit Uses COPs to Shift Pension Burden and Set a Few Records," *Bond Buyer*, Dec. 28, 2005; *In re* City of Detroit, 504 B.R. 191; Joshua C. Showalter, "The Consequences from Issuing Invalid Municipal Debt: Examining the Voidable Debt Issues in the Detroit

Bankruptcy and Puerto Rican Debt Crisis," *North Carolina Banking Institute* 21, no. 1 (2017): 195.

132. Karen Pierog, "Detroit Files Lawsuit Seeking to Void Pension Debt," *Reuters*, Jan. 31, 2014.

133. "SWAPS, COPS, Lingering Questions in Detroit Bankruptcy," ACLU Michigan (Feb. 5, 2014), https://www.aclumich.org/en/news/swaps-cops-lingering-questions-detroit-bankruptcy.

134. Bomey and Gallagher, "How Detroit Went Broke."

135. Ibid.

136. Ibid.

137. *In re* City of Detroit, 504 B.R. 191 (Bankr. E.D. Mich. 2013).

138. Some language in a Supreme Court decision from 1992, *New York v. United States*, suggested that state acquiescence does not necessarily render an act of the federal government constitutional against a federalism challenge. The *Detroit* court thought this was stray *dicta* and not important, given the clear holding that Chapter 9 was constitutional in United States v. Bekins. *In re* City of Detroit, 504 B.R. at 239–43 (discussing and "explaining some puzzling language in" New York v. United States, 505 U.S. 144 (1992).

139. Ibid., 254. Challengers tried to get an injunction in state court against filing but were beaten to the courtroom by the city's lawyers by a few minutes. Bomey & Gallagher, "How Detroit Went Broke."

140. The federal Constitution bars legislatures from passing laws "impairing the obligation contracts." U.S. Const. Art I., Sec. 10. The same basic right exists in the Michigan Constitution. Mich. Const. Art. IX, Section 24 ("No . . . law impairing the obligation of contract shall be enacted.")

141. Monica Davey, "Finding $816 Million, and Fast, to Save Detroit," *New York Times*, Nov. 7, 2014.

142. *In re* City of Detroit, 504 B.R. at 191–255.

143. Bomey, *Detroit Resurrected*; Kirk Pinho, "Rosen Talks about Detroit's Grand Bargain, the City's Future and Kwame Kilpatrick," *Crain's Detroit Business*, Jan. 22, 2017; "'Grand Bargain' in Detroit Exemplifies New Kind of Philanthropy," *Philanthropy News Digest*, Nov. 17, 2014, https://philanthropynewsdigest.org/news/grand-bargain-in-detroit-exemplifies-new-kind-of-philanthropy; Davey, "Finding $816 Million."

144. James M. Ferris, "Detroit's Grand Bargain: Philanthropy as a Catalyst for a Brighter Future," Center for Philanthropy and Public Policy, 10 (June 2017), http://cppp.usc.edu/wp-content/uploads/2017/08/IHI_Digital_2017.pdf.

145. Bomey and Gallagher, "How Detroit Went Broke."

146. *In re* City of Detroit, 524 B.R. 147 (Bankr. E.D. Mich. 2014); Notably, the city's plan of adjustment gave the holders of the COPs from the 2005 transaction a very low recovery rate because they thought there was a substantial chance a court would find them invalid because they were issued in excess of the city's debt limit. In the end, the holders eventually swapped them for some city assets the value of which is quite variable but which may end up providing them with a very substantial return. Bomey and Gallagher, "How Detroit Went Broke"; Alisa Priddle, "Why Detroit–Windsor Tunnel Plays Key Role in Bankruptcy Deal," *Lansing State Journal*, Sept. 10, 2014.

147. *In re* City of Detroit, 524 B.R. at 159–61.

148. Ibid., 255–58.

149. Ibid., 273–74.

150. "Summary of Plan of Adjustment," City of Detroit, Feb. 21, 2014, https://detroitmi.gov/Portals/0/docs/EM/Announcements/Summary_PlanOfAdjustment.pdf.

151. Orr asked the Obama administration for aid, but this was seen as impossible, given Republican control of Congress. Chris Isidore, "Detroit to Get $300 Million in Federal Help," *CNN Money*, Sept. 27, 2013.

152. President Obama was able to redirect some federal money using his executive authority, and also encourage some private investment in the City. Jackie Calmes, "$300 Million in Detroit Aid, but No Bailout," *New York Times*, Sept. 26, 2013.

153. Robert S. Chirinko, Ryan Chiu, and Shaina Henderson, "What Went Wrong? The Puerto Rican Debt Crisis, the 'Treasury Put,' and the Failure of Market Discipline," *CESifo* Working Paper Series 7558, March 2019.

154. Bomey, *Detroit Resurrected* (telling a heroic story of Orr's tenure).

155. Quinn Klinefelter, "Detroit's Big Comeback," National Public Radio Dec. 28, 2018; John Gallagher, "Detroit's Historic Bankruptcy and More Contributed to City's Revival," *Detroit Free Press*, July 18, 2018; John Gallagher, "Detroit's Reputation Is Rising, but Recovery Still Has a Long Way to Go," *Detroit Free Press*, Nov. 3, 2019; Christine Ferreti, "After Detroit Bankruptcy: Optimism, but 'Challenges Are Real,'" *Detroit News*, July 18, 2018. In the alternative, John Gallagher, "Detroit Can't Cherry-Pick Statistics, Ignore Inconvenient Facts," *Detroit Free Press*, Aug. 21, 2019).

156. For a summary, see Aurelia Chaudhury, Adam J. Levitin, and David Schleicher, "Junk Cities: Resolving Insolvency Crises in Overlapping Local Governments," *California Law Review* 107, no. 2 (Apr. 2019): 459.

157. Financial Oversight & Management Board for Puerto Rico v. Aurelius Investment, LLC, 140 S. Ct. 1640 (2020) (holding that members of the Financial Oversight Management Board for Puerto Rico were officers vested with primarily local duties, and were therefore not considered officers of the United States for purposes of the Appointments Clause); Puerto Rico v. Franklin Cal. Tax-Free Trust, 136 S. Ct. 1938 (2016) (holding that Chapter 9 of the Bankruptcy Code pre-empted a Puerto Rico statute that provided a special mechanism for public utilities to restructure their debt).

158. Puerto Rico Oversight, Management, and Economic Stability Act, Pub. L. No. 114–187, 130 Stat. 549 (2016) (codified at 48 U.S.C. § 2101) [hereinafter PROMESA].

159. I.R.C. § 936(a)(1) (1976) (repealed 1996).

160. 48 U.S.C. § 745 (1917) ("[A]ll bonds issued by the Government of Puerto Rico, or by its authority, shall be exempt from taxation by the Government of the United States, or by the government of Puerto Rico or of any political or municipal subdivision thereof, or by any State, Territory, or possession, or by any county, municipality, or other municipal subdivision of any State, Territory or possession of the United States . . . .").

161. Ibid. State income tax regimes generally exempt interest on bonds issued by in-state governments (either the state or local governments) making those bonds "double tax exempt," as they are exempt for in-state holders from both federal and state income taxes. Bonds can also be exempt from municipal income taxes, in the cities where those exist, making them "triple tax exempt," as they are exempt from federal, state, and local income taxes. Puerto Rico bonds are exempt from all three types of federal income tax for all holders, making them "triple tax exempt" in all states and cities.

162. Scott Greenberg and Gavin Ekins, "Tax Policy Helped Create Puerto Rico's Fiscal Crisis," Tax Foundation (June 30, 2015). While Congress repealed Section 936, they did not also repeal federal regulations like the minimum wage, which is much too high for Puerto Rico's economy, or the Jones Act, which increases shipping costs to and from the Island. Nelson A. Denis, "The Jones Act: The Law Strangling Puerto Rico," *New York Times*, Sept. 25, 2017; Nick Timiraos and Ana Campoy, "Puerto Rico's Pain Is Tied to U.S. Wages," *Wall Street Journal*, July 1, 2015,

163. Brian Glassman, "A Third of Movers from Puerto Rico to the Mainland United States Relocated to Florida in 2018," U.S. Census Bureau, Sept. 26, 2019, https://www.census.gov/library/stories/2019/09/puerto-rico-outmigration-increases-poverty-declines.html; Federal Reserve Bank of New York, "Report on the Competitiveness of Puerto Rico's Economy" (June 29, 2012), https://www.newyorkfed.org/regional/puertorico/challenges.html.

164. Antonio Flores and Jens Manuel Krogstad, "Puerto Rico's Population Declined Sharply after Hurricanes Maria and Irma," Pew Research Center, July 26, 2019.

165. Puerto Rico's public debt grew from $39.2B to $67.8B between FY 2005–2014. Moreover, in September 2016, Puerto Rico missed $1.5B of debt payments that came due. Government Accountability Office, "U.S. Territories: Public Debt Outlook" (Oct. 2017), https://www.gao.gov/assets/690/687546.pdf.

166. Mary Williams Walsh, "The Bonds That Broke Puerto Rico," *New York Times*, June 30, 2015.

167. A 2014 study by the GAO found that Puerto Rican statehood would affect 11 of 29 federal programs studied, which would result in billions of dollars more in funding for Medicare, Medicaid, SNAP, and SSI among others. "Puerto Rico: Information on How Statehood Would Potentially Affect Selected Federal Programs," Government Accountability Office, GAO-14-31 (Mar. 2014), https://www.gao.gov/assets/670/661334.pdf.

168. Nick Brown, "Puerto Rico Pension, Highway Agency Join Government in Bankruptcy," *Reuters*, May 22, 2017.

169. Act No. 91 of May 13, 2006 (codified at P.R. Laws Ann. tit. 13, § 12); Act No. 291–2006 of Dec. 26, 2006 § 1 (codified as amended at P.R. Laws Ann. tit. 13, §§ 11a-16); Act No. 56–2007 of July 5, 2007 (codified as amended P.R. Laws Ann. tit. 13, §§ 11a-16). Walsh, "The Bonds That Broke Puerto Rico."

170. Act No. 56, §3, *supra* note 168. See also, Andrew Scurria, "Puerto Rico Wins Approval of $18 Billion Bond Restructuring," *Wall Street Journal*, Feb. 4, 2019 (outlines COFINA's bond issuances, starting in 2007).

171. Act No. 56, §2, *supra* note 168 ("all the funds deposited therein on the effective date of this act and all the future funds that must be deposited in the FIA pursuant to the provisions of this law are hereby transferred to, and shall be the property of COFINA.").

172. Federal Reserve Bank of New York, *An Update on the Competitiveness of Puerto Rico's Economy* (July 31, 2014), 20–21; Chirinko, Chiu, and Henderson, "What Went Wrong?"

173. Chirinko, Chiu, and Henderson, "What Went Wrong?"

174. Michael Corkery and Mary Williams Walsh, "Puerto Rico's Governor Says Island's Debts Are 'Not Payable,'" *New York Times*, June 28, 2015.

175. Anne Krueger, Ranjit Teja, and Andrew Wolfe, "Puerto Rico—A Way Forward," June 29, 2015, http://www.gdb-pur.com/documents/PuertoRicoAWayForward.pdf, 1,16.

176. Puerto Rico v. Franklin Cal. Tax-Free Trust, 579 U.S. 115, 116, 130 (2016) ("The amended definition of 'State' excludes Puerto Rico for the single purpose of defining who may be a debtor under Chapter 9 of this title. . . . The pre-emption provision then imposes an additional requirement: The States may not enact their own municipal bankruptcy schemes. A State that chooses not to authorize its municipalities to seek Chapter 9 relief under the gateway provision is no less bound by that pre-emption provision. Here too, Puerto Rico is no less bound by the pre-emption provision even though Congress has removed its authority to provide authorization for its municipalities to file Chapter 9 petitions.") (quotation marks and citations removed).

177. Lin-Manuel Miranda even got involved, lobbying for the bill with a newly written rap he performed on the *Late Night with John Oliver* TV show. "Puerto Rico: Last Week Tonight with John Oliver," Apr. 24, 2016, Youtube, video, *Last Week Tonight*, https://www.youtube.com/watch?v=Tt-mpuR_QHQ.

178. David Skeel, "Notes from the Puerto Rico Oversight (Not Control) Board: 34th Pileggi Lecture," *Delaware Journal of Corporate Law* 43 (2019): 529, 533–34. The Supreme Court rejected a challenge to the constitutionality of the method of appointing members of the board. Financial Oversight & Management Board for Puerto Rico, 140 S. Ct. at 1640.

179. For instance, the Board did not have the power to enact labor law reform. Skeel, "Notes," at 538. Rather, the Board may choose between certifying the Governor's fiscal plan, or its own fiscal plan. Ibid., 534.

180. Ibid., 535.

181. Lauren Hirsch and Nick Brown, "Puerto Rican Power Utility Files for Bankruptcy," *Reuters*, July 2, 2017, https://www.reuters.com/article/us-puertorico-debt-prepa/puerto-rican-power-utility-files-for-bankruptcy-idUSKBN19O02F; Nick Brown, "Puerto Rico Files for Biggest Ever U.S. Local Bankruptcy," *Reuters*, May 3, 2017, https://www.reuters.com/article/us-puertorico-debt-bankruptcy/puerto-rico-files-for-biggest-ever-u-s-local-government-bankruptcy-idUSKBN17Z1UC.

182. Skeel, "Notes," 536–37.

183. Department of Homeland Security, *FEMA Approves More Than $500 Million in Assistance to Puerto Rico*, Oct. 24, 2017, https://www.dhs.gov/news/2017/10/24/fema-approves-more-500-million-assistance-puerto-rico.

184. Skeel, "Notes," 537–38 (discussing reforms to pensions and labor law).

185. Patricia Mazzei and Frances Robles, "Ricardo Rosselló, Puerto Rico's Governor, Resigns after Protests," *New York Times*, July 24, 2019.

186. Brad Setser, "Is There Still a Path that Returns Puerto Rico to Debt Sustainability?," Council on Foreign Relations (Mar. 25, 2019), https://www.cfr.org/blog/there-still-path-returns-puerto-rico-debt-sustainability.

187. Amended Title III Joint Plan of Adjustment of The Comm. Of P.R., In re: Fin. Oversight & Mgmt. Bd. for P.R., No. 17 BK 3283-LTS (D.P.R. 2020).

188. Ibid.

189. Michelle Kaske, "Puerto Rico Debt Plan at Risk as Economic Outlook Darkens," *Bloomberg Law*, March 20, 2020, https://news.bloomberglaw.com/bankruptcy-law/puerto-rico-debt-plan-at-risk-as-island-economic-outlook-darkens.

190. Maria Chuchitan, "Puerto Rico Gets Green Light to End Five-Year Bankruptcy," *Reuters*, Jan. 18, 2022.

191. Skeel, "Notes," 535.

192. David Dayen, "Don't Reward the Greedy Vulture Funds Who Recklessly Invested in Puerto Rico," *New Republic*, July 1, 2015.

193. Chuck Boyer, "Legal Uncertainty & Municipal Bond Yields: Market Spillovers from Puerto Rico," unpublished manuscript, July 8, 2019, https://www.brookings.edu/wp-content/uploads/2019/07/Boyer_PuertoRicoPrecedence_BrookingsDraft.pdf.

194. P.R. const. art VI, § 8 ("In case the available revenues including surplus for any fiscal year are insufficient to meet the appropriations made for that year, interest on the public debt and amortization thereof shall first be paid, and other disbursements shall thereafter be made in accordance with the order of priorities established by law.").

195. In fact, the legislation authorizing the creation of COFINA and the issuance of COFINA bonds was enacted around the same time that Puerto Rico was losing the benefits of Section 936 of the Internal Revenue Code. Serious attempts to reform Puerto Rico's fiscal situation only began substantially later.

196. Another major issue that emerged in the Title III case was about how protected secured creditors really are in municipal bankruptcy. The court held that the government did not have to pay secured creditors immediately due to the automatic stay and prohibitions on courts ordering governments to spend money or make policy changes. Assured Guar. Corp. v. Carrion (In re Fin. Oversight & Mgmt. Bd. for P.R., 919 F.3d 121 (1st Cir. 2019).

197. Moreover, PROMESA forbids courts from even considering challenges to the Board's certification decisions. Skeel, "Notes," 534 (citing to PROMESA Sec. 2126(e)).

198. Matthew Goldstein, "Judge in Puerto Rico's Debt Lawsuit Handled Major Financial Cases," *New York Times*, May 5, 2017.

Chapter 6

1. Julia Wolfe and Melat Kassa, "State and Local Governments Have Lost 1.5 Million Jobs since February," Economic Policy Institute, July 29, 2020, https://www.epi.org/blog/state-and-local-governments-have-lost-1-5-million-jobs-since-february-federal-aid-to-states-and-loc alities-is-necessary-for-a-strong-economic-recovery. Because population increased and the economy grew, returning to the same raw number of employees meant that state and local employment was much lower as a percentage of population and GDP.

2. Barb Rosewicz, Justin Theal, and Joe Fleming, "States' Financial Reserves Hit Record Highs," Pew, Mar. 18, 2020, https://www.pewtrusts.org/en/research-and-analysis/articles/2020/03/18/states-financial-reserves-hit-record-highs.

3. Michael Katz, "State Pensions Entered Pandemic in Worse Position Than in 2008," *Chief Investment Officer Magazine*, Aug. 20, 2020, https://www.ai-cio.com/news/state-pensions-entered-pandemic-worse-position-2008.

4. *Final Report*, State Budget Crisis Task Force, July 2014, https://www.volckeralliance.org/sites/default/files/attachments/state_budget_crisis_task_force.pdf.

5. Alicia H. Munnell and Jean-Pierre Aubry, "An Overview of the Pension/OPEB Landscape" (2016), Center for Retirement Research, Working Paper 2016–11, 8–11 https://papers.ssrn.com/sol3/papers.cfm?abstract_id=2847725.

6. Lucy Dadayan, "State Tax and Economic Review: 2020 Quarter 1," Tax Policy Center, Aug. 25, 2020, https://www.urban.org/research/publication/state-tax-and-economic-review-2020-quarter-1 (describing "freefall drop" in revenues and expected revenues in Spring 2020); Elizabeth McNichol and Michael Leachman, "States Continue to Face Large Shortfalls Due to COVID-19 Effects," Center for Budget and Policy Priorities, July 7, 2020, https://www.cbpp.org/research/state-budget-and-tax/states-continue-to-face-large-shortfalls-due-to-covid-19-effects.

7. Ryan Nunn, Jana Parsons, and Jay Shambaug, "Incomes Have Crashed. How Much Has Unemployment Insurance Helped?," Brookings Institution, May 13, 2020, https://www.brookings.edu/blog/up-front/2020/05/13/incomes-have-crashed-how-much-has-unemployment-insurance-helped.

8. South Dakota v. Wayfair, Inc., 138 S.Ct. 2080 (2018) (states may charge sales tax on sales made by out-of-state sellers even if that seller lacks physical presence in the state); Louise Sheiner and Sophia Campbell, "How Much Is COVID-19 Hurting State and Local Revenues?," Brookings Institution (Sept. 24, 2020); Danielle Moran, "How Wayfair and COVID Spurred a State Tax Bonanza," *Bloomberg*, Mar. 5, 2021 (describing huge boom in state sales tax revenue from online sales). States that did not take advantage of *Wayfair* to tax Internet-based sales saw larger sales tax revenue declines. Liz Farmer, "As of July 1, Florida Will Require Online Sellers to Collect 6% Sales Tax from Residents," *Forbes*, Apr. 21, 2021.

9. Jeff Lagasse, "Public Hospitals Are Compounding COVID-19 Budget Risks for Large Urban Counties, Moody's Finds," *Healthcare Finance Magazine*, Oct. 14, 2020, https://www.healthcarefinancenews.com/news/public-hospitals-are-compounding-covid-19-budget-risks-countrys-largest-urban-counties-moodys; Eleanor Lamb, "States Take Action as COVID-19 Chokes Revenue Streams," *Transport Times*, Nov. 20, 2020, https://www.ttnews.com/articles/states-take-action-covid-19-chokes-revenue-streams (describing losses in toll and fare revenue).

10. Bill Hammond, "New York's Medicaid Enrollment Surges to an All-Time High," Empire Center, July 29, 2020 https://www.empirecenter.org/publications/new-yorks-medicaid-enrollment-surges-to-an-all-time-high; Christina Dorfhuber et al., "Surviving the Pandemic Budget Shortfalls," Deloitte, Sept. 9, 2020, https://www2.deloitte.com/us/en/insights/economy/covid-19/state-budget-shortfalls.html (describing surge in demand for government services); Luz Lazo and Justin George, "In a Week, the Coronavirus Razed U.S. Transit and Rail Systems," *Washington Post*, Mar. 22, 2020 (describing effect on costs and farebox revenue for transit providers).

11. Patti Domm, "The $3.8 Trillion Municipal Bond Market, Rocked by the Coronavirus, Looks to Washington for Help," *CNBC*, Apr. 28, 2020 ("When credit markets started to seize up in March, the muni market was hit by massive outflows and it shutdown to new issues.").

12. Mary Williams Walsh, "Illinois Seeks a Bailout from Congress for Pensions and Cities," *New York Times*, Apr. 17, 2020.

13. Joe Gose, "Plunge in Convention Hotel Travel Puts Municipal Bonds at Risk," *New York Times*, Apr. 14, 2020; Emily Badger, "Transit Has Been Battered by Coronavirus. What's Ahead May Be Worse," *New York Times*, Apr. 9, 2020; Mallory Moench, "California Hospitals Lose Billions to Coronavirus," *San Francisco Chronicle*, June 3, 2020.

14. Erin Huffer and Aravind Boddupalli, "COVID-19's Effect on Employment Varies across States, Except in One Sector: Government Jobs," Urban Institute, May 22, 2020, https://www.urban.org/urban-wire/covid-19s-effect-employment-varies-across-states-except-one-sector-government-jobs; Barb Rosewicz and Mike Maciag, "How COVID-19 Is Driving Big Job Losses in State and Local Government," Pew, June 6, 2016, https://www.pewtrusts.org/en/research-and-analysis/articles/2020/06/16/how-covid-19-is-driving-big-job-losses-in-state-and-local-government.

15. Scott Cohn, "Cuts to Basic Services Loom as Coronavirus Ravages Local Economies and Sends States into Fiscal Crisis," *CNBC*, July 7, 2020, https://www.cnbc.com/2020/07/07/states-in-fiscal-crisis-cuts-to-basic-services-loom-due-to-pandemic.html; Louise Sheiner, "Why Is State and Local Employment Falling Faster Than Revenues?," Brookings Institution, Dec. 23, 2020, https://www.brookings.edu/blog/up-front/2020/12/23/why-is-state-and-local-employment-falling-faster-than-revenues/ (arguing that too-high estimates of lost revenue led to greater job losses).

16. Martin Z. Braun, "States Pull Back on Pension Payments as Virus Ravages Revenue," *Bloomberg*, July 31, 2020.

17. Dylan Matthews, "How the US Won the Economic Recovery: I Looked for a Country That Got the Economic Response to Covid-19 Right. I Found the US," *Vox*, Apr. 30, 2021; Adam Taylor, "How the $1.9 Trillion U.S. Stimulus Package Compares with Other Countries' Coronavirus Spending," *Washington Post*, Apr. 5, 2021; Martin Sandbu, "US Stimulus Package Leaves Europe Standing in the Dust," *Financial Times*, Mar. 14, 2021; Michael Rainey, "Covid Relief Bill Includes Major Tax Cuts," *Yahoo Finance*, Mar. 8, 2021.

18. Tracy Gordon, "Improving State Tax Collections Don't Let Congress Off the Hook on COVID-19 Relief," Tax Policy Center, Nov. 19, 2020, https://www.taxpolicycenter.org/taxvox/improving-state-tax-collections-dont-let-congress-hook-covid-19-relief; Michael Leachman and Elizabeth McNichol, "Pandemic's Impact on State Revenues Less Than Earlier Expected But Still Severe," Center on Budget & Policy, Oct. 30, 2020, https://www.cbpp.org/research/state-budget-and-tax/pandemics-impact-on-state-revenues-less-than-earlier-expected-but; "State Tax Revenue Rebound," *Wall Street Journal*, Nov. 16, 2020. There were, of course, differences across types of governments.

19. Mary Williams Walsh, "Virus Did Not Bring Financial Rout That Many States Feared," *New York Times*, Mar. 1, 2021; Kate Davidson, "Covid-19's Hit to State and Local Revenues Is Smaller Than Many Feared," *Wall Street Journal*, Feb 7, 2021.

20. Robert McClelland, "Will COVID-19 Cause a Decline in Property Taxes?," Tax Policy Center, June 30, 2020 (predicting property tax revenue would not fall); Marc Joffee, "Most Local Governments' Tax Revenues Haven't Been Hit Hard By COVID-19 Pandemic," *Reason Magazine*, Mar. 5, 2021 (noting that property tax revenue for most jurisdictions did not fall).

21. Lucy Dayadan and Kim S. Reuben, "Congress Needs to Understand State Tax Revenue Declines When Drafting COVID-19 Legislation," Tax Policy Center, Dec. 10, 2020, https://www.taxpolicycenter.org/taxvox/congress-needs-understand-state-tax-revenue-declines-when-drafting-covid-19-legislation (noting backward-looking nature of the property tax); Matthew Haag, "Remote Work Is Here to Stay. Manhattan May Never Be the Same," *New York Times*, Mar. 29, 2021 (discussing potential future commercial property tax revenue declines).

22. Jared Walczak, "State Aid in American Rescue Plan Act Is 116 Times States' Revenue Losses," Tax Foundation, May 27, 2021, https://taxfoundation.org/state-and-local-aid-american-rescue-plan/; Alan Greenblatt, "Stimulus Solves Most—But Not All—State and Local Budget Problems," *Governing*, Mar. 11, 2021; "State and Local Governments Do Not Need Half a Trillion in COVID Relief," Committee for a Responsible Federal Budget, Feb. 17, 2021 https://www.crfb.org/blogs/state-and-local-governments-do-not-need-half-trillion-covid-relief.

23. "What's in the Final Covid Relief Bill of 2020," Committee for a Responsible Federal Budget, Dec. 21, 2020, https://www.crfb.org/blogs/whats-final-covid-relief-deal-2020.

24. "American Rescue Plan Act of 2021," National Conference of State Legislatures, Mar. 9, 2021, https://www.ncsl.org/ncsl-in-dc/publications-and-resources/american-rescue-plan-act-of-2021.aspx.

25. Elliot Davis Jr., "The States Benefiting the Most from the Infrastructure Deal," *U.S. News & World Report*, Nov. 19, 2021.

26. Jimmy Vielkind, "New York State Coffers Swell, Riding Covid-19 Recovery," *Wall Street Journal*, June 20, 2021 (quoting E.J. McMahon).

27. Scott Shafer, "Flush with Cash, California Set to Send Billions in Rebates to Taxpayers," *KQED*, May 10, 2021, https://www.kqed.org/news/11872910/flush-with-cash-california-set-to-send-billions-in-rebates-to-taxpayers.

28. John Reitmeyer, "Deadline Looms as Budget Work Done in Private," *New Jersey Spotlight*, June 21, 2021 (noting New Jersey had in 2021 a $10B surplus); Yvette Shields, "Deadline Looms as Budget Work Done in Private," *Bond Buyer*, June 18, 2021 (discussing Illinois 2021 budget).

29. Jimmy Vielkind, "States Are Swimming in Cash Thanks to Booming Tax Revenue and Federal Aid," *Wall Street Journal*, Jan. 21, 2022.

30. Mark Muro, Eli Byerly-Duke, and Joseph Parilla, "The American Rescue Plan's Secret Ingredient? Flexible State and Local Aid, Brookings Institution, Apr. 2, 2021, https://www.

brookings.edu/blog/the-avenue/2021/04/02/the-american-rescue-plans-secret-ingredi
ent-flexible-state-and-local-aid/?utm_source=feedblitz.

31. Tricia Brooks and Andy Schneider, "The Families First Coronavirus Response Act: Medicaid
and CHIP Provisions Explained," Georgetown University Health Policy Institute, Mar. 2020,
https://ccf.georgetown.edu/wp-content/uploads/2020/03/Families-First-Coronaviurs-
Response-Act-Explainer-Brief-1.pdf. States receive different matching rates based on their
income levels; the change increased all of these match rates by 6.2%. Alayna Treene, "The
Growing Coronavirus Stimulus Packages," *Axios*, Mar. 19, 2020, https://www.axios.com/
coronavirus-stimulus-packages-compared-7613a16f-56d3-4522-a841-23a82fffcb46.html.

32. Matt Broaddus, "Families First's Medicaid Funding Boost a Useful First Step, but Far from
Enough," Center for Budget & Policy Priorities, Apr. 21, 2020, https://www.cbpp.org/blog/
families-firsts-medicaid-funding-boost-a-useful-first-step-but-far-from-enough. It also included changes to Supplemental Nutrition Assistance Program that gave states new flexibility
in their provision of food stamps.

33. Garrett Watson, Taylor LaJoie, Huaqun Li, and Daniel Bunn, "Relief Plan for Individuals and
Businesses," Tax Foundation, Mar. 30, 2020, https://taxfoundation.org/cares-act-senate-
coronavirus-bill-economic-relief-plan/; Sharon Parrott, Chad Stone, Chye-Ching Huang,
Michael Leachman, Peggy Bailey, Aviva Aron-Dine, Stacy Dean, and Ladonna Pavetti,
"CARES Act Includes Essential Measures to Respond to Public Health, Economic Crises, but
More Will Be Needed," Center for Budget & Policy Priorities, Mar. 27, 2020 https://www.
cbpp.org/research/economy/cares-act-includes-essential-measures-to-respond-to-public-
health-economic-crises.

34. This meant small states did much better than large ones on a per capita basis. See "The CARES
Act Provides Assistance for State, Local and Tribal Governments," United States Department
of the Treasury, 2020, https://home.treasury.gov/policy-issues/cares/state-and-local-gove
rnments; Parrott et al., "CARES Act Includes Essential Measure"; "How Much Each State
Will Receive from the Coronavirus Relief Fund in the CARES Act," Center for Budget &
Policy Priorities, March 26, 2020 https://www.cbpp.org/research/how-much-each-state-
will-receive-from-the-coronavirus-relief-fund-in-the-cares-act.

35. "Coronavirus Relief Fund Guidance for State, Territorial, Local, and Tribal Governments,"
United States Department of the Treasury, Sept. 2, 2020, https://home.treasury.gov/system/
files/136/Coronavirus-Relief-Fund-Guidance-for-State-Territorial-Local-and-Tribal-Gove
rnments.pdf.

36. Ibid.; Nick Grube, "States, Including Hawaii, Slow to Spend COVID-19 Relief Aid," *Honolulu
Civil Beat*, July 30, 2020, https://www.civilbeat.org/beat/report-states-including-hawaii-
slow-to-spend-covid-19-relief-aid/; Michael Leachman, "Good Reasons Why States Haven't
Yet Spent All Coronavirus Relief Funds," Center for Budget & Policy Priorities, June 25, 2020,
https://www.cbpp.org/blog/good-reasons-why-states-havent-yet-spent-all-coronavirus-rel
ief-funds.

37. Christopher J. Armstrong, Nicole M. Elliott, and Rich Gold, "Covid-19 Round 3 in
D.C.: CARES Act Summary," Holland & Knight, Mar. 27, 2020, https://www.hklaw.com/
-/media/files/insights/publications/2020/03/caresactsummarymarch272020.pdf?la=en.
The mass transit money was allocated based on pre-existing formula grant systems developed
by the Federal Transportation Administration based on population and transit miles. Kea
Wilson, "Federal Corona Bill Seems Generous to Transit. It's Not," StreetsBlog USA, Apr.
8, 2020, https://usa.streetsblog.org/2020/04/08/fede.ral-corona-relief-bill-seems-gener
ous-to-transit-its-not/ (noting this was particularly bad for New York City, which because its
subway system has more riders per mile than other systems, received far less per rider).

38. Josh Barro, "Why Mitch McConnell's State Bankruptcy Idea Is So Stupid," *New York Magazine*,
Apr. 26, 2020, https://nymag.com/intelligencer/2020/04/why-mitch-mcconnells-state-ban
kruptcy-idea-is-so-stupid.html; David Frum, "Why Mitch McConnell Wants States to Go
Bankrupt," *The Atlantic*, Apr. 25, 2020, https://www.theatlantic.com/ideas/archive/2020/
04/why-mitch-mcconnell-wants-states-go-bankrupt/610714.

39. Andrea Riguier, "As the Fed Steps into the Municipal Bond Market, Will It Be Enough?,"
MarketWatch, Apr. 4, 2020, https://www.marketwatch.com/story/as-the-fed-steps-into-the-
municipal-bond-market-will-it-be-enough-2020-03-31.

40. Bin Wei and Vivian Z. Yue, "The Federal Reserve's Liquidity Backstops to the Municipal Bond Market during the COVID-19 Pandemic," Federal Reserve Bank of Atlanta Policy Hub No. 05-2020 (May 2020), https://www.frbatlanta.org/-/media/documents/research/publicati ons/policy-hub/2020/05/28/the-federal-reserves-liquidity-backstops-to-the-municipal-bond-market-during-the-covid-19-pandemic.pdf, 3. There were also $5B a week in outflows from municipal money market funds. Ibid.

41. Finn Shuele and Louise Sheiner, "What's Going on in the Municipal Bond Market? And What Is the Fed Doing about It?," Brookings Institution, Mar. 31, 2020, https://www.brookings.edu/blog/up-front/2020/03/31/whats-going-on-in-the-municipal-bond-mar ket-and-what-is-the-fed-doing-about-it.

42. Jeanna Smialek, "Fed Backstops Corner of Municipal Debt Markets amid Calls for Support," *New York Times*, Mar. 20, 2020, https://www.nytimes.com/2020/03/20/business/econ omy/federal-reserve-money-markets.html.

43. Wei and Yue, "The Federal Reserve's Liquidity Backstops"; Reuters Staff, "Variable-Rate Muni Yields Fall in Wake of Latest Fed Action," *Reuters*, Mar. 23, 2020. This was done through the Money Market Liquidity Facility and the Commercial Paper Facility. Shuele and Sheiner, "What's Going on in the Municipal Bond Market?"

44. Huixin Bi and W. Blake Marsh, "Flight to Liquidity or Safety? Recent Evidence from the Municipal Bond Market," Kansas City Fed. Research Working Paper 20-19 (2020), 16.

45. See "Federal Reserve Takes Additional Actions to Provide up to $2.3 Trillion in Loans to Support the Economy," Board of Governors of Federal Reserve System, Apr. 9, 2020, https://www.federalreserve.gov/newsevents/pressreleases/monetary20200409a.htm#:~:text= The%20Treasury%20will%20provide%20%2435,appropriated%20by%20the%20CA RES%20Act ("Help state and local governments manage cash flow stresses caused by the coronavirus pandemic by establishing a Municipal Liquidity Facility that will offer up to $500 billion in lending to states and municipalities. The Treasury will provide $35 billion of credit protection to the Federal Reserve for the Municipal Liquidity Facility using funds appropriated by the CARES Act.")

46. Peter Conti-Brown, "Explaining the New Fed-Treasury Emergency Fund," Brookings Institution, Apr. 3, 2020, https://www.brookings.edu/research/explaining-the-new-fed-treasury-emergency-fund/; Skanda Amarnath and Yakov Feygin, "The Fed Can and Should Support State Government Efforts to Respond to COVID-19 Right Now," *Medium*, Mar. 15, 2020, https://medium.com/@skanda_97974/the-fed-can-and-should-support-state-gov ernment-efforts-to-respond-to-covid-19-right-now-5e5ecf7b7ed8.

47. "Federal Reserve Board Announces an Expansion of the Scope and Duration of the Municipal Liquidity Facility," *Board of Governors of Federal Reserve System*, Apr. 27, 2020, https://www.federalreserve.gov/newsevents/pressreleases/monetary20200427a.htm ("The MLF is es-tablished under Section 13(3) of the Federal Reserve Act, with approval of the Treasury Secretary.").

48. As Peter Conti-Brown argues, this is not really a legal requirement, as much as it is a polit-ical or prudential one. Conti-Brown, "Explaining the New Fed-Treasury Emergency Fund" (noting that Section 13(3) does require that debt be "indorsed or otherwise secured to the satisfaction" of the Fed, but this does not require not losing money ever). Another clause in Section 13, George Selgin, argues, means the Fed cannot take losses at all. George Selgin, "The Constitutional Case for the Fed's Treasury Backstop," Cato Institute, Apr. 13, 2020, https://www.cato.org/blog/constitutional-case-feds-treasury-backstops (noting that Section 13(3) (b)(i) requires the Fed to ensure "that the security for emergency loans is sufficient to protect taxpayers from losses.") However, the section is not very specific and seems to delegate au-thority to the Fed to determine what constitutes an adequate amount of risk of loss. In the face of this legal dispute and political skepticism about the Fed taking on too much risk, the Fed has been conservative in its beliefs about what losses it can take. The money from the CARES Act may have helped ease that concern.

49. Kellie Mejdrich and Victoria Guida, "Fed to Buy Municipal Debt for First Time, Underscoring Peril Facing Cities," *Politico*, Apr. 9, 2020, https://www.politico.com/news/2020/04/09/ fed-to-buy-municipal-debt-178222.

50. James Politi and Colby Smith, "Fed Extends Municipal Lending to Smaller US Cities and Counties," *Financial Times*, Apr. 27, 2020, https://www.ft.com/content/34a77027-72b9-4a6b-9aa4-7cf9a6fa56e5.

51. Skanda Amarnath, Alex Williams, and Arnab Datta, "How the Fed Jammed in a Penalty Rate Requirement for All Emergency Lending When It Didn't Have To," *Medium*, Sept. 18, 2020, https://medium.com/@skanda_97974/how-the-fed-jammed-in-a-penalty-rate-requirem ent-for-all-emergency-13-3-lending-when-it-didnt-3c4f5ba6a417 (citing Walter Bagehot's seminal work *Lombard Street*, which argues that as a lender of last resort, central banks should "lend freely, at a penalty rate, against good collateral" during a crisis); Walter Bagehot, *Lombard Street: A Description of the Money* (1906), 56–57 ("the final Bank reserve must lend freely. Very large loans at very high rates are the best remedy for the worst malady of the money market.")

52. "Municipal Liquidity Facility," Board of Governors for Federal Reserve System, Aug. 11, 2020, https://www.federalreserve.gov/newsevents/pressreleases/files/monetary2020081 1a1.pdf; Rich Saskal, "Fed Lowers Interest Rates for Municipal Liquidity Facility," *Bond Buyer*, Aug. 11, 2020, https://www.bondbuyer.com/news/federal-reserve-lowers-interest-rates-for-municipal-liquidity-facility.

53. "Municipal Liquidity Facility," Board of Governors, 1 ("Eligible Notes are tax anticipation notes (TANs), tax and revenue anticipation notes (TRANs), bond anticipation notes (BANs), revenue anticipation notes (RANs), and other similar short-term notes issued by Eligible Issuers, provided that such notes mature no later than 36 months from the date of issuance.).

54. Wei and Yue, "The Federal Reserve's Liquidity Backstops."

55. Ibid.

56. Bi and Marsh, "Flight to Liquidity or Safety?," 2.

57. David Hammer, "Munis in Focus: 2020 Municipal Market Update," Pimco, Sept. 11, 2020, https://www.pimco.com/en-us/insights/investment-strategies/featured-solutions/munis-in-focus-2020-municipal-market-update (noting narrow spreads on highly rated municipal bonds but wider ones for lower-rated municipal securities).

58. "Illinois to Sell Debt in First Deal with Fed's Muni Liquidity Facility," *Reuters*, June 2, 2020, https://www.reuters.com/article/us-usa-illinois-fed/illinois-to-sell-debt-in-first-deal-with-feds-muni-liquidity-facility-idUSKBN239328.

59. Amanda Albright and Danielle Moran, "New York's MTA Becomes Second to Tap Fed as Banks Demand Higher Yields," *Bloomberg*, Aug. 18, 2020, https://www.bloomberg.com/news/articles/2020-08-18/ny-mta-becomes-second-to-tap-fed-as-banks-demand-higher-yields.

60. In July 2020, Governor Murphy signed into law the New Jersey COVID-19 Emergency Bond Act that authorized the issuance of $9.9B of bonds. See Jenna Cantarella and Holly Horsley, "NJ Passes COVID-19 Emergency Bond Act," *JDSupra*, July 20, 2020, https://www.jdsupra.com/legalnews/nj-passes-covid-19-emergency-bond-act-63538/. The state Republican Party sued to prevent Murphy from issuing the bonds and took the case to the New Jersey Supreme Court. Samantha Marcus, "GOP Fight to Stop Murphy from Borrowing $9.9B for State Budget Hits N.J. Supreme Court Wednesday," *NJ.Com*, Aug. 5, 2020, https://www.nj.com/coronavirus/2020/08/gop-fight-to-stop-murphy-from-borrowing-99b-for-state-budget-hits-nj-supreme-court-wednesday.html. The New Jersey Supreme Court, however, held that the Act did not violate the state constitution. N.J. Republican State Comm. v. Murphy, 236 A.3d 898 (2020).

61. Wei and Yue, "The Federal Reserve's Liquidity Backstops."

62. Andrew Haughwout, Benjamin Hyman, and Or Shachar, "The Option Value of Municipal Liquidity: Evidence from Federal Lending Cutoffs during COVID-19," Federal Reserve Bank of New York, draft paper, 2021, https://papers.ssrn.com/sol3/papers.cfm?abstract_id= 3785577.

63. Ibid.

64. Senator Elizabeth Warren, "Senators Warren, Van Hollen, Cortez Masto Urge Mnuchin and Powell to Provide Greater Financial Assistance to State and Local Governments," July 14, 2020, https://www.warren.senate.gov/newsroom/press-releases/senators-warren-van-hol

len-cortez-masto-urge-mnuchin-and-powell-to-provide-greater-financial-assistance-to-state-and-local-governments; Senator Elizabeth Warren, "Warren, Colleagues Warren, Colleagues Urge Fed to Reconsider Arbitrary Population Requirements That Lock Most Cities and Counties Out of CARES Act Budget Help," Apr. 18, 2020, https://www.warren.senate.gov/newsroom/press-releases/04/18/2020/senators-demand-fed-revisit-municipal-prog ram; Aaron Klein and Camille Busette, "Improving the Equity Impact of the Fed's Municipal Lending Facility," Brookings Institution, Apr. 14, 2020, https://www.brookings.edu/resea rch/a-chance-to-improve-the-equity-impact-of-the-feds-municipal-lending-facility.

65. Nick Timiaros, "Fed to Lower Rates for Cities, States Seeking Short-Term Loans," *Wall Street Journal*, Aug. 11, 2020 (lowering the interest rate spread by 50 bps); Politi and Smith; *supra* note 50 (expanding the program to smaller US cities).

66. Nick Timiaros and Kate Davidson, "Mnuchin Declines to Extend Several Fed Lending Programs," *Wall Street Journal*, Nov. 19, 2020.

67. That said, the statute explicitly states that the Fed retains all the powers it had under 13(3) pre-CARES Act. This arguably included the right to set up something like the MLF.

68. Haughwout et al., "The Option Value of Municipal Liquidity," 4 (noting that the MLF helped low-rated issuers by promoting credit risk sharing).

69. Jim Saksa, "States Need Money. The Fed Has It. Politics May Be an Obstacle," *Roll Call*, June 26, 2020), https://www.rollcall.com/2020/06/26/states-need-money-the-fed-has-it-polit ics-may-be-an-obstacle/.

70. Another group of advocates argued that the Fed should use its major intervention into the municipal bond market to fundamentally change the nature of that market, encouraging the creation of a market with a wider set of buyers for bonds. Their arguments were much like the arguments for the Build America Bonds program discussed in the previous chapter. They argued that the state-based nature of municipal bond markets often makes markets for bonds very thin. Further, state-specific markets harm price discovery, as the few state-based municipal bonds funds end up buying almost all the bonds in the state, reducing the degree to which the bond market will punish irresponsible states and cities. The fact that the Fed didn't end up buying many municipal bonds rendered these types of reforms impossible, but I will return to their logic when I discuss the interest tax exemption for municipal bonds in Chapter 11. David Beckworth, "Skanda Amarnath, Yakov Feygin, and Elizabeth Pancotti on Municipal Bond Market Intervention and the CARES Act as Responses to COVID-19," Mercatus Center, Apr. 1, 2020, https://www.mercatus.org/bridge/podcasts/04012020/ska nda-amarnath-yakov-feygin-and-elizabeth-pancotti-municipal-bond-market.

71. See, e.g., Barb Rosewicz and Mike Maciag, "How COVID-19 Is Driving Big Job Losses in State and Local Government," PEW Trust, June 16, 2020, https://www.pewtrusts.org/en/research-and-analysis/articles/2020/06/16/how-covid-19-is-driving-big-job-losses-in-state-and-local-government.

72. Committee For a Responsible Federal Budget, "What's in the Final."

73. Emily Cochrane, "Divided Senate Passes Biden's Pandemic Aid Plan," *New York Times*, Mar. 6, 2021; "Fact Sheet: The American Rescue Plan Will Deliver Immediate Economic Relief to Families," United States Department of the Treasury, Mar. 18, 2021; CBPP Staff, "American Rescue Plan Act Will Help Millions and Bolster the Economy," Center for Budget and Policy Priorities, Mar. 15, 2021 https://www.cbpp.org/research/poverty-and-inequality/american-rescue-plan-act-will-help-millions-and-bolster-the-economy.

74. Michael Lachman and Elizabeth McNichol, "Despite Improved State Fiscal Conditions, Serious Challenges Remain, Including for Localities, Tribal Nations, and Territories," Center for Budget and Policy Priorities, Feb. 26, 2021, https://www.cbpp.org/research/state-bud get-and-tax/despite-improved-state-fiscal-conditions-serious-challenges-remain.

75. See Jordan Weissman, "Biden Wants to Give States $350 Billion. Do They Still Need It?," *Slate*, Feb. 12, 2021, https://slate.com/business/2021/02/state-budgets-relief-bill-congr ess-covid.html; Andrew Prokop, "The Debate over State and Local Aid in Biden's Stimulus Bill, Explained," *Vox*, Mar. 1, 2021, https://www.vox.com/22301420/congress-pandemic-rel ief-state-local-aid.

76. Holland and Knight Public Policy & Regulation Group, "American Rescue Plan Act of 2021: Summary," Mar. 11, 2021, https://www.hklaw.com/-/media/files/insights/publicati ons/2021/03/americanrescueplankeyprovisions.pdf?la=en.

77. Rachel Siegel and Andrew Van Dam, "U.S. Economy Grew 5.7 Percent in 2021, Fastest Full-Year Clip since 1984, Despite Ongoing Pandemic," *Washington Post*, Jan. 7, 2022.

78. Goldman Sachs Asset Management, "Municipals in 2021: The Sun Also Rises," Jan. 8, 2021, https://www.gsam.com/content/dam/gsam/pdfs/us/en/articles/muni-market-monthly/2021/Muni_Outlook_2021.pdf?sa=n&rd=n.

79. Social Security Act §602(c), As Amended through P.L. 117–2, Enacted March 11, 2021.

80. The statute also included language barring states from putting aid directly into their pension funds. Social Security Act §602(c)(2)(B) As Amended through P.L. 117–2, Enacted Mar. 11, 2021. But this language does not include the "directly or indirectly" clause from the tax provision, so it mostly seems to require some weird accounting, rather than placing any real limitation on state behavior.

81. Social Security Act §602(c)(2)(A); Paul Bonner, "Federal Aid Could Hobble New State Tax Cuts and Credits," *Journal of Accountancy*, Mar. 17, 2021, https://www.journalofaccounta ncy.com/news/2021/mar/federal-coronavirus-aid-could-hobble-new-state-tax-cuts-cred its.html.

82. Dept. of Treasury, Coronavirus State and Local Fiscal Recovery Funds Interim Final Rule, 31 CFR Part 35, RIN 1505-AC77 at 85–95, May 10, 2021; Daniel Hemel, "Treasury's Noble Effort to Save the Net Tax Revenue Provision, Substance over Form" May 10, 2021, https:// substanceoverform.substack.com/p/treasurys-noble-effort-to-save-the.

83. Ohio v. Yellen, 2021 U.S. Dist. LEXIS 90274 (S.D.Ohio 2021) (finding that the challenge had a substantial likelihood of success on the merits).

84. Tony Romm, "Ohio Attorney General Sues Biden Administration over $1.9 Trillion Stimulus," *Washington Post*, Mar. 17, 2021.

85. Titus Wu, "Judge: Feds Can't Prohibit Ohio's Use of COVID-19 Relief Funds for Tax Cuts," *Columbus Dispatch*, July 2, 2021.

86. Brian Chappatta, "With $350 Billion, States Won't Hold America Back This Time," *Bloomberg*, Mar. 15, 2021, https://www.bloomberg.com/opinion/articles/2021-03-15/stimulus-che cks-states-won-t-hold-america-back-this-time?sref=nNOdD5kh.

87. John V. Miller, "Munis Remain Steady as Credit Recovery Gains Steam," Nuveen, Apr. 13, 2021, https://www.nuveen.com/en-us/insights/municipal-bond-investing/municipal-mar ket-update; Goldman Sachs Asset Management, "Outperformance during a Global Yield Surge," Apr. 2021, https://www.gsam.com/content/dam/gsam/pdfs/us/en/fund-literat ure/investment-commentary/muni_commentary_quarterly.pdf?sa=n&rd=n.

88. Yvette Shields, "Chicago Public Schools Awash in Federal Cash Inches Closer to Investment Grade," *Bond Buyer*, Apr.5, 2021.

89. Rachel Hinton, "Pritzker Touts State's First Credit Rating Upgrade in Decades: 'Illinois Is Making a Major Comeback,'" *Chicago Sun-Time*, June 29, 2021.

90. Brian Chapatta, "Illinois Owes Georgia Voters a Debt of Gratitude," *Bloomberg Opinion*, Apr. 5, 2021 https://www.bloomberg.com/opinion/articles/2021-04-05/illinois-owes-georgia-voters-a-debt-of-gratitude-on-borrowing-costs. This is despite Illinois voters' decision in November 2020 to reject a constitutional amendment allowing the state to pass a progressive income tax, a decision that would have brought in a substantial amount of revenue.

91. See, e.g., Thomas Breen, "New Haven's School Challenge: How to Spend All That Federal Money," *CT Mirror*, Apr. 17, 2021 ("New Haven's typically cash-strapped school system has a big challenge, and a big opportunity: Figuring out how to spend $136 million in pandemic-induced federal relief over the next few years without getting hooked on the short-term dough.")

92. Keith M. Phaneuf, "Lamont: Pouring Budget Surpluses into Pensions Means Big Savings Next Year," *CT Mirror*, July 7, 2022.

93. Jim Tankersly, "Biden Signs Infrastructure Bill, Promoting Benefits for Americans," *New York Times*, Nov. 15, 2021.

94. Katie Lobosco, "What Biden's Infrastructure Law Has Done So Far," *CNN.Com*, Feb. 27, 2022.

95. The Week Staff, "A Big Bet on Amtrak," *The Week*, Sept. 5, 2021 (quoting Jeff Davis of the Eno Center saying that the money managed by the secretary of transportation is "way more than any other transportation secretary has ever been given.")

Chapter 7

1. Either you are convinced by one side of this debate or another. "Fear the Boom and Bust: Keynes vs. Hayek, The Original Rap Battle!," Jan. 24, 2010, Emergent Order, YouTube, video, https://www.youtube.com/watch?v=d0nERTFo-Sk. For what it is worth, much of this book takes a pretty explicitly Keynesian approach to macroeconomic questions. But it is still, I hope, useful to those who do not.
2. One could, I suppose, have an accelerationist attitude toward crises, believing that debt crises are good because they make jurisdictions adopt needed policy changes that they would have not have absent a default or near-default. Holding this opinion about default crises in general requires a very strong set of assumptions about how politics works in both good times and bad (as well as a belief that sacrifices necessary to get post-crisis policy changes are worth the costs). A more conventional understanding, that budget crises are unfortunate and sad, involving many bad things—service cuts, tax increases, layoffs during recessions, declining ability to borrow and invest, bad precedents for future leaders, depressed civic confidence—is wiser.
3. David Gamage and Darien Shanske, "Tax Cannibalization and Fiscal Federalism in the United States," *Northwestern University Law Review* 111, no. 2 (Feb. 2017): 295, 300.
4. Juan J. Cruces and Christoph Trebesch, "Sovereign Defaults: The Price of Haircuts," *American Economic Journal: Macroeconomics* 5, no. 3 (July 2013): 85 ("restructurings involving higher haircuts are associated with significantly higher subsequent bond yield spreads and longer periods of capital market exclusion").
5. Alicia H. Munnell and Jean-Pierre Aubry, "An Overview of the Pension/OPEB Landscape" (2016), Center for Retirement Research Working Paper 2016-11, 8–11 https://papers.ssrn.com/sol3/papers.cfm?abstract_id=2847725.

Chapter 8

1. "IMF Lending," International Monetary Fund, Mar. 27, 2020, https://www.imf.org/en/About/Factsheets/IMF-Lending (discussing conditionality of IMF lending, and noting that "[a] country's return to economic and financial health ensures that IMF funds are repaid so that they can be made available to other member countries.").
2. Jared Walczak, "State Aid in American Rescue Plan Act Is 116 Times States' Revenue Losses," Tax Foundation, May 27, 2021, https://taxfoundation.org/state-and-local-aid-american-res cue-plan/; Michael Leachman, "Fiscal Relief Needed Now to Stop Massive State Job Loss from Becoming Permanent," Center on Budget and Policy Priorities, May 15, 2020, https://www.cbpp.org/blog/fiscal-relief-needed-now-to-stop-massive-state-job-loss-from-becom ing-permanent.
3. Julia Rock, "This Last-Minute Provision Blocks GOP Govs from Using Stimulus Money to Subsidize Tax Cuts," *Newsweek*, Mar. 17, 2021, https://www.newsweek.com/this-last-minute-provision-blocks-gop-govs-using-stimulus-money-subsidize-tax-cuts-1576676 (discussing state and local tax cut limitation in state and local aid provision of the ARP as part of Democratic Party's broader anti–tax cut belief).
4. National Federation of Independent Business v. Sebelius, 567 U.S. 519 (2012).
5. Eloise Pasachoff, "Conditional Spending after NFIB v. Sebelius: The Example of Federal Education Law," *American University Law Review* 62, no. 3 (2013): 577.
6. Ibid., 596–600.
7. National Federation of Independent Business v. Sebelius, 567 U.S. at 581.
8. Pennhurst State School & Hospital v. Halderman, 465 U.S. 89 (1984).
9. For instance, there was a serious but ultimately unsuccessful challenge to an effort by New Jersey to borrow during the height of the COVID-19 recession. However, in New Jersey Republican State Committee v. Murphy, 243 N.J. 574 (2020), the New Jersey Supreme Court blessed a state law that approved borrowing to cover a shortfall in revenue due to the recession.

It held that such borrowing was allowed under a "disaster" exception in the state's debt limit, but that before borrowing, the governor or the state treasurer needed to certify that it was made necessary by the fiscal harm created by the disaster that is the COVID pandemic.

10. "Truth and Integrity in State Budgeting: Preventing the Next Fiscal Crisis," Volker Alliance, Dec. 12, 2018 https://www.volckeralliance.org/truth-and-integrity-state-budgeting-prevent ing-next-fiscal-crisis ("Cash-based accounting, widely used by state governments, allows expenditures to be recognized only when bills are paid. This permits a government to commit to significant spending in one year but not reflect that decision until future years, when the payments are actually made.")

11. Ibid.

12. Some governments use something called the "encumbrance" system of accounting in budgeting to capture some issues like this. Betty T. Yee, "State of California Accounting Standards and Procedures for Counties, 2022 Edition," California State Controller's Office, https://www.placer.ca.gov/DocumentCenter/View/37788/Accounting-Standards-and-Pro cedures-for-Counties-ASP—2022-Edition-PDF.

13. "Governor Ducey Announces That Arizona Owns Capitol Buildings Again," Office of Governor Doug Doucey, Jan. 14, 2019, https://azgovernor.gov/governor/news/2019/01/ governor-ducey-announces-arizona-owns-capitol-buildings-again ("Arizona will finally own our state Capitol building again, reversing one of the of most infamous budget gimmicks of the Great Recession, paying off debt and saving taxpayers more than $100 million."); Tim Murphy, "Arizona Wants to Buy Back State Capitol It Inexplicably Sold," *Mother Jones*, Jan. 11, 2012, https://www.motherjones.com/politics/2012/01/arizona-wants-buy-back-state-capitol-it-inexplicably-sold/ (explaining transaction); Jennifer Steinhauer, "In Need of Cash, Arizona Puts Offices on Sale," *New York Times*, Sept. 25, 2009.

14. Julie Roin, "Privatization and the Sale of Tax Revenues," *Minnesota Law Review* 95 (2011): (2011) (describing sale and leaseback arrangements among other balanced budget and debt limit avoidance techniques).

15. *The Daily Show with Jon Stewart*, "Arizona State Capitol Building for Sale," Comedy Central, Sept. 15, 2009, https://www.cc.com/video/9v8aeq/the-daily-show-with-jon-stewart-ariz ona-state-capitol-building-for-sale (mocking Arizona's budget gimmicks).

16. Roin, "Privatization and the Sale of Tax Revenues."

17. E. J. McMahon, "Taking Control: How the State Can Guide New York City's Post-Pandemic Fiscal Recovery," Manhattan Institute, Sept. 24, 2020, https://www.manhattan-institute.org/ guiding-nyc-out-of-covid-budget-crisis; New York City Charter § 1516 ("The tax rates shall be such to produce a balanced budget within generally accepted accounting principles for municipalities.").

18. The case for the constitutionality of this proposed condition is stronger still because jurisdictions that have high levels of nonbonded "debt" (due to things ranging from sale-and-leaseback arrangements to underfunded pensions) have less capacity to borrow to finance new infrastructure. Better state accounting would serve the same ends as the tax exemption, promoting state spending on infrastructure.

19. There are other ideas Congress could attach to a bailout bill. For instance, Congress could also commit to aiding the reconstruction and reform of state rainy day funds, encouraging states to save in advance of recessions, as Brian Galle and Kirk Stark advocate. Brian Galle and Kirk J. Stark, "Beyond Bailouts: Federal Tools for Preventing State Budget Crises," *Indiana Law Journal* 87, no. 2 (Spring 2012): 599.

20. For a discussion of the exemption for municipal securities, see "Investor Bulletin: The Municipal Securities Market," Securities and Exchange Commission, Feb. 1, 2018, https:// www.sec.gov/oiea/investor-alerts-and-bulletins/ib_munibondsmarket.

21. Christine Sgarlata Chung, "Municipal Securities: The Crisis of State and Local Government Indebtedness, Systemic Costs of Low Default Rates, and Opportunities for Reform," *Cardozo Law Review* 34 (Apr. 2013): 1455.

22. Ibid. Chung's argument that the Tower Amendment should be repealed would be particularly powerful if reforms were passed alongside a federal state-aid package during a fiscal crisis. The argument in favor of the Tower Amendment is weakest when the federal government is

providing aid. Requiring disclosures alongside future bond issuance can be understood as a way of reducing the likelihood that bailouts will be needed in the future.

23. Coronavirus Aid, Relief, and Economic Security Act, Pub. L. 116–136, tit. VI, §601(b)(2), 134 Stat. 281, 502 (2020).

24. "Coronavirus Relief Fund: Frequently Asked Questions," United States Department of the Treasury, Oct. 19, 2020, https://home.treasury.gov/system/files/136/Coronavirus-Relief-Fund-Frequently-Asked-Questions.pdf.

25. "FAQs: Municipal Liquidity Facility," Federal Reserve Bank of New York, Oct. 5, 2020, https://www.newyorkfed.org/markets/municipal-liquidity-facility/municipal-liquidity-facility-faq ("States, Cities, and Counties may use the proceeds of Eligible Notes sold to the SPV under the MLF to purchase the notes of, or otherwise assist, any of their political subdivisions or other governmental entities as described above.").

26. Clayton P. Gillette, "Dictatorships for Democracy: Takeovers of Financially Failed Cities," *Columbia Law Review* 114, no. 6 (2014): 1373, 1377 (describing Rhode Island and Michigan takeover laws).

27. Charles K. Coe, "Preventing Local Government Fiscal Crises: The North Carolina Approach," *Public Budgeting and Finance* 27, no. 3 (Fall 2007): 39<I/BT> (describing North Carolina's much-admired system of state oversight).

28. Ibid., 41 (describing different systems of state oversight).

29. Gillette, "Dictatorships,"1375–79.

30. McMahon, "Taking Control" ("FCB played a critical role in the city's recovery from the brink of bankruptcy 45 years ago"); Annie McDonough, "Why New York Is Relying on Commissions to Make Policy," *City and State*, Apr. 4, 2019 ("The Emergency Financial Control Board, which saved the day in the fiscal crisis in New York City back in the 1970s"); Vincent J. Cannato, "The Man Who Saved NY," *New York Post*, Aug. 8, 2011. That said, some think it represented an unwanted turn away from social democracy and toward austerity. Kim Phillips-Fein, *Fear City: New York's Fiscal Crisis and the Rise of Austerity Politics* (New York: Metropolitan Books, 2017).

31. Mike DeBonis, "After 10 years, D.C. Control Board Is Gone But Not Forgotten," *Washington Post*, Jan. 30, 2011, https://www.washingtonpost.com/local/after-10-years-dc-control-board-is-gone-but-not-forgotten/2011/01/30/AB5485Q_story.html.

32. See, generally, Nathan Bomey, *Detroit Resurrected: To Bankruptcy and Back* (W.W. & Company, Inc., 2017).

33. David Skeel, "Notes from the Puerto Rico Oversight (Not Control) Board: 34th Pileggi Lecture," *Delaware Journal of Corporate Law* 43 (2019): 529,.

34. Yvette Shields, "Former Michigan Governor, Flint Emergency Managers Face Criminal Charges over Water Crisis," *Bond Buyer*, Jan. 14, 2021 (describing criminal charges against the governor of Michigan, and Flint's emergency managers, for actions that caused lead to appear in Flint's water supply); Curt Guyette, "Why Is the Law That Spawned Flint's Water Catastrophe Still Standing?," *Detroit Free-Press*, Apr. 4, 2019 (blaming the emergency manager law for the catastrophe in Flint); Chad Livengood, "In Detroit and Flint, Two Tales of Emergency Management," *Crain's Detroit*, Apr. 29, 2018 (comparing Detroit and Flint experience with emergency managers).

Chapter 9

1. Lee Bucheit et al., "Revisiting Sovereign Bankruptcy, Committee on International Economic Policy and Reform," Brookings Institution, 2013, https://www.brookings.edu/wp-content/uploads/2016/06/CIEPR_2013_RevisitingSovereignBankruptcyReport.pdf (discussing long debate over sovereign bankruptcy).

2. 11 U.S.C. §109(c).

3. David A. Skeel Jr., "Is Bankruptcy the Answer for Troubled States and Cities," *Houston Law Review* 50, no. 4 (Apr. 2013): 1064.

4. Vincent Buccola, "The Logic and Limits of Municipal Bankruptcy Law," *University of Chicago Law Review* 86, no. 4 (June 2019): 817; Laura N. Coordes, "Gatekeepers Gone

Wrong: Reforming the Chapter 9 Eligibility Rules," *Washington University Law Review* 94, no. 5 (2017): 1191.

5. Michael W. McConnell and Randal C. Picker, "When Cities Go Broke: A Conceptual Introduction to Municipal Bankruptcy," *University of Chicago Law Review* 60 (1996): 450–54; Clayton P. Gillette and David A. Skeel Jr., "Governance Reform and the Judicial Role in Municipal Bankruptcy," *Yale Law Journal* 125 (2016): 1150, 1237.

6. Clayton P. Gillette, "How Cities Fail: Service Delivery Insolvency and Municipal Bankruptcy," *Michigan State Law Review* 2019 (2019): 1238–48.

7. Ibid., 1237–40.

8. Gillette, "How Cities Fail," 1245–48.

9. The notion of equality of creditors has long been a central tenet of American bankruptcy law. David A. Skeel Jr., "The Empty Idea of 'Equality of Creditors,'" *University of Pennsylvania Law Review* 166 (2017): 700.

10. Richard M. Hynes and Steven D. Walt, "Pensions and Property Rights in Municipal Bankruptcy," *Review of Banking and Financial Law* 33 (2014): 609, 613.

11. Ibid., 618.

12. For a discussion of the use and the need for disclosure of statutory lien provisions for general obligation bonds, see National Federation of Municipal Analysts, "White Paper on General Obligation Bond Payments: Statutory Liens and Related Disclosures," Dec.2017 (discussing statutory lien provisions in California, Colorado, Idaho, and Rhode Island).

13. Juliet Moringiello, "Goals and Governance in Municipal Bankruptcy," *Washington and Lee Law Review* 71, no. 1 (Winter 2014): 403, 413–14.

14. Adam J. Levitin, "Bankrupt Politics and the Politics of Bankruptcy," *Cornell Law Review* 97, no. 6 (Sept. 2012): 1399.

15. Editorial Board, "Chicago's Puerto Rican Bonds," *Wall Street Journal*, Jan. 31, 2020; Mark Glennon, "Why Nobody But Bond Buyers Should Like Chicago's Latest Deal—Wirepoints Original," *Wirepoints*, Jan. 19, 2020, https://wirepoints.org/why-nobody-but-bond-buyers-should-like-chicagos-latest-deal-wirepoints-original/; "Chicago Refunds an Additional $673 Million with Sales Tax Bonds," Civic Federation, Dec. 7, 2018, https://www.civicfed.org/civic-federation/blog/chicago-refunds-additional-673-million-sales-tax-bonds. These bonds have features that make them a little less problematic than COFINA, but more problematic than the original "Big MAC" bonds. On the plus side, like "Big MAC" bonds but unlike COFINA, the bonds were authorized by the state government, not the issuing government. However, like COFINA and unlike the Big Mac bonds, it is not clear that Chicago issued these bonds to overcome a temporary liquidity crisis or as part of a broader set of structural reforms. Rather, it appears they were just trying to get lower interest rates on new debt by taking some of the revenue that supported ordinary general obligation (GO) bonds and giving it to a new set of bondholders. However, Chicago, as the first big user of sales tax securitization bonds, used the revenues to pay down some GO debt, complicating the analysis. "Chicago's Bonds Aren't Akin to Puerto Rico's," *Wall Street Journal*, Feb. 12, 2020.

16. Aurelia Chaudhury, Adam J. Levitin, and David Schleicher, "Junk Cities: Resolving Insolvency Crises in Overlapping Local Governments," *California Law Review* 107, no. 2 (Apr. 2019): 459, 525 n.271.

17. The same was true for the original UDC structure, which gave the UDC time to complete apartment buildings which then generated revenue.

18. Ibid, 470–77.

19. Emma Brown, "Michigan Legislature Approves $617 Million Bailout Package for Detroit Schools," *Washington Post*, June 9, 2016.

20. Chaudhary, Levitin, and Schleicher, "Junk Cities," 483–84.

21. Anna Gelpern, "Bankruptcy, Backwards: The Problem of Quasi-Sovereign Debt," *Yale Law Journal* 121, no. 4 (2012): 888; David A. Skeel Jr., "States of Bankruptcy," *University of Chicago Law Review* 79, no. 2 (2012): 677, 680; Steven L. Schwarcz, "A Minimalist Approach to State 'Bankruptcy,'" *UCLA Law Review* 59, no. 2 (Dec. 2011): 322; Jeb Bush and Newt Gingrich, "Better Off Bankrupt," *Los Angeles Times*, Jan. 27, 2011; David Skeel, "Give States a Way to Go Bankrupt," *Weekly Standard*, Nov. 29, 2010,

22. Josh Barro, "Why Mitch McConnell's State Bankruptcy Idea Is So Stupid," *New York Magazine*, Apr. 26, 2020; David Frum, "Why Mitch McConnell Wants States to Go Bankrupt," *The Atlantic*, Apr. 25, 2020; John Wagner, "McConnell Takes Flak after Suggesting Bankruptcy for States Rather Than Bailouts," *Washington Post*, Apr. 23, 2020.

23. Barro, "Why Mitch McConnell's State Bankruptcy Idea Is So Stupid."

24. For the reasons discussed in Chapter 5, I find this argument particularly unpersuasive. Pensioners generally—although not always—have done better than other unsecured creditors in Chapter 9 bankruptcies.

25. Vincent S. J. Buccola, "An ex ante Approach to Excessive State Debt," *Duke Law Journal* 64, no. 2 (2014): 235 (describing the application of Chapter 9 to states).

26. Mobile v. Watson, 116 U.S. 289 (1886).

27. Ibid., 291.

28. Ibid., 304.

29. 103 U.S. 358, 365 (1881).

30. Clayton P. Gillette, "Saving Cities or Exploiting Creditors? State Diversion of Municipal Assets," *Fordham Urban Law Journal* 48 (2021); 753, 758.

31. Jed Rubenfeld, *Revolution by Judiciary: The Structure of American Constitutional Law* (Cambridge, MA: Harvard University Press, 2005), 67–68.

32. This line of cases has been cited in later opinions, but in very different contexts. In Missouri v. Jenkins, 495 U.S. 33, 55 (1990), the Court cited them to discuss a related but different issue, the power of a federal court to issue an order overriding a state tax limitation. In Gomillion v. Lightfoot, 364 U.S. 339, 344 (1960), the Court cited them for the proposition that state legislative changes to municipal boundaries could violate the constitution if doing so otherwise violated the Constitution.

33. Gillette, "Saving," 763–74.

34. 316 U.S. 502 (1942).

35. U.S. Trust Co. of N.Y. v. New Jersey, 431 U.S. 1 (1977) (finding the repeal of a 1962 bond agreement by New York and New Jersey violated the Contract Clause).

36. Where a single level of government issues both the sales tax bonds and the GO bonds, as in the Puerto Rico COFINA case, the question becomes a bit harder.

37. Williams v. Mayor, 289 U.S. 36 (1933); Hunter v. City of Pittsburgh, 207 U.S. 161 (1907).

38. Gomillion, 364 U.S., at 339–47 (changing borders of Tuskegee, Alabama, to intentionally exclude African Americans is unconstitutional); Board of Education v. Grumet, 512 U.S. 687 (1994) (drawing special school district boundaries intentionally to include only members of a particular religious group violates the First Amendment's ban on state establishment of religion).

39. As long as it is consistent with the state's own constitution, of course.

40. Wolff, 103 U.S., at 365.

41. Ibid., 366.

42. Gillette proposes that courts facing Contract Clause challenges to "Big MAC" style bonds should distinguish between proper and improper diversions of revenue by looking at legislative motive. Gillette, "Saving," 755. Removing a city's power to tax to harm bondholders intentionally violates the Contract Clause, he argues, while other changes to municipal taxing power should not. As a policy matter, this is not too far from what I suggested earlier in this chapter as something Congress could do as part of reform of municipal bankruptcy law. But it is hard to shoehorn this idea into the Constitution. The text of Contract Clause does mention motive. Nor would it be easy for a court operating in a constitutional register to be clear about what is and what is not okay.

43. And, indeed, the New York Court of Appeals did not invalidate the MAC bonds. Quirk v. Municipal Assistance Corporation, 41 N.Y.2d 644 (1977).

Chapter 10

1. Elaine S. Povich, "State Income Tax Revenue Is Increasingly Volatile," *Governing*, Oct. 14, 2014, https://www.governing.com/news/headlines/state-income-tax-revenue-is-increasingly-volatile.html; "State and Local Revenues," Urban Institute, n.d., https://www.urban.org/

policy-centers/cross-center-initiatives/state-and-local-finance-initiative/state-and-local-backgrounders/state-and-local-revenues#state.

2. Brian Galle and Kirk J. Stark, "Beyond Bailouts: Federal Tools for Preventing State Budget Crises," *Indiana Law Journal* 87, no. 2 (Spring 2012): 601–602.

3. David Gamage and Darien Shanske, "Tax Cannibalization and Fiscal Federalism in the United States," *Northwestern University Law Review*, 111 (2017): 300.

4. Gamage and Shankse, "Tax Cannibalization," 303.

5. Ibid; Michael Keen, "Vertical Tax Externalities in the Theory of Fiscal Federalism," International Monetary Fund, Working Paper No. 97/173, 1997, https://www.imf.org/en/Publications/WP/Issues/2016/12/30/Vertical-Tax-Externalities-in-the-Theory-of-Fiscal-Federalism-2446.

6. Gamage and Shanske, "Tax Cannibalization," 303. And that is before factoring in the inefficacies that result from people leaving jurisdictions due to high taxes, a subject of much debate. Enrico Moretti and Daniel J. Wilson, "The Effect of State Taxes on the Geographical Location of Top Earners: Evidence from Star Scientists," *American Economic Review* 107, no. 7 (July 2017): 1858 (star scientists mobility patterns heavily influenced by taxes); Cristobal Young, *The Myth of Millionaire Tax Flight: How Place Still Matters for the Rich* (Stanford, CA: Stanford University Press, 2018) (detailing how despite the propensity for the rich to migrate, actual levels of migration are limited).

7. Gamage and Shanske, "Tax Cannibalization," 303.

8. Jan M. Rosen, "Tax Watch: The Likely Forms of New Taxes," *New York Times*, Dec. 19, 1998 ("Lawrence Summers . . . explained in a quip why the United States had not adopted a value-added tax so far. 'Liberals think it's regressive and conservatives think it's a money machine.' If they reverse their positions, the V.A.T. may happen, he said.").

9. See Alicia H. Munnell and Jean-Pierre Aubry, "An Overview of the Pension/OPEB Landscape" (2016), Center for Retirement Research Working Paper, 2016-11.

10. James E. Spiotto, "When Needed Public Pension Reforms Fail or Appear to Be Legally Impossible, What Then? Are Unbalanced Budgets, Deficits and Government Collapse the Only Answer?," Hutchins Center on Fiscal and Monetary Policy, May 30, 2018, https://www.brookings.edu/wp-content/uploads/2018/04/Spiotto-J.-v8.pdf; W. Gordon Hamlin Jr. et al., "Embracing Shared Risk and Chapter 9 to Create Sustainable Public Pensions," *MuniNet Guide*, Apr. 16, 2018, https://muninetguide.com/creating-sustainable-public-pensions/; Mary Williams Walsh, "Stepping Up with a Plan to Save American Cities," *New York Times*, Nov. 11, 2013; James E. Spiotto, "Unfunded Pension Obligations: Is Chapter 9 the Ultimate Remedy? Is There a Better Resolution Mechanism?," Chapman & Cutler, June 2013, https://s3.amazonaws.com/s3.documentcloud.org/documents/816158/public-pension-discussion-series-james-e-spiotto.pdf.

11. Brian Tumulty, "How to Deal with Insolvent Public Pension Systems," *Bond Buyer*, July 16, 2018.

12. Amy Monohan, "Statutes as Contracts? The 'California Rule' and Its Impact on Public Pension Reform," *Iowa Law Review* 97 (2012): 1029, 1032.

13. In Chapter 5, I discussed this aspect of the *Detroit* case.

14. The rule was first articulated by the Supreme Court of California in the case of Allen v. City of Long Beach, 45 Cal.2d 128 (Cal. 1955) and was discussed in Chapter 5.

15. Lydia Wheeler and Joyce E. Cutler, "California High Court Upholds Limits to Public Pension Benefits," *Bloomberg Law*, July 30, 2020, https://news.bloomberglaw.com/employee-benefits/california-high-court-upholds-limits-to-public-pension-benefits.

Chapter 11

1. Chad Stone, "Fiscal Stimulus Needed to Fight Recessions," Center on Budget and Policy Priorities, Apr. 16, 2020, https://www.cbpp.org/research/economy/fiscal-stimulus-needed-to-fight-recessions (discussing contrast between relatively calm period of the Great Moderation of the '80s, '90s, and early 2000s with the wild swings since).

2. David Schleicher, "Stuck! The Law and Economics of Residential Stagnation," *Yale Law Journal* 127, no. 1 (2017), 78, 81–86.

3. Ibid., 86–111.

4. Ibid., 111–14 (discussing debate over causes of declining mobility).

5. Kyle F. Herkenhoff, Lee E. Ohanian, and Edward C. Prescott, "Tarnishing the Golden and Empire States: Land-Use Restrictions and the U.S. Economic Slowdown," *Journal of Monetary Economics* 93 (2018): 89–109 ("U.S. labor productivity would be 12.4 percent higher and consumption would be 11.9 percent higher if all U.S. states moved halfway from their current land-use regulation levels to the current Texas level."); David Albouy and Gabriel Ehrlich, "Housing Productivity and the Social Cost of Land-Use Restrictions," *Journal of Urban Economics* 107 (2018): 101("Observed land-use restrictions raise housing costs by 15 percentage points on average, reducing average welfare by 2.3 percent of income on net."); Chang-Tai Hsieh and Enrico Moretti, "Housing Constraints and Spatial Misallocation," *American Economic Journal: Macroeconomics* 11 no. 2 (2019): 1–39 (finding that perfect mobility would lead to an increase in growth rates of 87% and a GDP 8.9% higher, and that simply reducing New York, San Francisco, and Silicon Valley's zoning restrictiveness to the national average would lead to 3.7% higher GDP); Bryan Caplan, "Hsieh-Moretti on Housing Regulation: A Gracious Admission of Error," EconLib, Apr. 5, 2021, https://www.econlib.org/a-correction-on-housing-regulation/ (showing that Hsieh and Moretti's growth calculation should have led to an estimate of annual GDP 36% higher under full mobility, and 14% higher in the three city estimate); Devin Michelle Bunten, "Is the Rent Too High? Aggregate Implications of Local Land-Use Regulation," draft paper, 2017, https://papers.ssrn.com/sol3/papers.cfm?abstract_id=2980048 ("Welfare and output would be 1.4% and 2.1% higher, respectively, under the planner's allocation" than it is with land use regulation.).

6. Schleicher, "Stuck!" 117–22.

7. Ibid., 125–27.

8. Sage Belz and Louise Shiner, "Tax Exemption Offsets Lack of Competition in Municipal Bond Markets," Brookings Institution, July 23, 2018), https://www.brookings.edu/blog/up-front/2018/07/23/tax-exemption-offsets-lack-of-competition-in-municipal-bond-market.

9. Daniela Pylypczak-Wasylyszyn, "What Are Build America Bonds?", *Municipal Bonds,* June 24, 2015, https://www.municipalbonds.com/education/what-are-build-america-bonds.

10. The Tariff Act of 1894 created a federal income tax with no exemption for interest on municipal bonds. George E. Lent, "The Origin and Survival of Tax-Exempt Securities," *National Tax Journal* 12, no. 4 (1959): 301, 302. In Pollock v. Farmers' Loan & Trust Co., 157 U.S. 429, 586 (1895), the Supreme Court held, among other things, that the federal government could not tax interest income from state and local bonds because of the Tenth Amendment. But following the passage of the 16th Amendment in 1913, which allows taxation for income "from whatever source derived" and the weakening of the doctrine of intergovernmental tax immunity, the constitutional basis for the exemption of state bond interest from federal income taxes became less certain. U.S. Constitution, Amendment XVI; Kyle Richard, "Towards a Standard for Intergovernmental Tax Immunity Between the Several States," *Tax Law* 70 (2017): 869, 869–92 (discussing changes in the doctrine of intergovernmental tax immunity. Seventy-five years after the passage of the 16th Amendment, the Court made clear that the holding in *Pollock* that the federal government could not tax interest on state and local debt was no longer good law. South Carolina v. Baker, 485 U.S. 505, 607–11 (1988) (reversing bond-specific holding in *Pollock*).

11. Lent, "The Origin and Survival of Tax-Exempt Securities," 305–11 (discussing efforts by Harding, Coolidge and Roosevelt administrations to repeal the exemption); Lucille Derrick, "Exemption of Security Interest from Income Tax in the United States," *Journal of Business* 19 (1946); Franklin Delano Roosevelt, "Message from the President of the United States," Hearings on H.R. 3790, Committee on Finance, U.S. Senate, 76th Cong., Feb. 21, 1939, at 3–5 https://www.finance.senate.gov/imo/media/doc/76HrgSalary.pdf (calling for exemption).

12. Michael A. Livingston, "Reform or Revolution? Tax-Exempt Bonds, the Legislative Process, and the Meaning of Tax Reform," *U.C. Davis Law Review* 22 (1989): 1165, 1172–1206 (describing efforts between 1968 and 1986 to repeal or reform the tax code's municipal bond provisions) President Reagan's initial proposal included the elimination of the exemption for private activity bonds. See John E. Petersen, "Examining the Impacts of the 1986 Tax Reform Act on the Municipal Securities Market," *National Tax Law Journal* 40 (1987): 39.

13. "Municipal Securities Provisions of H.R. 1, the 'Tax Cuts and Jobs Act,'" Municipal Securities Rulemaking Board, Jan. 2018, http://www.msrb.org/Market-Topics/~/media/20AB21E90 C3E4103885B4E8670B1F1E8.ashx.

14. One thing to note is that the value of the exemption changes radically over time due to other changes in federal tax law. Over the course of the history of the income tax, top tax rates increased and fell over time, peaking at 94% during World War II and seeing a trough of 28% after the Tax Reform Act of 1986. The value the exemption provides to bond purchasers is based on tax rates, and therefore these broader changes have changed the size of the subsidy to state and local governments. Other tax changes, like 2017's changes to the state and local tax exemption, can increase value of the exemption as well. See Carla Fried, "The Tax Law Gives Municipal Bonds a New Allure," *New York Times*, Feb. 23, 2018, https://www. nytimes.com/2018/02/23/business/the-tax-law-gives-municipal-bonds-a-new-allure.html. This book obviously can't review all tax changes over the course of American history, but it is worth remembering the context in which the exemption exists.

15. Daniel Bergstresser and Randolph Cohen, "Changing Patterns in Household Ownership of Municipal Debt: Evidence from the 1989–2013 Surveys of Consumer Finances," Brookings Institution, July 2015, https://www.brookings.edu/wp-content/uploads/2016/07/MFC_ allpapers.pdf, at 1 (describing increasing ownership of municipal bonds by top 0.5% of income distribution).

16. Scott Greenberg, "Reexamining the Tax Exemption of Municipal Bond Interest," Tax Foundation, July 21, 2016, https://taxfoundation.org/reexamining-tax-exemption-munici pal-bond-interest; Calvin H. Johnson, "Repeal Tax Exemption for Municipal Bonds," *Tax Notes* 117 (2007): 1259 (arguing that the exemption is inefficient).

17. In places with municipal income taxes, municipal bonds can be "triple tax exempt," exempt from federal, state, and local income taxes. Kent Thune, "Taxation of Municipal Bond Funds," *The Balance*, Oct. 29, 2019, https://www.thebalance.com/taxation-of-municipal-bond-funds-2466708. As discussed in Chapter 6, Puerto Rico's debt is triple tax exempt everywhere in the country, by federal statute.

18. Bergstresser and Cohen, "Changing Patterns in Household Ownership of Municipal Debt" (discussing how tax exemption leads to municipal bonds being largely held by rich domestic individuals). Tax reform in 1986 ensured that rich individuals were the major purchasers of municipal bonds, by reducing the benefits banks got from holding bonds (by curbing the practice of writing off interest payments on money borrowed to purchase municipal bonds). Matthew R. Marlin, "Did Tax Reform Kill Segmentation in the Municipal Bond Market?," *Public Administration Review* 54 (1994): 387; James M. Poterba, "Tax Reform and the Market for Tax-Exempt Debt," *Regional Science & Urban Economy* 19 (1989): 537. There is an exception for bonds issued by small municipalities. See "Bank Qualified Bonds," WM Financial Strategies, last visited Sept. 25, 2021, http://www.munibondadvisor.com/BQBonds.htm (describing continued ability of banks to deduct 80% of the carrying cost of bonds issued by small local governments).

19. Dep't of Revenue of Kentucky v. Davis, 553 U.S. 328, 329 ("The intrastate funds absorb securities issued by smaller or lesser known municipalities that the interstate markets tend to ignore").

20. Daniel Garrett, Andrey Ordin, James W. Roberts, and Juan Carlos Suárez Serrato, "Tax Advantages and Imperfect Competition in Auctions for Municipal Bonds," National Bureau of Economic Research Working Paper No. 23473, 2017, https://www.nber.org/papers/w23 473 (finding that exemption reduces borrowing costs by increasing participation of investors, therefore reducing power of lenders).

21. Graciela L. Kaminsky and Carmen M. Reinhart, "On Crises, Contagion, and Confusion," *Journal of International Economy* 51 (2000) (distinguishing between linkages and "true" or informational contagion risks).

22. Jonathan William Welburn, "Crises beyond Belief," RAND Working Paper Series, Working Paper WR-1221 (Jan. 2018), https://www.rand.org/content/dam/rand/pubs/working _papers/WR1200/WR1221/RAND_WR1221.pdf. See also Laura Kordes and Matthew Pritsker, "A Rational Expectations Model of Financial Contagion," *Journal of Finance* 57 (2002): 769.

23. Ronald I. McKinnon, "Monetary Regimes, Government Borrowing Constraints, and Market-Preserving Federalism: Implications for EMU," in *The Nation State in a Global/Information Era: Policy Challenges*, ed. Thomas Courchene (Kingston: John Deutsch Institute For the Study of Economic Policy, 1996), 101, 110. ("Thus foreigners, who would not receive the tax advantage, do not buy them, and the market becomes narrowly 'on-shore' in U.S. dollars. This makes it easier for the U.S. Federal government to ignore bankruptcies in any one state or locality, that is, no bailout, because such a bankruptcy does not impair the country's international credit rating and, possibly, the credit standing of the other states.")

24. Clayton P. Gillette, "Fiscal Federalism, Political Will, and Strategic Use of Municipal Bankruptcy," *University of Chicago Law Review* 79, no. 1 (2012): 281, 304 (reviewing literature on contagion from New York and Orange County fiscal crises and concluding that "the empirical evidence about fiscal pollution from local distress is mixed but offers some support for the presence of contagion.").

25. Rabah Arezki et al., "Are There Spillover Effects from Munis?," International Monetary Fund, Working Paper No. WP/11/290, 2011.

26. A counterpoint should be noted. Perhaps, as Robert Inman argues, domestic ownership of debt makes bailouts more likely, as the losers are not foreigners, but domestic residents who can vote. Robert P. Inman, "Transfers and Bailouts: Institutions for Enforcing Local Fiscal Discipline with Lessons from U.S. Federalism," in *Fiscal Decentralization and the Challenge of Hard Budget Constraints*, eds. Jonathan Rodden, Gunnar Eskelund, and Jennie Litvack (Cambridge, MA: MIT Press, 2003), 58. But the state-specific nature of municipal bond ownership makes it unlikely that there is mass support across the country on behalf of creditors who are heavily concentrated in one jurisdiction.

27. There is another case against the exemption based on the effect of defaults. That bonds are held by in-state residents means that defaults harm the local economy, as locals are the ones that lose money. However, most municipal bonds are held as parts of diversified state-based funds, which are themselves parts of more broadly diversified individual portfolios held by rich investors. So any one governmental default is unlikely to have too large an effect on the balance sheets of individual holders.

28. Lynne Funk, "Billions Pulled from Funds as Investors Flee Munis," *Bond Buyer*, Mar. 19, 2020, https://www.bondbuyer.com/news/billions-pulled-from-funds-as-investors-flee-munis; Jeremy R. Cooke, "Municipal Borrowers Flee Auction Securities Market," *Seattle Times*, Mar. 22, 2008, https://www.seattletimes.com/business/municipal-borrowers-flee-auction-securities-market.

29. Leah Brooks and Zachary Liscow, "Infrastructure Costs," *American Economic Journal: Applied Economics* (forthcoming 2022), https://www.aeaweb.org/articles?id=10.1257/app.20200398&from=f.

30. Alon Levy, "Why American Costs Are So High (Work-in-Progress)," *Pedestrian Observations*, Mar. 3, 2019, https://pedestrianobservations.com/2019/03/03/why-american-costs-are-so-high-work-in-progress; Alon Levy, "Why It's So Expensive to Build Urban Rail in the U.S.," *Bloomberg*, Jan 26, 2018; Tracy Gordon and David Schleicher, "High Costs May Explain Crumbling Support for U.S. Infrastructure," *Real Clear Policy*, Mar. 30, 2015.

31. Kirk J. Stark, "Rich States, Poor States: Assessing the Design and Effect of a U.S. Fiscal Equalization Regime," *Tax Law Review* 63 (2010): 957, 993–94.

Chapter 12

1. Daniel J. Hopkins, *The Increasingly United States: How and Why American Political Behavior Nationalized* (Chicago: University of Chicago Press, 2018); David Schleicher, "Federalism and State Democracy," *Texas Law Review* 95 (2017): 763.

2. One might think that state governments' lack of authority over important areas of policy like monetary policy leads to a lack of voter interest in state politics. But this does not make much sense on further reflection. To start, there is variation in how much policy different states make, but no real variation in the degree to which state elections are determined by national level partisanship. And state and local governments do a lot right now. Policing, housing policy,

healthcare, transportation, and so on are hardly obscure, unimportant issues. The lack of state party competition is best explained as a result of changes in party organization and media.

3. Hopkins, *The Increasingly United States*; Steven Rogers, "National Forces in State Legislative Elections," *Annals of American Academy of Political & Social Science*, Aug. 17, 2016, 207.

4. Schleicher, "Federalism and State Democracy," 775 (discussing literature on second-order elections).

5. Hopkins, *The Increasingly United States.*

6. Christopher S. Elmendorf and David Schleicher, "Informing Consent: Voter Ignorance, Political Parties, and Election Law," *University of Illinois Law Review* (2013): 363, 370–80.

7. Morris P. Fiorina, *Retrospective Voting in American National Elections* (New Haven: Yale University Press, 1981), 89–105.

8. Elmendorf and Schleicher, "Informing Consent," 370–80.

9. Nonpartisan local elections can be even worse, at least in bigger jurisdictions. If party labels provide only a little information in state and local elections, removing them often means voters have even less to go on.

10. Schleicher, "Federalism and State Democracy," 780–86; David Schleicher, "Why Is There No Partisan Competition in City Council Elections? The Role of Election Law," *Journal Law and Policy* 23, no. 4 (2007): 419.

11. The inability of state and local politicians to appeal to a mass electorate infects all sorts of state and local policy areas. Take land use, one of the most important issues for local governments. Even as well-known mayors in cities like New York and San Francisco have sought to increase housing supply, city councils have used their authority over land use to stop necessary construction. The result is a housing crisis that does not serve future residents or renters well, but serves the interests of groups that dominate low-information council primary elections: heavily invested homeowners who would rather not put up with increased traffic or see new housing supply drive down the price of their homes. Why are homeowners dominant even in majority-renter cities like New York City? Politicians need homeowners, who vote regularly. Other groups—renters, employers—are less influential in city council elections. The only people who pay attention are those with interests very different from those of the broader populace. David Schleicher, "City Unplanning," *Yale Law Journal* 122, no. 7 (2013) (discussing systematic pro-restriction bias of city councils); Michael Hankinson and Asya Magazinnik, "The Supply-Equity Trade-Off: The Effect of Spatial Representation on the Local Housing Supply," 2020, draft paper, http://mhankinson.com/documents/supply_equ ity_working.pdf.

12. Sarah Anzia, *Timing and Turnout: How Off-Cycle Elections Favor Organized Groups* (Chicago: University of Chicago Press, 2014).

13. Pengjie Gao, Chang Lee, and Dermot Murphy, "Financing Dies in Darkness? The Impact of Newspaper Closures on Public Finance," *Journal of Financial Economics* 135, no. 2 (2020): 445–67.

INDEX

For the benefit of digital users, indexed terms that span two pages (e.g., 52–53) may, on occasion, appear on only one of those pages.

Notes: Tables and figures are indicated by an italic *t* and *f* following the page/paragraph number.